RECENT ITALIAN CINEMA

Spaces, Contexts, Experiences

RECENT ITALIAN CINEMA
Spaces, Contexts, Experiences

Tiziana Ferrero-Regis

t

Published by
Troubador Publishing Ltd
5 Weir Road, Kibworth Beauchamp
Leicester, LE8 0LQ
Tel: 0116 229 2299
Email: books@troubador.co.uk
Web: www.troubador.co.uk

Series Editor
Professor George Ferzoco
University of Bristol, UK

ISBN: 9781848760851

Typesetting: Troubador Publishing Ltd, Leicester, UK

To my parents, Morgana and Craig

CONTENTS

PREFACE

For decades, the emphasis by Anglo-American critics and researchers of Italian cinema has been on close textual readings of a selected number of films that could be analysed following the paradigm of the auteur theory. A failure to recognise changes in mass culture, audiences, instances of production, and distribution and technology has resulted in the inability to appreciate Italian cinema of the period 1980–2000 beyond a few films that could still be classified according to grand theories.

Italian cinema literature started to appear in Italy in the middle of the 1990s, especially works by Mario Sesti and Vito Zagarrio, who have strenuously tried to make sense of contemporary Italian cinema. Their works began to open up complex questions in the area of film studies, and raised the possibility of writing a book that could suggest new areas of inquiry.

This book owes its framework and analysis to the specific direction in film studies undertaken by academics such as Tony Bennett, Toby Miller, Tom O'Regan and Albert Moran at Griffith University, Brisbane, Australia at different times between the late 1980s and 2000. There is, of course, a recognition of the legacy of Italian cinema literature by international scholars; however, this rich work on Italian auteurs (past and present) has somehow produced a backlash which has stymied different approaches to Italian cinema. It has also locked Italian cinema into an equation in which the absence of recognisable grand auteurs indicated the absence of a national cinema altogether.

Recent Italian Cinema does not address all the questions and issues about current Italian cinema. This book merely scraps the surface of a complex system of film production, distribution and exhibition which has a significant and multifaceted history. This history often enriches current film practices, but more than often it is onerous. *Recent Italian Cinema* attempts to open up fields of inquiry whose analysis could transcend traditional theoretical stereotypes.

Tiziana Ferrero-Regis
Brisbane, February 2008

ACKNOWLEDGEMENTS

There are many people that I would like to thank for their help and suggestions. I am very grateful to the following for their reading of earlier versions of the manuscript, and who offered essential advice and supportive comments: Albert Moran, Jason Jacobs and Tony May. Tom O'Regan has provided an invaluable viewpoint on early material during his mentorship of a reading and writing group at Griffith University, while he was director of the Australian Key Centre of Media and Cultural Policy; Mike Levy, Griffith University, for supporting the project through the provision of a small fund; Pat Hoffie for letting me off my duties at the Queensland College of Art during the late stage of writing; Adriana Diaz for her efficient work as research assistant, and Sue Jarvis and Cori Stewart for their copy-editing of the manuscript and for their intelligent suggestions, and, last but not least, the series editor, George Ferzoco and Jane Rowland at Troubador.

I would also like to offer my thanks to people who have agreed to be interviewed at various times during the research: Luca Bigazzi, Enzo Monteleone, Kiko Stella, Maurizio Colombo (Marketing director at Medusa Film in 2000), Carole-Andrè Smith (Marketing director Cinecittà Studios), Luciana Castellina (director of Italia Cinema in 2000), Diana Tocci (ANICA), Franco Imperiali and Simonetta Quatrini (Cineteca Luigi Chiarini, Scuola Nazionale di Cinema, Rome), Giampietro Mazzoleni, Franca Sozzani, editor, Vogue Italy. I would like to acknowledge especially the friendship of Annabella Miscuglio and her hospitality.

Finally, I would like to thank my husband, Craig, and my daughter, Morgana, for their love, patience and support.

Tiziana Ferrero-Regis
Brisbane, February 2008

INTRODUCTION

Recent Italian Cinema does not offer impressionistic and lyrical reflections about Italian films that seek some intrinsic meaning and teleological truth. Nor does it provide a complete survey of Italian cinema in the period 1980–2006. Rather, the aim of this book is to address a number of questions about Italian cinema of the last twenty years, bringing an interdisciplinary knowledge to the study of a cinema that eschews traditional definitions and categories, and challenges critical assumptions about a film industry that is struggling to find a new direction. In doing so, *Recent Italian Cinema* offers a transverse analysis of the Italian cinema industry in its dealings with national and international film production, and of the themes and issues that have emerged in films produced during the period 1980–2006.

The book approaches this goal in two ways. Culturally, it situates Italian cinema within the historical contingencies of the 1980s and 1990s, two decades characterised by a new consumerism and a collective retreat to the domestic space in opposition to the exhilarating years of 1968–69 and the exhaustion of the 1970s. A specific preoccupation with history and memory emerges in many films of the last two decades of the century, signalling a work of mourning for collective political and social experiences and a shared national history by new directors. Industrially, it locates recent Italian cinema within changes in filmmaking practices that occurred after the economic collapse of the film industry and the Cinecittà studios in the middle of the 1970s, followed by the advent of commercial television from the late 1970s onwards.

Cultural and political shifts are explored through an investigation of the Resistance and 1968 as myths which were created in the second half of the century and shattered in the late 1970s by a conservative backlash. Films by Gabriele Salvatores, Nanni Moretti, Daniele Luchetti, Guido Chiesa,

Davide Ferrario, Gianni Amelio, Mimmo Calopresti and other directors are discussed with regard to their impact on the construction of a postwar myth of democracy, and the disillusionment about that myth which subsequently emerged. The common referents for these directors are the Resistance, terrorism, 1968 and Fascism, and the ways in which these events have affected contemporary Italy. These films are part of discursive histories of ways in which the figure of the partisan, the notion of victim/perpetrator and revolutionaries have been represented throughout the history of Italian cinema. For each one of these issues there is a story to be told, and *Recent Italian Cinema* glimpses at these stories in the attempt to create a continuity between past and present cinema. Moreover, the cinema of the late 1980s and 1990s has a very specific generational address and milieu of production in that it found its audience through common historical references which affected both the films themselves and how the films were made. The country's recent history thus becomes a way for a new generation of directors to generate audience recognition, compensating for the lack of stars or generic conventions.

The year 1999 closed a decade of confused and contradictory approaches to filmmaking. The Academy Awards to Tornatore, Salvatores and Benigni, and the box office success of *Il postino* (Michael Radford, 1995) created a paradox in which success abroad did not correspond with the positive domestic reception of Italian cinema. Apart from the Oscar® directors, Italian filmmakers found difficult to find any kind of distribution process, let alone an efficient system. In addition, the scarcity of funding, infrastructure and investments in quality scripts and the pre-production phase corresponded with a parallel lack of ideas and aesthetic innovation. Thus the 1990s were characterised by the 'flat photogram' (Zagarrio 2001, p. 11), a simplistic aesthetic accompanied by banal stories. Very few films emerged at the tip of the iceberg, and their visibility depended on different circumstances. They either made it into the international circuit through film festivals and special niche screenings, or they were lucky enough to be cherry-picked by the Hollywood distribution system.

In the 1990s, the domestic market share for Italian films oscillated between 21.9 and 23.6 per cent (European Observatory on the Audiovisual Industry, Strasburg, 2000). The year 2000 was the worst: Italian film production decreased and imports of European films also diminished from 104 in 1999 to 84 in 2000; however, imports of US films increased from 178 the previous year to 212 (Associazione Nazionale Industrie Audiovisive e Multimediali, ANICA, 2000). Italian cinema's market share dropped to a record low of 17 per cent, and the then president of the Associazione Nazionale Industrie Audiovisive e Multimediali (ANICA), Fulvio Lucisano, called for a restructuring of the industry, suggesting that the existing heavily subsided funding system be abandoned. Yet in 2000, films such as *Placido Rizzotto* (Pasquale Scimeca), *I cento passi* (Marco Tullio Giordana), *Pane e tulipani* (Silvio Soldini) and *Domenica* (Wilma Labate) were released. These were quality films, either highly praised or successful at the box office. Two fundamental questions must be asked: the first concerns the fact that Italian cinema as national cinema is in reality reduced to a niche market in its own territory, while the second relates to what Italian audiences do with domestic films. It is clear that it is no longer possible to separate national cinemas from the grip that the American film industry has on world markets in terms of imagination and modes of production, distribution and exhibition. It is thus only by examining the multiple layers of description and analysis which take into account the presence of Hollywood that we can come to an understanding of what recent Italian cinema is.

WHAT NATIONAL CINEMA?

There are more questions about what constitutes a national cinema than certainties. Is it the nationality and language of its makers? Does the nationality of its production practices or the institutional funding system define an Italian film as a 'film of national cultural interest'? What is the role of its political and cultural contexts, or specific genres, motifs, history, star system and locations? Like literature, cinema has always aspired to have a global dimension. It is not possible to speak of a national cinema without taking into consideration its relation to the international circulation of the audiovisual product. Historically, the concept of national cinema was mobilised as a way to prescribe what a national cinema should be, especially in comparison to Hollywood. Higson (1989) maintains that a national cinema should be measured according to its relationship with its audiences, that it should be looked at in terms of the way audiences make sense and use the film, as well as with regard to sites of production and consumption, which include dynamics of distribution and exhibition. Thus, a national cinema today is no longer purely the projection of national character or a series of ways by which we can understand and read this projection in film; rather, it encompasses industrial infrastructures, production, distribution and exhibition companies, sets of meanings, unity or disunity of texts, aesthetics, contents, imaginary coherence, and so on.

The most significant problem arises from the poor local distribution of Italian films. This problem was already understood by Pier Paolo Pasolini when he declared:

> Distribution, distribution, distribution – that's the issue … the whole business of people saying to European producers that you just need to make film audiences want to see is complete crap. There are American movies that should not be in 100 theatres, ghastly movies with terrible reviews that no one cares about, but because a major has the muscle they get them onto those screens. (Pasolini in Miller et al. 2001, p. 148)

Thus the question of the visibility of domestic films to domestic audiences must take into consideration the presence of Hollywood's distribution subsidiaries in the European territory, and thus within national boundaries. American distributors, which operate in vertically integrated networks with Hollywood studios, dictate what goes on screens – even when a local film is successful (Miller et al. 2001, p. 148). A good example is Daniele Luchetti's latest film *Mio fratello è figlio unico* (2007), which

topped the box office for over a month in both Rome and
restricted to fewer screens, displaced by the release of *Spide*

Other questions concerning national cinemas are connected to genre, form and content. I want to concentrate on a few examples in which genre, form and content come to play an important part in the domestic and international circulation of films. Recent Italian filmmaking covers a large spectrum, with many variables that range from the experimental cinema of Roberta Torre, Ciprì and Maresco, and Bruno Bigoni to the comedy of Paolo Virzì, and the existentialism of Gianni Amelio and Mario Martone (see table in Bichon 2000, p. 122). As a way of illustrating the complexity of defining Italian national cinema today and the predicament of art cinema, I will look at the work of some Italian directors at opposite ends of a range of possibilities that come into play when speaking of Italian national cinema content and form. Their work is also emblematic of the interconnections between commercial cinema and art cinema, especially when we evaluate the expectations that art cinema creates in audiences, both nationally and internationally.

Gabriele Muccino and Daniele Luchetti enjoy commercial success in Italy. However, Muccino has been enlisted by Columbia to work in the United States, while Luchetti's films remain confined within national boundaries. Neither Muccino nor Luchetti fall into the category of art cinema or commercial cinema, as these groupings are traditionally understood. They both make good quality films which appeal, for different reasons, to the Italian public. They represent the 'median' quality films that constitute the backbone of the film industry; however, there is an expectation, internationally, that European national films are equal to art cinema. Muccino explores the boundaries of sentimental relationships in contemporary Italy, while Luchetti's films have a national flavour as they tap into the national imaginary through national history. Incidentally, Muccino's success in Italy is linked with that of the production company Fandango, which literally took off with the domestic box office success of *L'ultimo bacio* (2001), and has since become an international production and distribution company, with interests stretching as far as Australia.

Following his success as a director and writer, Columbia called Muccino to direct *The Pursuit of Happyness* (2004) in the United States. A second film, *Seven Pounds*, is in the pre-production phase at the time of writing. Muccino's most successful Italian films as director and writer, *L'ultimo bacio* (which was picked up by Miramax for international distribution) and *Ricordati di me* (2003), adopt the narrative transparency of continuity storytelling which is typical of Hollywood features, pointing to the adoption of the romantic comedy by Muccino, in which social and individual problems are displaced on to love and sex. His films follow a formula based on a concatenation of many stories and events, a narrative structure used also in *Crash* by Paul Haggis (2004), in which the main characters of each story are drawn together at the end of the film, providing a final closure with a happy ending for at least one of the stories. In *The Pursuit of Happyness*, this narrative gimmick is used to separate the phases of Chris Gardner's (Will Smith) life as he goes from being a compassionate, caring father – but a loser according to American parameters of success – to a position in which his mathematical abilities and humanity make him the most successful student/apprentice in a large US brokerage firm. Interestingly, *L'ultimo bacio* has been remade in the United States (*The Last Kiss*, Tony Goldwyn, 2006) with a script written by *Crash*'s Paul Haggis.

The failure of some of the relationships in Muccino's films spices the story with a flavour akin to art cinema, while the happy endings of other relationships provide for a cathartic and pleasurable closure. Thus Muccino's similarity to and difference from Hollywood not only appeal to Italian audiences, as Elsaesser (in Higson 1989, p. 39) stresses: 'Hollywood can hardly be conceived ... as totally other, since so much of any nation's film culture is implicitly "Hollywood', but it also interests Hollywood's movie moguls. This is because difference is not resistance, and capitalism allows for heterogeneity to serve the free market as it constantly negotiates between homogeneity and difference.

On the other hand, Daniele Luchetti's films remain confined to a specific culture and territory; however, they offer resistance at the level of the culture that animates them. Luchetti's work can be taken as a metaphor for a country which has systematically suppressed the most advanced instances of democratisation and which has experienced a profound social change between the end of Fascism and globalization, with very few resources that could make the transition easy. Luchetti's films directly reference national history (*Domani accadrà*, 1988), corruption (*Il portaborse*, 1991), the Resistance (*I piccoli maestri*, 1998), 1968 and terrorism (*Mio fratello è figlio unico*, 2007); thus they deal with issues that are typically national. *Il portaborse* and *Mio fratello è figlio unico* have topped the domestic box office, but Luchetti has not made inroads internationally because: 'Distributors' take-up of foreign film material for art-house circulation frequently excludes the culturally specific.' (Crofts 1992, p. 58) This explains why, for example, Amelio's films are carefully sifted through by international distribution: *Lamerica* (1994) was seen outside Europe only at niche festivals, while *Ladro di bambini* (1991) made Amelio an international *auteur*. Equally, Nanni Moretti's material has hardly crossed European boundaries (and in some cases the French–Italian borders).

Nanni Moretti in fact represents a third example of directors who deal with realism, politics and sentiments. His films are very popular in France, but they have had limited circulation in the United States. Despite the fact that the rights of his film *La stanza del figlio* (2000) were bought by Miramax after it won the Palm d'Or in Cannes in 2001, the film was not nominated as Best Foreign Film at the Academy Awards, as Miramax decided to invest in a domestic picture, *In the Bedroom* (Todd Field, 2001), with a similar storyline to Moretti's film.[1] Like Daniele Luchetti's films, Nanni Moretti's cinema is deemed too local for the American market. On the other hand, Nanni Moretti has always found support and funding in France from the pan-European producer and distributor Canal Plus. Here he won two Palm d'Or – for *Caro Diario* (1993) and *La stanza del figlio* – and was nominated for *Aprile* (1998). From *Cahiers du cinema* to *Liberation* and *Positif*, Moretti has been considered by French film critics for his political commitment as the only director who offered resistance to

Berlusconi (Manin 1994, p. 33); however, Nanni Moretti's favour with French audiences and critics might be due to the peculiarity of his navel-gazing films, so close to much of French cinema of the 1980s and 1990s. Julie Delpy's latest film, *Deux jours à Paris* (2007), is clearly influenced by Moretti's self-obsessive vitriolic comedy.

Nanni Moretti's films are categorised within the parameters of art cinema, which operates within the variables of art, culture, quality and national identity (Neale 1981, p. 11), and these discourses have 'historically been mobilised against Hollywood ... and used to justify various nationally specific national economic systems of support and protection' (Higson 1989, p. 41). However, in recent times the traditional opposition between art and entertainment has collapsed in the European Union's attempt to circulate its audiovisual product on a wider scale, especially on the US market and at international film festivals. Art film thus becomes a portmanteau term. It is a fact that by the 1990s there was a greater fluidity in the boundaries between commercial and art cinema. Thus Muccino's realistic portraits of the contemporary Italian middle class have benefited from a more fluid, 'contaminated' understanding of art cinema internationally, while following conventional narrative structures.

The Italian comedy comes closer to a national cinema, in the sense that 'comedies do *not* travel well' (Moretti 2001, p. 4). According to cultural historian Franco Moretti, language is the single most important feature of comedies, as jokes and many other ingredients of comedy are weakened by translation. Interestingly, laughter arises out of implicit understandings that are common to a culture and history, so they disappear or weaken when translated into another language and culture. Moretti surveyed the top box office films in the period 1986–1995 and noticed that every single national hit was a comedy.[2] In this regard he writes:

> This fixation – which began in the sixties, and apparently will never end – must have something to do with that mix of aggression and anxiety that psychoanalysis has recognized in laughter, and that is so typical of the emotional cosmos of the *commedia all'italiana*. It's the grimace of a culture structurally

unsure about its position in the world: the last of the 'advanced' countries, arrogantly showing its teeth to what is left of the past – or the first of the 'backward' ones, populistically bent on 'decrowning' those placed above it? (Moretti 2001, p. 4)

Thus a question arises: to what extent are we prepared to accept that Vanzina's and Pieraccione's films, and Aldo, Giovanni and Giacomo's comedies, are the true representations of Italian imaginary and thus national cinema? Interestingly, we are always prepared to associate the national spirit with the sublime and a canon of *auteurs*, but tend to disregard popular genres so that the bulk of popular cinema, with its stars, goes uncharted. None of the cinemas produced in the period 1980–2006 can be enunciated as central to national representations, but they all made up the problematic notion of national cinema. Popular comedies were successful at the local box office, but did not circulate to prestigious international film festivals. Period films froze the past into 'mausoleumification' (Hayward 1993, p. 7), which ossified Italian cinema into a past that was no longer culturally active or relevant. On the other hand, while *auteur* films barely recovered their production budgets in the domestic market, they were presented to prominent international festivals where they won many international awards and were raised to cult status.[3] Thus it is increasingly difficult to say what constitutes Italian national cinema, as many Italian films work within the Hollywood's formal system of narration, and Italian audiences have enjoyed Hollywood films for decades. Art cinema never achieved national popular success in the domestic market, although it created expectations of how national Italian cinema should be perceived abroad. It would follow that a national cinema – whether successful or not – is a compromise between artistic qualities and popular cinema.

Pierre Sorlin (1996) has offered an interesting analysis of Italian national cinema from the point of view of what generations of audiences have done with, and how they have related to, Italian cinema. This angle is a welcome departure from authorial analyses that assemble separate films and individual directors through a concentration of textual analysis, in search of teleological truths about what film means.[4] As Moretti (2000, p. 57) states, the problem of these close textual analyses is that they necessarily depend on very small canons because only few of them are really significant, and thus we should start looking at Italian film production as a whole to be able to write about histories and patterns.

Despite his different approach, when in the last chapter Sorlin comes to recent cinema he still applies some of the prejudices that grew around a cinema that refuses dominant discourses about film. In the past, Italian cinema produced body of works that could be identified with specific moments in the country's cultural history and politics, and with industrial systems: early historical epics, Fascist film, neorealism and art cinema. However, from the end of the 1970s there were no trends that could be identified, other than the constant presence of television. Also, the theorisation of production of spectatorship in the 1980s continues to be afflicted by a preoccupation with aesthetics and film as a reflection of Italian society and culture.

The renewal of Italian cinema studies has been produced by some fundamental texts in the Italian language from 1994. Mario Sesti and Vito Zagarrio are the most important authors and editors who have attempted to open new fields of inquiry to crucial elements such as political economy, technology, global film, film and television and so on.[5] Clearly the influence of globalisation has inspired and allowed the interpenetration of film studies with critical cultural studies and political economy that detail the conditions under which a text is produced. Sesti's and Zagarrio's merits rest in their attempt at reconstituting a taxonomy of Italian films, genres, directors, themes. This reconstruction becomes a methodology in itself as it attempts to write a quantitative history and to create a collective system of recent Italian films.

GEOPOLITICS OF FILM

The definition of national cinema then starts to take form in relation to the methodology employed in its analysis. This book proposes a consideration of the country's cinema as an ecosystem for a transversal reading of information. In this way, every element is in relation: territory of encounters; place within geographical boundaries; and political, economic and textual accounts of Italian cinema. The analysis of the intimate connection between communication and the human negotiation of physical space is critical because, since the advent of cinema in the last part of the nineteenth century and of television in the 1940s and 1950s, the visuality of space has increased, and the moving image now constitutes a rich archive of spatial experience over more than a century (Moran 2004, p. 2).

Two key issues demonstrate the analysis animating this study. The first is that whatever the genre or occasion of filmmaking, moving images and sounds of screen spaces are resources for the development of an anthropology of place, in which spaces intersect with off-screen flows and circulation of other spaces. The second issue is related to the way in which particular films function as maps within wider spaces and locations, and thus territorialise the places where they are engaged. This intersection between space and film can be regarded as relating to a diverse sense of how space and place are part of the experience of film in everyday life. What kinds of spaces are being created by cinema and what kinds of effects do these spaces in turn have on film? Indeed, film has constantly been produced for, and has been engaged at, particular locations.

Peppino Ortoleva (1996) identified three different meanings of media geography, which can aptly be applied to film geography. The first is the *geography of networks*, which in Ortoleva's theorisation corresponds to the distribution of television networks on the territory. In the case of cinema, a geography of networks can be established by looking at the various ramifications of, and collaboration between, production companies and individual professionals along the peninsula. Thus the *geography of production* can be linked to the geography of networks so that it is possible to understand which cities and regions are the most active and how they relate to the geography of *international* production. Last, there is the *geography of content*, which deals with location and identities and allows us to see what areas are marginalised or excluded. This is particularly significant in the case of Mediterranean cinema, whose new artistic output in recent years has allowed the Mediterranean area to move from the margins of cultural production to a more central position. Thus *Recent Italian Cinema* offers a reading of different experiences of space, mapping out the economic geography of Italian film through local, national, regional and international production, and a geography of content representing Italy's position in the spaces of regional and global public culture.

In recent years, the field of screen studies has included specific studies on screen genres, space and the representation of specific places in film. There is now a wealth of literature about cinema and the city that approach film through its link to space.[6] Central to much scholarship on space and film is Henri Lefebvre's (1991) conceptual innovation of Marxism that extends Marxist analysis of the modes of labour production to the social production of space. The spatial organisation of the industry, the shaping of cities by cinema as a cultural practice,[7] space in films – the space of the shot and of narrative setting – as well as the relationship between different spaces in films and the position of Italian cinema in global film all contribute, following Lefebvre, to a process of production of space, not only of labour and technology but also through representation in visual images.

Within this relatively new research field, *Recent Italian Cinema* ilustrates how physical and social landscapes have been mediated through the screen institutions, just as physical geography has helped shape the screen institutions and the screen culture. The geopolitics of cinema is thus a useful way to understand how recent Italian cinema has negotiated its space of production and distribution in the domestic and international markets and how this is reflected in film representation. *Recent Italian Cinema* is not the sum of individual films, but a collective system informed by cultural, historical and industrial geopolitics.

IDEOLOGICAL AND INDUSTRIAL FUNCTIONS OF THE HISTORY FILM

A second element that comes into play when mapping a national cinema is its relationship to national history. Like the British heritage film (see Higson 1993), the commodification of Italy's national past is an important element in the articulation of versions of that past that could be marketed internationally and thus succeed economically. However, cinematic reconstructions of history also create an important space for playing out contemporary anxieties and fantasies of national identity, class and power. Higson draws on Benjamin's idea of historical materialism: the past is articulated in moments of danger that affect tradition, its content and its receivers (Benjamin 1969, p. 255). Anxieties brought up by change can be articulated in a nostalgic mode, where the past is colonised aesthetically. For instance, landscape shots that 'fall out of the narrative' (Higson 1993, p. 117), and are consumed as the lost object of desire, are fundamental elements for the international commercial success of Italian history films.

To make Higson's statement explicit, it can be said that the history film could accommodate two functions: the industrial, tied to its circulation on national and international markets; and the political, subtextually linked to contemporary national issues. These two functions can easily be traced from the very beginning of cinema, exactly because of cinema's temporal contingency with processes of nation-making or of modernisation and industrialisation, and thus with shifts in the historical imaginary. These two functions can either exist at the same time in one film, or separately in a single movie – and the latter is usually the nationally sensitive historical film, which then only appeals to the domestic audience.

Patterns in which the past emerges as a central concern in cinematic representation can be observed in the history of all Western national cinemas, starting with early American cinema, to the French *film de qualité* the Australian period film, British heritage film and to the obsession with recent past in New German Cinema. In every case, the representation of the past created an important imagined space in which national anxieties were played out. They were a cultural response to moments of change or unstable and socially deprived environments. For this reason, the restaging of the past on the screen becomes a public site, the function of which is to question unresolved national tensions. In this way, these films mobilise and reconstruct identity, and thus recreate simultaneously their audience and a new film culture. At the same time, in all of the historical cinematic representations of these national cinemas there was a strong economic-industrial element related to issues of audience-seeking and export. They occupied a space in the international image market. This is, for instance, a strong element in the high-budget costume films in which a commodified past is presented as a form of exotic spectacle for the international audience.

Since the origin of cinema, Italian history films have presented both characteristics. One function of the history film was related to the industry and the expansion of its market, both domestic and international. As history films accommodated a range of cultural elements, including high art, they contained essential elements for success in the international market. The second function pertained to the sphere of politics and ideologies, where cinema had assumed the function of modern creator of myths and propaganda. History films could induce a profound identification and recognition in Italian audiences, primarily because of their subject-matter, history and the simultaneous national preoccupations embedded in the films.

Not only have these two functions of the history film been retained in recent Italian filmmaking, they have traversed the entire history of the Italian national cinema. The intertextuality, the visual spectacle and the lasting popularity of these films are elements that have always attracted investments from producers. Thus the expectations of the history film in the Italian cinema industry has always been placed in its economic function – that is, helping to create a recovery from the cyclical crises of the Italian film industry.

It is certainly possible to say that the Italian history film codified a certain set of practices with spectacular and epic characters which, at least in their more external configuration, still remain in contemporary cinematic production. By 1914, the development of this specific set of conventions peculiar to Italian history films had become the paradigm of both new economic and industrial developments in the film industry, and of the demand for a more extensive and consolidated emergent middle class audience.

The history film is a remarkably stable product in the history of Italian cinema. It creates patterns and discourses related to domestic nationalism, as well as to phenomena of high-budget productions. To exemplify this, in the 1950s history films relied on international co-productions and famous stars in order to ensure a large audience, but the peplum stories related to a past that no longer had historical relevance. This loss of contact with history and reality in history films certainly refers to the loss, in the 1950s, of the cultural relevance of classicism in Italian popular culture. The historical epics of the 1950s were, first, directed to an essentially low-class public, and second, as Brunetta (1998, p. 574) points out, the aura of history functioned in deflecting censorship, so that it justified the progressive uncovering of the female body. With their simplistic narratives, history films in the 1950s were taken as a mere exploitation of the genre. By contrast, Luchino Visconti's films *Senso* (1954) and *Il gattopardo* (1963) moved between imaginary tales of romance and a background of real historical events related to the Risorgimento and Italian unification. These films not only were the perfect blueprint for the nineteenth century historical novel, but they were constructing the past according to contemporary sentiments on the Left which attributed to the failure of the Resistance the same features as those involved in the failure of the Risorgimento.[8] Thus Visconti's films embedded contemporary cultural values, nevertheless adding visual spectacle to pleasurable narratives.

Similarly, the intensifying representations of Fascism during the 1970s said more about the present than about the past. The decade 1970–80 was another period of profound social and political conflict when fears of an imminent Fascist coup were fuelled by the strategy of tension put in place by the secret services. True to their political and industrial functions, films such as Bernardo Bertolucci's *Il conformista* and *Novecento*, (1970 and 1976 respectively), Federico Fellini's *Amarcord* (1973) and Liliana Cavani's *Il portiere di notte* (1974) expressed these anxieties alongside enjoying international success and awards.

Some elements of the classical form of history films (costume dramas) have remained in the Italian production up to the 1990s. The works of

Paolo and Vittorio Taviani and Franco Zeffirelli are perhaps the most exemplary representatives of this form. In their films, the use of costumes and attention to period detail, the hiring of international stars (a result of international funding) and the deployment of big and lavish sets are consciously exploited as elements recognisable by an international audience. However, these films are not exemplary of recent Italian cinema, and other than Zeffirelli's *Jane Eyre* and *Tea with Mussolini*, Italian costume films (period films) produced between 1988 and 1999 have rarely been successful on the international market, and have seldom been appreciated by the domestic audience. The discourse of the New Italian cinema has been constructed around another set of texts which deal more closely with individual existential memory. These texts have implications in connection with contemporary reality and raise questions related to generational issues which emerge in the form of memory as a general mourning for the loss of the Italian political radical past. Because of their address to a specific audience, their exploration of and return to *grand événements* and biography, and their symbolic function of sites of memory, a central part of *Recent Italian Cinema* presents the exploration of contemporary history films as the fundamental cultural preoccupation of the generation of 1968.

STRUCTURE OF THE BOOK

Chapter 1 provides an overview of the economic structure of the film industry, through its modes of production, distribution and exhibition. For nearly two decades, most Italian films have been produced outside box office returns, through a practice of subsidy and co-financing between many institutional and private entities. Thus Italian cinema had to define its mode of production and use-value of films in a different way. This chapter maps out in a practical way key moments and terms useful for understanding the current organisation of Italian cinema.

    Chapter 2 offers an analysis of Italy's current position in the global context of film production and circulation. The New International Division of Cultural Labour (NICL) (Miller et al. 2001) is a useful theoretical and practical tool in the examination of the relationship between the Italian film industry and international instances of production. The chapter presents a historical overview of Cinecittà and the renaissance of the studio in the late 1990s, thanks to a program of restructure that guaranteed its comeback on the map of international film production. The chapter addresses some aspects of Italian postwar cinema, in particular the 1950s and 1960s, because recent cinema cannot be separated from political, cultural and industrial transformations that occurred at this time. Recent Italian cinema is in fact a product of the changes in the economic infrastructures of the film industry, that was inevitably influenced by other major changes in technology and the industry at an international level.

The Piedmont region is one of the most active regions outside Rome and Milan in terms of promoting and branding its cultural products. Having secured the 2006 Winter Olympics, the city of Turin has undergone six years of cultural and architectural make-up, propped up by twenty years of long-sighted policy investing in cultural public life. Thus **Chapter 3** presents a case study of Turin as a creative city, examining its economic and cultural policy in connection with the urban entity by presenting the interplay of industry and image. The chapter then discusses broad themes to do with representation and cultural contexts in the depiction of Turin in several films produced between 1999 and 2005. The case study is a blueprint for other similar localised studies of clusters of film production in Naples, for example, or Milan, whose analysis would be most welcome in conjunction with the television industry.

Part II is concerned with the historical re-mapping of cultural and political elements affecting screen contexts. **Chapter 4** analyses how the hegemony of a specific political discourse in the postwar period can be taken into account to explain the enduring disdain of Italian critics toward the cinema of the late 1980s and 1990s. Cinema in Italy has always enjoyed considerable cultural prestige, not least because of the cultural policy of the Italian Communist Party (PCI) which included intellectuals in the representation of reality of rural and proletarian life. The currency of cinema in Italian cultural life decreased with its absorption by television in the 1980s. Essentially, film critics failed to recognise the need for media theory and for a reconceptualisation of film criticism and the role of the film critic.

Chapters 5 and 6 explore the space that historical revisionism occupies in Italian culture and the prominence of specific events in the cinema of the 1990s and early 2000s. These chapters offer an account of how, in a period of relative economic recovery and restoration of a new social and political conservatism, the Resistance, the Holocaust, 1968 and terrorism became a major preoccupation in Italian cinema. By arguing that such preoccupation with history and historical representations was a strategy for directors to legitimate themselves with an audience who shared the symbolic references of 1968, these two chapters describe a struggle over the interpretation of national history.

Finally, Part III examines the interplay of industry and image through the examination of two main aesthetic elements: the enclosed space and the landscape. In **Chapters 7 and 8** the reader returns to one of the two central subjects of the book, that is, how space highlights and mediates human experience of place. The intimate screen – the film for television – kept the film industry going in times of decline. This area of production is mostly unknown, as most of the films have never been discussed, criticised or reviewed, and often they were made but never circulated. The aesthetic of interiors is intimately bound to the scarcity of the means of production and to the production model imposed by television. But the claustrophobia of enclosed spaces crosses also to films with higher production values, perhaps to indicate the closure of horizons and possibilities after Tangentopoli and the entrance of Berlusconi into political life. On the other hand, the landscape film is surveyed through representations and structures concerning the Mediterranean region, which is also seen as a repository for tradition and renewal. Franco Cassano's Meridian thought is a useful tool for analysing the renewed interest in Mediterranean landscape by local directors and international production alike.

NOTES

Introduction

1. The Oscar® for Best Foreign Film was won in 2001 by *No Man's Land*, a Bosnian film in co-production with Italy, France and Belgium. Similarly to Salvatores' *Mediterraneo*, and Benigni's *La vita è bella*, this is a tragicomic war story.

2. This data is confirmed by Bagella (2000).

3. See Gianni Amelio's *Lamerica*, which did not recover its production budget, but was raised to cult status by Leftist critics.

4. Given that the United States is the country of close reading, it is not surprising that most of the texts about Italian cinema come from that country. See, for example Millicent Marcus's *After Fellini* (2002) and Giorgio Bertellini's collection *The Cinema of Italy* (2004). William Hope's *Italian Cinema: New Directions* (2005), and Gaetana Marrone's *New Landscapes in Contemporary Italian Cinema* (1999) are multi-authored studies and therefore do not offer a strong overarching conclusion as to what recent Italian cinema is, rather they continue to privilege trends in genres and *auteurs*. The third edition of Bondanella's *From Neorealism to Present* (2001) covers Italian cinema to the Second Millennium, but still privileges a reading of Italian cinema based on genres and authorship. A welcome departure that opens up the relationshio between Italian cinema and global cineama is *Italian Neorealism and Global Cinema* (2007), edited by Ruberto and Wilson, which examines the impact and influences of Italian neorealism on world cinema.

5. See Mario Sesti's *Nuovo Cinema Italiano* (1994); Sesti's edited collection *La 'scuola' italiana* (1996); Vito Zagarrio's *Cinema italiano anni novanta* (1998) and his two edited collections *Il cinema della transizione* (2000) and *La meglio gioventù* (2006).

6. See P. Ortoleva (1996) in the area of Italian media; David B. Clarke (1997) and Mark Shiel and Tony Fitmaurice (2001) on cinematic cities; Allen J. Scott (2000) on the cultural economy of cities; Ben Goldsmith and Tom O'Regan (2005) on global spaces of film production; Philip Cooke and Luciana Lazzaretti on local cultural development; and finally the already mentioned pivotal texts on global Hollywood by Toby Miller et al. (2001, 2005).

7. See the intimately bound relationship between Rome and Cinecittà, or Los Angeles and Hollywood.

8. Nonetheless, *Senso* fell under the axe of censorship provoking polemics in the Leftist community of critics who condemned Visconti for his definite departure from neorealism. By virtue of the accumulation of interpretations and critiques, *Senso* is today a canonical text.

PART I

NATIONAL, GLOBAL, LOCAL

1. ROLLING AWAY FROM THE CENTRE

The years of thoughtless happiness in the 1950s economic boom, followed by the brief period of exhilarating ideologies in 1968, are a pale memory. Exhaustion settled in the 1970s, and the brief second economic miracle of the 1980s reframed the post-terrorism period into a time of individual consumerism and self-referential representations of society. Localism re-emerged and grew in the 1980s with the political phenomenon of the Lega Nord. Since then, politics have been in a perennial state of chaos, with the deconstruction of the traditional party system after Tangentopoli, the inquiry into corruption of the public sector and the political class.[1]

Political change was achieved for the first time in 1996. However, internal factious in-fighting has persisted on both the left and right, making the second Berlusconi government between 2001 and 2006, ironically, the most stable in Italian postwar history. Between 2000 and 2007, the liberalisation of the European frontiers has produced massive migration from Eastern to Western Europe.[2] This has happened in an extraordinarily short time. The shift to the Euro dollar and the triple acceleration of the expansion of knowledge, technology and markets, which creates a false idea of global citizenship, have impoverished Italy, in particular affecting the lower classes and igniting deep racist sentiments and resistance to globalisation. Also, this combination of technological and economic changes under capitalism – what David Harvey (1990) labelled the 'time-space compression' – has created political and economic inequality, both globally and locally.

Between the end of 2004 and 2005, the Italian Gross Domestic Product (Prodotto Interno Lordo – PIL) collapsed to – 0.5 per cent; between 2000 and 2005, the increase in gross salary was among the lowest in Europe,[3] and in the year between 2002 and 2003, Italian families lost 1,896 Euros in their purchasing power, calculated on an average yearly income of 24,896 Euros. Italy's national economic growth has a direct consequence on the country's film industry because funding in the sector is tied to the PIL's performance. Thus impoverishment has not only had disastrous effects on individual purchasing power, but also directly on subsidies to the film industry, as well as in the rest of the cultural sector, including academic research, art and festivals which have all suffered funding cuts by the state.

Professionals in the cinema sector lament a lack of generational change instigated by specific state interventions and policy. From the middle of the 1970s, a structural and economic crisis of the Italian film system set in. At the end of the 1980s, filmmakers, referring to the collapse of the Italian film industry, also lamented the fragility of the industry, plagued by too many films "produced and abandoned". Therefore there is a sense of continuity between the 1980s and the second millennium in the fact that, despite cyclical small increases in production and distribution, and occasional box office successes, the Italian cinema industry is becoming a niche industry in its own country.

This chapter maps the period 1980–2006, from the decentralisation of film production that occurred in the 1980s to the development of film commissions in the late 1990s. It considers how decentralisation in the industry contributed to new modes of production, and consequently to a small recovery in the late 1980s. The chapter will present data related to production, distribution and exhibition, and current infrastructures, and will retrace the strategies adopted by the filmmakers to reach an increasingly fragmented audience as they worked in an industry that was progressively resembling a cottage industry.

"NEW" AS A RHETORICAL TROPE

The first institutional legitimation of the New Italian cinema came from France. In 1988, Jean A. Gili wrote in *Positif* that the first signs of renewal in Italian cinema started to appear in the films *Domani accadrà* (Daniele

Luchetti, 1987) and *La maschera* (Fiorella Infascelli, 1987) (Gili 1988, p 39). It was in fact at the 1988 Cannes Film Festival, in the section *Un certain regard*, that Luchetti's history film made a favourable impression on the audience. Words such as *jeune* (young) and *nouveau* (new) Italian cinema started to circulate internationally.

In the period 1988–96, Italian critics made a number of awkward attempts to define Italian cinema as neorealism, minimalist and *carino* (cute); thus the expression "new" was increasingly used by Italian critics (Quaresima 1991; Sesti 1994, 1996; Masoni and Vecchi 1995; Bo 1996; D'Agostini 1996). The numerous films produced in this period were made by new directors who worked in various styles, and were concerned with a range of themes. What puzzled the critics was that Italian cinema had developed variegated forms of expression that could not be related to revered and traditional paradigms of aesthetic criticism. In the critical literature, two specific terms were deployed: *nuovo* and *giovane* (new and young). Both words have been used in film studies in the past to designate avant-garde movements; prominent examples of such usage include neorealism, French Nouvelle Vague, the New American Cinema, the New German Cinema, the young generation of German filmmakers and the young generation of Chinese directors.

When *Nuovo Cinema Paradiso* (Giuseppe Tornatore, 1988) won the Cannes Film Festival, in 1989, the most important Italian producers called for a restructuring of the industry after a decade of chaotic decentralisation (Bruzzone 1989). There were two reasons for this, and both were essentially economic. On the one hand, in view of the unification of the European market (with the forthcoming Maastricht Treaty of 1992), the Italian film industry had to regain a competitive position in order to access European funds and strike co-production deals. On the other hand, it was necessary to return to international markets, and in particular the American market. Hence the enshrinement of Tornatore, Salvatores and Amelio in the auteurist pantheon became a necessary strategy to legitimise and make sense of the increase in domestic production. The international authentication of the three directors was fuelled by intense debate at home. For example, in the cases of *Cinema Paradiso* and *Mediterraneo*, Italian

': some exulted, but others claimed that the Americans
. unreal, provincial and anachronistic Italy, a country that
₋ponded to the American popular imaginary – that is, the stereotype
of a country of Sicilian migrants, artists and clumsy soldiers, suspended
between their dreams and reality (Morandini 1990; Masoni and Vecchi
1995; Grassi 1997). Nevertheless, like the New German directors'
contribution to the German film industry, the international success of
Nuovo Cinema Paradiso, Mediterraneo (1991), *Ladro di bambini* (1992)
and *Il Postino* (1995) started to put Italian cinema back on the international
stage and contributed to the relative revival of the industry. The word
"new" was therefore used as a rhetorical trope to designate an objective
condition: that recent Italian cinema spoke of new themes, and was largely
practised by new directors. Chapter 4 further analyses the interlocking
between film criticism and the emergence of a new cinema in the 1990s.

ACTORS

Actors are an important element of identification for audiences. Two
discourses relate to the power of stars. The first is that, once they cross into
the category of stars, their power and influence construct a popular
discourse of cinema. The second discourse relates to the political economy
of cinema, in that the presence of a star in a film guarantees returns on
investments. Since silent film, stars have established themselves as
economic entities, becoming more and more involved in the pre-
production phase selling a concept to investors. Much of the past glory of
Italian cinema in its own market was due to the phenomenon of *divismo*
(star system), which in the 1950s and 1960s was propelled by American
uptake of national popular actors and actresses to work in the United
States. In the early 1950s, three Italian actresses landed in New York for a
week devoted to Italian cinema. Silvana Mangano, Marina Berti and
Eleonora Rossi Drago brought their style of simplicity and 'elegant
matriarchy' (Caratozzolo 2006, p. 63) to New York, conquering American
women, and leaving a permanent mark on what Americans considered to be

the Italian look that was still remembered in 1965 in an article in the magazine *Time* (Caratozzolo 2006, p. 63).

Popular gossip and film magazines followed scandals involving directors and stars, from Rossellini's relationship with Ingrid Bergman to Sophia Loren and Carlo Ponti's adulterous relationship. Alberto Sordi, Vittorio Gassman and Marcello Mastroianni played an active symbolic role in the psyche of Italians as they became associated with the everyday man or with the existentialism of famous directors (Mastroianni as alter ego of Federico Fellini). Sophia Loren, Gina Lollobrigida, Silvana Mangano and Claudia Cardinale represented the typical Mediterranean beauty in national and international imaginaries. These actors and actresses exited their film roles and, as they increasingly became public figures, audiences became interested in their lives. But with the film crisis in the 1980s, there were no stars to replace the ageing celebrities. Audiences found it difficult to even remember the names of new actors and actresses. Enzo Montaleone commented in 2000 that:

> If you ask around the name of an Italian actor or director, they still tell you Sophia Loren, Mastroianni, Fellini. Two are dead, and one has not been working for long time. But these names still echo in the air. At the moment there is a group of new actors and actresses, who are thirty/forty years old, but the public ignore their existence because they never saw one movie with them. The films do not go on television.[4]

Television replaced cinema in the creation of celebrity in Italy. Almost every single comedian, after a stint in television where they established their popularity, crossed into cinema and then crossed again into television to market their films and to reinforce their celebrity status. Gossip and current affairs magazines such as those owned by the group Rcs Mediagroup (formerly Rcs Rizzoli), *Visto*, *Oggi* and *Novella*, and *Eva Express* owned by Hachette Rusconi, generate interest mainly around national television personalities linked to reality programs. As Marshall (2001) puts it, the 'television celebrity is configured around conceptions of familiarity' (2001, p. 119), whereas the film celebrity encapsulates the glamour of film, and thus plays at a distance. With cinema having lost its aura, Italian gossip magazines' endorsement of television popular personalities and starlets became an integral part of the media world that interpreted and mediated culture for audiences.

Nevertheless, a few new actors who started working in the 1980s were able to establish a career in the 1990s. Thanks to networks between directors and places of production (which is the topic for the following section), some actors worked on many films set in different parts of Italy, and thus had a continuous screen presence. Silvio Orlando, Diego Abatantuono, Claudio Bisio, Laura Morante, Claudio Amendola, Valeria Bruni Tedeschi, Enrico Lo Verso and Luigi Lo Cascio are among those who started acting in the late 1980s or early 1990s, while in the cinema of the second millennium, young new actors are emerging to incarnate doubts and passions of a new generation. These are Fabio Troiano, Nicola Vaporidis, Primo Reggiani and Anita Caprioli – all working in comedies or teenage films from either emerging or established directors.

Some actors have been able to embody cultural types which were repeated in various films, thus eliciting identification or pleasure in audiences. Stefano Accorsi's alluring personality builds on his look which is appealing to those aged 30 to 40, and especially to young women. He is the symbol of perennial youth, or of the typical adolescent who does not want to grow up. Accorsi played his first character in Pupi Avati's *Fratelli e sorelle* (1992). After participating in a television advertisement and in Wilma Labate's *La mia generazione* (1996), it was *Jack Frusciante è uscito dal gruppo* (1996), a film that typifies Accorsi as representative of his own generation, which launched him to a wide public. He is the main character in Luchetti's *I piccoli maestri* (1997), *Radiofreccia* (Ligabue, 1998) and *Ormai è fatta* (Enzo Montaleone, 1999). He played a character obsessed with pornography in Moretti's *La stanza del figlio* (2001), and was in the lead role in both *Le fate ignoranti* (Ferzan Ozpetek, 2001) and *L'ultimo bacio* (Gabriele Muccino).

Margherita Buy had already acted in *Domani accadrà* (Daniele

Luchetti, 1987), but made a breakthrough in Sergio Rubini's *La stazione* (1990), produced by Domenico Procacci. She has mainly played characters of fragile or rich spoilt woman. Since her role as a betrayed bourgeois wife in Ozpetek's *Le fate ignoranti* (2000), Margherita Buy has acted in another film by Ozpetek (*Saturno contro*, 2007), in *Caterina va in città* (Paolo Virzì, 2003) and with Carlo Verdone in *Manuale d'amore* (Giovanni Veronesi, 2005), always in roles of betrayed wife or a woman entangled in disastrous relationships. Margherita Buy is one of the most prolific actresses of the last twenty years, having acted in 39 films to date.

The most recent male stars of Italian cinema are Alessio Boni, who plays Matteo the troubled policeman in *La meglio gioventù* (Marco Tullio Giordana, 2003), and Riccardo Scamarcio, who plays Matteo's son in the same film. Alessio Boni comes from a background in theatre, having studied with Luca Ronconi. After participating in television series and working in theatre, he was discovered by Marco Tullio Giordana, who cast him in two films. Riccardo Scamarcio studied drama at the National School of Cinema in Rome and worked in several small-budget films, but it is through his role in *Tre metri sopra il cielo* (Luca Lucini), adapted from the best-seller with the same title, that he has become an idol for younger audiences. His most recent stint was a steamy sex scene with Monica Bellucci in *Manuale d'amore – 2* (Giovanni Veronesi, 2007).

The only two actresses with an international reputation are Valeria Golino and Monica Bellucci. Valeria Golino started her career with Lina Wertmuller and then acted in *Piccoli fuochi* (Peter Dal Monte, 1985) and other films until she moved to Hollywood. Here she was cast in *Rain Main* (Barry Levinson, 1988) as Tom Cruise's girlfriend, and in 2002 in *Frida* (Julie Taymor, 2002) as Lupe Marin, the first wife of Mexican artist Diego Rivera. But it was in Italy that Valeria Golino was offered parts as a main character, in *Le acrobate* (Silvio Soldini, 1997) and in *Respiro* (Emanuele Crialese, 2002). Monica Bellucci started her career as a model, and moved into acting with a small role in *Vita coi figli* (Dino Risi, 1990). She played in other small roles before playing one of the vampire seductresses in *Dracula* (Francis Ford Coppola, 1992). Giuseppe Tornatore's *Malena* (2000), distributed by Miramax, launched her on to the international stage, especially thanks to her archetypal Mediterranean look which continues the stereotype represented by Sophia Loren that is so fixed in national and international imaginary.

FROM LOCAL TO NATIONAL TO REGIONAL CINEMA

Cinema production in Italy started with localised infrastructures. The first cinematic cities were Turin, Naples and to a lesser extent Milan and Rome, but soon cinema shows spread in regional cities such as Bergamo, Varese, Florence, Genoa, Udine and in the countryside (Bernadini 1978). Production companies grew out of photographic studios and subsequently converged with exhibitors and the system of film exchange. Like the development of cinema in the United States, distribution was the most important element of an industry that needed a stable structure. Between 1907 and 1908, a shift occurred when local producers/exhibitors could no longer sustain the rapid growth of the demand and thus ensure the circulation of new products. Thus the emergence first of the exhibitor/distributor and then the professional distributor marked the beginning of a proper industrial structure.

With the creation of the Istituto Luce in 1925 and then Cinecittà in 1937 in Rome, Italian film production shifted and became concentrated in Rome, with failed attempts to establish other production centres in different parts of the peninsula. Mussolini well understood the potential of cinema in terms of imaginary and industry; thus film became the first national cultural industry, with a production arm directly controlled by those in power in Rome. Basically, the Fascist regime supervised and financed the entire industry. After the war, Rome and Cinecittà became intimately bound thanks to the arrival of Hollywood and its star system, which transformed Cinecittà from a national film studio to an international production epicentre. The fortunes of Italian films in this period are tied to those of Cinecittà. In the meantime, Milan established itself as the centre of advertising production (Ortoleva 1996, p. 191).

The production of genre films, the core activity of the film industry, was radically upset by the industry crisis of the mid-1970s. The decline of the spaghetti Western, the police genre and the Italian comedy corresponded with an increase in the production of soft-porn comedies, which had emerged in the late 1960s and continued through to the middle of the 1980s. The centre of production for these films was still Rome.

Important factors that coalesced to create the crisis were the restriction of production opportunities (three major studios in Cinecittà closed down or relocated overseas after Hollywood pulled out), the absence of a generational change of producers, directors and technicians, the restriction and marginalisation of spaces for film reviews in weekly magazines, the loss of a dialogue between critics and filmmakers, the technological backwardness of exhibition sites and the lack of an effective policy on broadcasting and film funding.[5] This was not only an Italian scenario: the international mass media system was also under pressure during the 1970s.

The crisis provoked the collapse of vertically integrated production. A process of decentralisation started, which produced what the Italian film historian Gian Piero Brunetta called '*polverizzazione della produzione*' (Brunetta 1991, p. 625), a fragmented archipelago of production scattered throughout the peninsula. There were two reasons for the shift from a vertical to a horizontal mode of production. The first has to do with the unpredictability of the Italian market and the inability of the Italian film industry to compete with US economies of scale. Thus the fragmentation served – as it did in many other European national cinemas – as a strategy for achieving production flexibility. Flexibility meant that directors, writers, cinematographers, producers, actors and other professionals could work in different productions in various capacities and in different locations/cities. This network of production came together on an *ad hoc* basis, scattering *de facto* film production throughout the peninsula, without appropriate policy that could sustain the shift. Hence Brunetta's metaphor of '*polverizzazione*', an archipelago of production.

The second reason – the growth of local television networks, with the consequent creation and reinvention of local economies based on advertising agencies and connected creative services – is strictly related to the first. In this scenario, a new generation of directors and professionals survived throughout the cinema crisis, trained and were ready for a generational change that came about in the late 1980s. Organised in independent cooperatives, from the early 1980s many production companies have been operating in specific territories (regional capitals) and have been able to create small creative clusters of professionals. European Union audiovisual policy has taken into particular account 'the development of countries and regions with low productive capacity and/or of small geographical and linguistic areas',[6] supporting the development of film production especially in the south of Italy.

Davide Ferrario, originally form Bergamo, moved to Turin simply because he likes the place,[7] and has now directed three films in the city. Guido Chiesa is also based in Turin, while Gabriele Salvatores' company Colorado Film and Silvio Soldini's Monogatari operate in Milan. Domenico Procacci's Fandango and Nanni Moretti's vertically integrated Sacher are based in Rome. Sacher is a point of reference for other directors such as Daniele Luchetti. Francesca Archibugi is based in Rome, while Tuscany is home to Roberto Benigni, Francesco Nuti, Leonardo Pieraccioni and Cinzia T.H. Torrini. The couple Daniele Ciprì and Franco Maresco, Roberta Torre, Pasquale Scimeca and Dante Majorana work in Sicily, while Mario Martone, Pappi Corsicato, Antonietta De Lillo, Antonio Capuano and Giuseppe Gaudino are based in Naples. Among these, many other independent filmmakers and professionals such as actors, screenwriters, cinematographers rotate and exchange collaborations with different companies and directors/producers, establishing a creative network throughout the Italian peninsula. As an example, Enzo Monteleone, originally from Padua, worked as screenwriter on Salvatores' early films, but also collaborated with Cinzia T.H. Torrini before moving to Rome, where he took up directing. Luca Bigazzi, director of cinematography for Amelio on several films, has also worked with many other filmmakers based in various locations throughout the peninsula.

Some actors and directors are associated in the national cinematic imaginary with specific geographical networks. For example, Diego Abatantuono acted in many films by Gabriele Salvatores which addressed the public mainly from a post-1968 leftist Milanese entourage, while actor Silvio Orlando has worked in three films set in Turin (two with Ferrario and one with Calopresti), but also in films produced by Rome-based companies, in particular Nanni Moretti's Sacher. Nanni Moretti's autobiographical films and characters identify with an anti-establishment intelligentsia.

Production flexibility in a transnational context also means economic returns to the domestic film industry. For example, *Dopo mezzanotte* (2003), which was a domestic audience success, is a small-budget film that relied on Davide Ferrario's own investment earned from a Miramax contract. He spent four months in New York writing a film that was never made. When he returned to Turin, he had enough money to make *Dopo mezzanotte*. There is thus a two-way relationship between national and global at a micro-level that has some effects on the ups and down of the film industry, as we will see in the case of Cinecittà in Chapter 2.

In the 1980s, despite the emergence of small clusters of production scattered along the peninsula, the financial centre was still Rome, because this is the centre of state bureaucracy. Daniele Segre spoke about his experience in seeking funding through the Article 28 in the mid 1980s for his film *Manila paloma bianca* (1992), pointing out that it was difficult to access funding without living in Rome because one had to network and go from office to office to follow up applications (Martini 1987a, p. 45). However, slowly the decentralisation of cultural policy started to take place. Following the appearance of multiple centres of production, since the end of the 1990s the Ministry for Heritage and Cultural Activities has beefed up its incentives for film productions and set up regional film commissions. The result is that there are now more possibilities for accessing public funding, and therefore a more dynamic and multifaceted cinema is emerging that is able to work at the local, national and international levels, maintaining and expressing regional cultural differences and diversifying its product in terms of genre, budget-range, production arrangements and locations. In the past directors who were typically linked to specific locations now set their films where they can find convenient infrastructure and subsidies. For example, Cinzia T.H. Torrini, who worked predominantly in Tuscany in the 1980s, has made two films in Piedmont, and Dario Argento has also produced in the region. Despite the limitations of distribution in the national context, Italian cinema of the third millennium promises to be one of the most creative in the country's history.

FILM COMMISSIONS

In 2000 the Italian film commissions became operational, although some had been instituted since 1997. They are supported by public institutions and their role is to promote the region, provide assistance – often free of charge – and supply all information necessary to assist audiovisual production (including ancillary industry such as the production of documentaries, shorts, music videos and advertising) in the territory. The aim is to promote the territory, whether in Italy or abroad, inducing film producers to take advantage of the urban and natural landscape, and of professional resources typically linked to a specific place. The film commissions create a network between local industries, producers and professionals, and regional institutions. There are currently 24 film commissions scattered along the peninsula. Some are regional, some are local - for example, the Arezzo Film Commission (Tuscany), the Italian Riviera Film Commission (Liguria), the Capri Film Bureau (Campania) and the Portofino Film Commission, which is funded by the Fondazione Mediterraneo, Genoa City Council and Sestri Levante Council. Local film commissions are clearly set up to take advantage of specific natural and urban environments. Each commission has specific aims linked directly to the culture of a place. For example, the Bologna Film Commission directs its efforts to researching and supporting emerging talents, while CinemaRomaCittà, partly funded by Cinecittà Holding, is committed to events with an international focus. Table 1.1 lists the film commissions up to 2007. The Italian Film Commission, a division of the Italian Trade Commission, has been set up in Los Angeles, operating as promotion office for the Italian audiovisual industry. Its aim is to coordinate international production in various Italian locations in collaboration with the local film commission. It also sponsors the Los Angeles Italian Film Awards, which began in 1998 to promote Italian cinema in the United States.

TABLE 1.1 FILM COMMISSIONS TO 2007

Northern Italy	Central Italy	Southern Italy
Bologna Film Commission	Abruzzo Film Commission	Alberobello Puglia Film Commission
Emilia Romagna Film Commission	Arezzo Film Commission	Calabria Film Commission
Film Commission Torino	Piemonte Lazio Film Commission	Campania Film Commission
Friuli Venezia Giulia Film Commission	Lucca Film Commission	Capri Film Commission
Genova Set Film Commission	Marche Film Commission	Catania Film Commission
Italian Riviera Commission	Roma Cinema Film Commission	Sardegna Film Commission
Lombardia Film Commission	Umbria Film Commission	Sicilia Film Commission
Veneto Film Commission	Toscana Film Commission	Siracusa Film Commission

Source: Italian Film Commission (2007).

CULTURAL POLICY AND CINEMA

During Fascist rule, Italy was one of the first countries to create a ministry for the cultural sector. At this time, a large part of the cultural legislation was to support heritage. However, there were provisions that supported creativity, copyright interests and the commissioning of art in public buildings (2 per cent) (Council of Europe/ERI/Carts 2002). A key turning point in Italian cultural policy occurred in 1970 and 1971 after the creation of regions as autonomous administrative entities. This created a demand for more decentralisation which remained unfulfilled by the state. At this stage, the main objectives of cultural policy were the protection and preservation of heritage. However, new economic emphasis on the production of immaterial goods and services in the 1980s was fundamental to eliminating the last barriers to innovation and decentralisation (Council of Europe/ERI/Carts 2002). In 1998, the left government headed by the first (ex)-communist prime minister since 1947, Massimo D'Alema, instituted the Ministry for Heritage and Cultural Activities. Its role was to include cinema, copyright, media and the performing arts within the definition of culture and heritage. Thus, from an understanding of the cultural industry as a *society of spectacle*, intimately connected with localised places of exhibition (whether cinematic or artistic), the concept of culture shifted to the *society of information*, which included the activity of all the mass media creating the media space, and finally to the *global society*, which creates a virtual space for individualised consumption, dislocation of means of production and activities. Only in the early 1990s was the need for a program of innovation and transformation in cultural policy recognised, and between 1998 and 2000 all cultural activities became rationalised and overseen by the Department of Cultural Heritage, which extended its function to cultural activities (Associazione per l'economia della cultura 2005). Until then, legislation and regulation in cultural matters were extremely fragmented. In fact, one of the objectives of the reorganisation of cultural policy is to drive and control the process of decentralisation, rather than leaving this to spontaneous arrangements. In fact, much of the debate around cultural policy involved the dichotomy of devolution versus centralism.

There is no definition of culture in Italy, but because of the country's active involvement in international organisations, Italy agreed upon the European Union's definition of culture. This covers heritage, archives, libraries, visual arts, architecture, performing arts, books and the press, and cinema and audiovisual. Thus the definition of cultural industries in Italy rests on a list of activities which includes 'cinema, audiovisual production, performing arts, music, publishing and printing, music industry, cultural tourism and design' (Presidenza del Consiglio dei Ministri, Commissione per la garanzia dell'informazione statistica 2004). In 1999, there were around half a million people employed in the cultural sector.

Italian cultural policy was also biased by the dilemma between protection and enhancement which was seen as exploitation of cultural heritage. However, from the 1990s both the state and the regions have invested considerably in the sector, recognising the importance of actively promoting Italian cultural assets, while private investments have decreased. Some regions of the north and centre of Italy, specifically Piedmont, Umbria and Marche, have increased their investments in the cultural industry, while regions in the continental south, despite the fact that they are rich in cultural heritage, have decreased their expenditure, exposing once more the geographical imbalance between north and south in terms of cultural investments and consumption.

The cultural policy system works through four levels of government – state, regions, provinces and municipalities – with different levels of activities and responsibilities. For example, provinces are active in coordinating public cultural institutions (for example, libraries), while municipalities oversee the direct management of museums, archives, libraries, municipal theatres and so on. The state is the only responsible for the protection of heritage.

The 1990s was the decade in which the challenge to reform television, cinema and the rest of the audiovisual sector was most felt, especially because of the drop in national production and audience attendance. In relation to audiovisual resources, the duopoly Rai and Mediaset continued to collect 90 per cent of the resources and the public, thanks to large investments of advertising and sponsorship. Cinema attracts the largest slice of public funding (267 billion lira in 1990, which decreased to 189 in 2000, with an average of 170 billion lira yearly in the 1990s).[8]

Laws concerning cinema have been passed as law-decrees, and they are all modifications and amendments to the 1965 law on cinema, Law 1213, the so called Legge Corona. The law *Interventi urgenti in favore del cinema* (Urgent intervention in favour of the cinema) that was passed in 1994 (the first substantial modifications after 29 years) emphasised the difference between 'national' feature films and film with national cultural interest. In the first case, all films (with the exception of pornographic films) could access state grants up to 70 per cent of the budget, with a ceiling of 8 billion lira, while the second category of films could be financed up to 90 per cent of their budget by public funding. Films with particular artistic qualities could also access the quality bonus, a heritage from the 1950s and 1960s. Under the new law, the Italian look was defined by the use of a series of indicators, such as language, Italian settings, nationality of the director, main characters and the rest of the crew, post-production (it must be carried out in Italy) and themes (the film must be relevant to Italian culture). The famous art. 28 in the legistaltion (which I will discuss in another section) was replaced by art. 8.

Two important innovations were introduced in 1998 (Law 122) with the new amendments to the 1994 law. The first was the introduction of new regulations for television to broadcast European film and fiction for more than 50 per cent in their monthly schedule, of which 10 per cent must be given to independent producers. The definition of 'independent' is borrowed from the European Union legislation, which regards a producer as independent when the company or individual is not affiliated to a television network or has not worked for three years for only one broadcaster. The second innovation was the introduction of a 10 per cent quota of television advertising income for the production and purchase of European programs. From 1999, Rai was obliged to reserve at least 20 per cent from its licence fees to the production of European works. These redirections of income produced an improvement in local production, especially for television fiction[9] which has now replaced American fiction in prime time.

A new legislative decree was passed in February 2004. It operates through the Commission for Cinematography, overseen by the Ministry for Cultural Assets and Activities. Two sub-commissions operate in different stages of the funding submission. One assesses films in the project stage under the rubric of 'Film of National Cultural Importance', as well as the requisites necessary to establish that a film is an art film, while the second sub-commission verifies whether a work is consistent with the original project presented. Importantly, the new decree admits companies from countries that belong to the European Union to the same benefits that Italian companies enjoy, as long as most of the activities linked to the production of the film are carried out in Italy. A new fund for film production, distribution and exhibition continues to be managed by the Banca Nazionale del Lavoro.

HOW TO MAKE A FILM

There are several bodies and agencies that can be accessed to obtain subsidies. State subsidies, regional funds, transnational co-productions, European funds such as the successive MEDIA I (1991–95), MEDIA II (1996–2000) and MEDIA PLUS (2000–06), the European development SCRIPT, television production and pre-sales are ways to secure funding coordinated by small production companies. In this way, the producer becomes mainly the executive producer, or a packager, and films are almost always organised around the producer–director–actor or writer–producer–director triangulation. The use of European and state policies in the last ten years has been a method of broadening the financial base and the circulation of Italian films on the larger European market. State and European subsidies are related because securing support from one of the funds available at European level facilitates the film receiving national subsidies.

In the 1980s, with a total absence of regulations, the duopoly Rai-Fininvest financed almost all film production. At the end of the 1980s, this duopoly broke down when Cecchi Gori formed Penta with Berlusconi. Penta was to oversee all the cycles, from production to distribution, marketing of musical scores, audiovisual distribution and production with American partners through its arm Pentapictures, based in Los Angeles. Basically, with the acquisition of the publishing house Mondadori, Berlusconi came to control almost all the Italian cultural production, and in particular he controlled the life-cycle of a film. Many directors produced with Penta, from Salvatores to Benigni to the Taviani brothers.

History films, a stable product in Italian film history, could access both European funds and national funds, as they fell under the classification of film of 'national cultural interest'. European Union cultural policy is based on the article 128 of the Institutive Treaty of the European Union, which was adopted with the Maastricht Treaty in 1992. Interestingly, Article 128 stresses the importance of the improvement and diffusion of 'historical and cultural knowledge of European people'. The MEDIA Program reiterates the same concept in its objectives:

> The action of the community is double: it intends, on the one hand, to use the audiovisual sector to reaffirm the cultural prestige of 'old Europe'; on the other, to stimulate market spaces for a European cinema and television industry with such characteristics that could compete on the international market. (Per fare spettacolo in Europa 1996, p. 31)

The two expressions 'historical and cultural knowledge' and 'cultural prestige of Europe' are explicitly constructed around established categories of high culture, commonly related to art and history as means to human knowledge and achievement, consciousness and identity. From the symbolic allusion to antiquity embedded in history films at the turn of the twentieth century, these markers of European cultural prestige were transformed and translated in the art film in the 1960s. The parameters that the European Community cultural policy sets today are designed to achieve this notion of quality, defined against historical value. In other words, the marketing of history and nostalgia is set in the policy, and many European directors – not only Italian – have benefited from these rhetorical tropes to access European funding. The spate of history films produced in Italy in the 1990s (all films achieved a status of 'film of national cultural interest') benefited from Eurimages or MEDIA funds. In this way, the history film in Italy served a double function: one had to do with reacting against external threats and painful ideas, restoring some sort of self-worth; the second related to deliberate thematic choices in order to access both national and European funding.

Article 28 was instituted in 1965 to fund films with artistic intentions and was very little used in the 1970s, but after the crisis it became a staple in film production. The '28', as it notoriously became known among young directors, was used to fund first feature films, becoming a proper production structure. In the 1980s, few of the films produced with the 28 reached a regular distribution and exposure in theatres. There are very few films that were able to repay the loan from the state. Those which did include Salvatore Piscicelli's *Immacolata e Concetta* (1979) and *Le occasioni di Rosa* (1981), and Nanni Moretti's *Ecce Bombo* (1978). Between 1966 and 1985, 174 films were produced with the 28, with an increase in the 1980s (Martini 1987a, p. 38). Among the best films produced with the 28 were the Tavianis' *I sovversivi* (1967), Vittorio Orsini's *I dannati della terra* (1969), Giuliano Ferrara's *Il sasso in bocca* (1970), Marco Tullio Giordana's *Maledetti vi amerò* (1979) and Antonietta De Lillo's *Una casa in bilico* (1984). Many of the films produced with the 28 were supported by Gaumont distribution and two films, both produced in 1986, signalled the beginning of a new interest by US distributors in Italian cinema. These films were Cinzia Torrini's *Hotel Colonial* (1986) (Columbia distribution) and Peter Del Monte's *Piccoli fuochi* (20th Century Fox). In 1994, Article 28 was substituted with Article 8, but the conceptual framework remained unchanged.

PRODUCTION

If we take the Hollywood studio system as a paradigm, the only companies in Italy that have ever come close to it, with an integrated system of production, distribution and exhibition, were Titanus and Lux, both operating in the 1950s, Cecchi Gori group in the 1990s and Medusa Film in the second millennium. In the 1980s, as we have seen, films were produced either through the duopoly Rai-Fininvest or through a combination of television and state funding. State subsidies for first feature films were provided through the Article 28. These elements defined the Italian cinema mode of production in the period 1980–90, and conceptualised it in terms of political economy and narrative strategies. In that decade, high labour costs influenced the number of shooting weeks, which were reduced from an average of eight/nine weeks to six or seven, and imposed cuts to the number of professionals on set. Producers opted mainly for an executive role, which meant managing money found elsewhere. Basically, there were very few production companies that invested capital directly. The trend that emerged in the period 1980–85 was that of a very fragmented industry. Table 1.2 highlights that production companies produced an average of one film each, indicating that companies were formed around specific projects mainly to protect the director's creative work and rights.

In the same period, the production companies with the most consistent number of films were Dania and Capital, which then became CG Silver and then Cecchi Gori. Some of the companies listed below specialised in popular, low-budget comedies (Cecchi Gori, Italian International Film, Filmauro). Other companies specialised in the soft-porn genre, especially linked to the couple Lino Banfi-Edwige Fenech (Dania, Medusa and Filmes) (Martini 1987b, pp. 23–24). Many of the companies with single productions disappeared from one year to the next, confirming their opportunistic creation (see Table 1.3).

This situation continued throughout the 1990s, more than doubling the number of production companies from 200 to more than 500 in 2000 (see Figure 1.1). At the same time, some groups that functioned like majors – as

TABLE 1.2 FILMS PRODUCED BY PRODUCTION COMPANIES, 1980–85

Year	No. of films produced	No. of production companies
1980–81	87	63 (plus Rai)
1981–82	109	78 (plus Rai)
1982–83	112	84 (plus Rai)
1983–84	104	73 (plus Rai)
1984–85	97	81 (plus Rai)

Source: Adapted from *Cineforum*, no. 3, March 1987.

they took up also distribution and the audiovisual market – consolidated. With the already mentioned Penta, which became Medusa Film in 1995, Cecchi Gori became the most important player on the Italian scene. However, data collected in 2004 confirm that the majority of Italian production companies are small, artisan-like enterprises, as the companies employing between one and four people constitute 65.4 per cent of the total of production companies (*Il mercato cinematografico italiano, 2000–2004).* In a capitalist economy, this small-scale system of production implies that artisanal production 'lies outside the dominant system' (Pam Cook, quoted in

TABLE 1.3 AVERAGE NUMBER OF FILMS PRODUCED ANNUALLY BY EACH PRODUCTION COMPANY

Production company	No. of films produced each year (average) in the period 1980–85
Dania	6/7
Capital (Cecchi Gori)	5
International Italian Film	3
Clemi	3
Dean	3
Filmauro	2/3
Faso	1/6
Ama	2
Opera	2

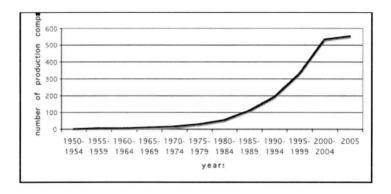

FIGURE 1.1 THE GROWTH IN THE NUMBER OF PRODUCTION COMPANIES
Source: Il mercato cinematografico italiano, 2000–2004 Cinecittà Holding

Elsaesser, 1989, p. 42), requiring support through patronage or from state institutions.

Three factors indicate a partial recovery of the Italian cinema system. Towards the end of the millennium, the figure of the producer as investor and talent-scout that was lost in the 1970s re-emerged. Second, a whole new generation of professionals – screenwriters, cinematographers, directors and actors – reinvigorated the industry. The third factor was the series of reforms kicked off by the centre-left government which, despite their inadequacy in the face of the acceleration of the global communication system and of the emergence of multiple delivery platforms, contributed to bringing Italian cultural policy to the level of other European nations, namely France and Great Britain.

Table 1.4 indicates investments in 2005 and 2006 production with 100 per cent Italian capital. It must be noted that films considered to be produced in these two years have benefited from public subsidy in previous years. The most important factor to note from Table 1.4 is that private investments grew more than public subsidies, which leads to two observations. The first is that regulations and the new law on cinema are still largely inadequate *vis-à-vis* the industry; the second is that Italian cinema is slowly shifting from a subsidised system to a capitalist mode of production because of the concentration of media and other delivery

TABLE 1.4 INVESTMENTS IN 2005 AND 2006 PRODUCTION WITH 100 PER CENT
ITALIAN CAPITAL

Production	2006	2005	Difference 2006/05
Films produced	90	68	+22
Films of national cultural interest (financed)	15	6	+9
Films produced with funds from Art. 8	2	6	−4
Films produced with OPS* funds	4	2	+2
Total films produced with state subsidies	21	14	+7
State investments in films produced (million €)	37.1	21.8	+15.3
Private investments (million €)	150.5	130.3	+20.2
Total investments with 100 per cent Italian capital (million €)	187.6	152,1	+35.5
Average investment per film (million €)	2.08	2.24	−0.16

*OPS stands for Opere Prime e Seconde (First and Second Features)

Source: *Ufficio Studi/CED ANICA*

platforms, even though a system of indirect subsidy such as tax incentives for investments in cinema has still yet to be implemented. In 2006, Italian state funds represented less than 20 per cent of the total investments. As a comparison, in 2006 French public funding, whose regulations subsidise through a system of direct funds and indirect incentives, amounted to around 49 per cent of the total investments in the film industry.

However, to the total public subsidies for films produced in 2006 indicated in the table there needs to be added nearly 48 million Euros in films which in 2006 have received finances from the three funds and from the script development fund, but which have not yet started production. Thus in 2006 the total investment by the Italian state in cinema was close to 85 million Euros. In the period 2000–04, state subsidies have increased 76.35 per cent, with the highest proportion of the funds distributed to films of national cultural interest, representing an average of 87 per cent on the total of state subsidies.

Currently, the average cost of a film produced with 100 per cent Italian capital is two million Euros, one-third of the average cost of a French film, and this amount has been stable for the last five years.[10] Co-productions provide a higher financial base, which in turn allows for higher production values. At present, the average cost of a film in co-production arrangements is eight million Euros.

INDEPENDENT PRODUCERS 1: COLORADO FILM

Colorado Film, founded in 1986, is synonymous with Gabriele Salvatores, Maurizio Totti and Diego Abatantuono. Since it began, Colorado has produced all Salvatores' films, often with exceptional success – as the Oscar for *Mediterraneo* demonstrates. *Kamikazen* (1987), *Puerto Escondido* (1992) and *Sud* (1993) were produced in collaboration with Cecchi Gori. Colorado Film has also made television advertising, shorts and video clips.

Gabriele Salvatores has distinguished himself since the early 1970s as the founder of Teatro dell'Elfo in Milan, which attracted a large public, especially the left-wing intelligentsia of the student movement. After a slow start with a debatable film, *Kamikazen – Ultima notte a Milano*, Salvatores' breakthrough as a film director arrived with *Marrakech Express* in 1989, which is the first of a series of films based on Salvatores' authorial elements: men's friendship, the theme of the trip as escape and generational solidarity. The group of films that followed – *Sud*, *Nirvana* (1997), *Denti* (2000) and *Amnesia* (2001) – is a collection of experiments in different genres and modes of narration.[11] With *Io non ho paura* (2003), the film adapted from Niccolò Ammaniti's book, Salvatores found again his way to the top of the box office. This was a co-production with Medusa, with a budget of three million Euros (Vivarelli 2004, pp. 88–89). The film was distributed in the United States by Miramax. In his latest film, *Quo Vadis, Baby?* (2006), Salvatores experiments with film noir, adapting Grazia Verasani's book of the same title. The book was published by the newly founded (2004) Colorado Noir book unit, confirming the tendency among independent producers to integrate film production with ancillary activities such as publishing to ensure they retain copyrights from successful books that can be translated into film scripts.

Around Colorado, a group of actors formed who partly came from the Teatro dell'Elfo and partly from the Milanese tradition of cabaret. Among these actors are Claudio Bisio, Paolo Rossi and Gigio Alberti. Silvio Orlando, who also works with Nanni Moretti and Davide Ferrario – thus establishing a triangular connection between Milan, Turin and Rome – joined the group as the main character in *Sud*. However, early Salvatores films were centred around the persona of Diego Abatantuono, also from the Milanese cabaret entourage. After acting and collaborating in Carlo Vanzina's popular comedies in the early 1980s (*I fichissimi, Viulentemente, Eccezzziunale veramente*), in which he played a vulgar, fake southerner, and Castellano and Pipolo's flop *Attila, flagello di Dio* (1982–83), Diego Abatantuono had two years off from working until Pupi Avati rescued him with a role in *Regalo di Natale* (1986). Salvatores' *Turné* (1990) typecast Abatantuono as a disillusioned, tragicomic character, which was to become his trademark in subsequent films with the Milanese director. Abatantuono's merit was his creation of a new cinematic comedian impersonating the *italiano medio* (everyday Italian) with a Milanese accent, in contrast with the Romanesque accent of Alberto Sordi, Vittorio Gassman or Carlo Verdone, thus catering for the specific Milanese audience. In 2002, Diego Abatantuono founded Colorado Café, a 'factory' for new comedians who perform at the Teatro dell'Erba in Milan and whose performances are also broadcast on television in a program called *Colorado Café*.

Colorado Film operates through two offices, in Milan and Rome. Ancillary activities of Colorado Film include the talent scout agency Moviement (headed by Maurizio Totti), which manages, among others, Monica Bellucci, Christophe Lambert, the athlete Giorgio Rocca and some soccer players.

INDEPENDENT PRODUCERS 2: FANDANGO

In the late 1980s, Domenico Procacci founded a cooperative called Vertigo with Renzo Rossellini, son of Roberto, and other colleagues. In 1990, Procacci produced Sergio Rubini's *La stazione*, under the name of Fandango. The film was a box office hit. Procacci continued to produce small-budget films with young directors, which received good audience and critical reception. The company's profile rests on the production of quality films, either commercial or *d'autore* (*auteur* films). In 1992, Domenico Procacci began working with Australian *auteur* Rolf De Heer by acting as executive producer on almost all of his films (*Bad Boy Bubby*, *Epsilon*, *Dance Me to My Song*, *The Tracker* and *Alexandra's Project*). Procacci's choice to work with Rolf De Heer stems from De Heer's own production practices, conceptually similar to Procacci's approach to production. The Australian director has produced and directed predominantly low-budget films, thanks to an integrated approach to filmmaking that results from carefully chosen locations, filming in sequence, using small, familiar, multi-skilled crews working in flexible ways and, most importantly, the fact that De Heer is himself the scriptwriter, producer and director (Ferrero-Regis 2004, pp. 88–89).

Despite the confrontational story, Procacci presented *Bad Boy Bubby* at the Venice Film Festival, where it won the Jury Prize. *Alexandra's Project*, a suburban thriller, was selected for the Official Competition at the 2003 Berlin festival even before delivery (Ferrero-Regis 2004, pp. 88–89). The Australian adventure did not stop at Rolf De Heer, as Procacci picked up the distribution rights for other Australian features, carving a niche market for Australian art films in Italy. These films were *Looking for Alibrandi*, *He Died with a Felafel in His Hands* (which Procacci also co-produced), *The Goddess of 1967*, *Angel Baby* and *Lantana*. In Australia, Domenico Procacci also began a working relationship with Antonio Zeccola, the owner of a chain of cinemas, Palace, who had also become a producer, and as well had been the organiser of a national Italian Film Festival since 2000. Domenico Procacci's dealings with the Australian film industry proved so successful that in 2002 he launched the company Fandango Australia, promising to co-produce films in Australia using domestic and European finance.[12] According to Procacci, 'working with Australia means to work in English and that means potentially to have a very large market' (Cosolovich 2002). Partners in Fandango Australia are directors Rolf De Heer and Richard Lowestein, and producers Sue Murray and Bryce Menzies.

Two films helped Fandango to launch into multi-million Euro revenues: in 1998, *Radiofreccia*, directed by the popular Luciano Ligabue, topped the box office and in 2001 Gabriele Muccino's *L'ultimo bacio*, which took 18 million Euros at the Italian box office, literally launched Muccino and Fandango into the international arena.

Film distribution started in 2000 with *Il partigiano Johnny*, by Guido Chiesa, followed by the Australian box office hit *Lantana* (Ray Lawrence). Revenues from feature films have enabled Procacci to turn his attention to documentaries, which deliver prestige to the company. In the process of branding the *factory* Fandango, the company has been diversifying in publishing and music labelling, through which Procacci can control book and music copyrights. Fandango is based in Rome, where it has opened Café Fandango as a selling point for the company's production (films, publishing, music). Café Fandango also organises talks and forums about cinema.

INDEPENDENT PRODUCERS 3: SACHER FILM

Io sono un autarchico (1976) and *Ecce Bombo* (1978) paved the way for Nanni Moretti to become an accomplished filmmaker. When in 1987 Nanni Moretti and Angelo Barbagallo founded Sacher Film, Moretti was already known in Europe, as he had won the Silver Bear at the 1986 Berlin Film Festival with *La messa è finita* (and had already received favourable reviews by *Cahiers du cinéma* for *Ecce Bombo*). Sacher Films started its production activities in 1987 with three films directed by Carlo Mazzacurati (*Notte italiana*), Daniele Luchetti (*Domani accadrà*, 1988) and Moretti (*Palombella rossa*, released in 1989). Daniele Luchetti had worked for long time in advertising and casting for television before becoming an assistant director on *Bianca* (1984) and *La messa è finita* (1985), both directed by Nanni Moretti. Mazzacurati had also worked in television as screenwriter. With the creation of Sacher Film, Moretti aspired to produce medium budget films with good production values targeted to the Italian market.

Both *Notte italiana* and *Domani accadrà* were presented at the Cannes Film Festival and favourably impressed the French critics who inaugurated the definitions 'new' and 'young' Italian cinema. With *Caro Diario* Nanni Moretti achieved international reputation, as the film was awarded the Palm d'Or in 1994 and distributed widely. Mimmo Calopresti's film *La seconda volta* (1995) had already obtained funding via Article 28 when Moretti and Barbagallo came on board and secured additional funding from the French La Sept Cinéma, Canal Plus and Italian public channel Rai Uno. The film, released in 1996, was Sacher's most successful film to date. With the release of the film and Moretti's own *Caro Diario*, in the period 1994–97 Sacher Film was the production company in Italy with the best ratio between budget and revenues (*Il settore cinematografico italiano*, 1998, p. 148).

Nuovo Sacher, a cinema dedicated to showing independent Italian and foreign films unable to make it in the mainstream circuit, opened in 1991. Since 1996, Moretti has hosted a festival of shorts, the Sacher Festival, and from 1997, with the founding of the distribution company Tandem, Moretti and Barbagallo came to control the whole system of film production, distribution and exhibition. Finally, Nanni Moretti was appointed artistic director of the Turin Film Festival, which is dedicated to art cinema and independent films. Compared to similar festivals, the Turin International Film Festival lacked glitz and never received due consideration from the mainstream media, although it is well respected among professionals. After only two days in as director, Moretti stepped down, reportedly due to tensions and disputes about his appointment among some of the organisers of the festival. Nevertheless, Moretti returned to direct the festival in the hope of drawing international attention to the event. This recent appointment confirms Moretti as the Italian mentor of independent and art cinema.

DISTRIBUTION AND EXHIBITION

By the end of the 1970s, the consumption of film on television replaced second- and third-run cinemas, usually located in the outer suburbs and accessed by the lower classes. From four tickets per capita on average in 1981, tickets sales fell to 2.2 per capita in 1985. To the disappearing audience, exhibitors responded with rising ticket prices. Historically, both distribution and exhibition have been fragmented – and they are both crucial phases in the life of a film. The disorganisation of the exhibition system was consequently one of the elements that contributed to the decline of cinema attendance in the 1970s, and later favoured the opening of exhibition theatres operated by the American majors whose practice of market saturation with many prints ensures large revenues. Distribution and exhibition are thus two elements that must be discussed together to understand how global concentration in both results in the marginalisation of local films.

As an example, at the end of the 1970s, one of the important causes of falling admissions was the theatres' technological backwardness. Low levels of investment by Italian exhibitors held back modernisation and the refurbishment of theatres, and it was not until the end of the 1980s that improvements in the quality of exhibition sites contributed to a growth in admissions. Even in 1992, only the big cities like Milan and Rome had multi-screen complexes: screens equipped with Dolby systems or with a 70mm projection were still below European averages. The improvement in technology in cinema theatres was mainly due to Hollywood major distribution and exhibition companies' investments in Europe in the 1980s. The arrival of special effects and big-budget films warranted US upgrade of European theatres. For example, majors like Warner Bros invested in new picture theatres in decentralised areas of Italy.[13]

The first Romano Prodi government (1996–98) accelerated deregulation in theatre exhibition; thus first-run cinemas and multiplexes started to function on a full scale in city centres and outer suburbs. In this period, it is possible to note the emergence of three major players in the sector. Arco (De Pedys) owned 195 screens over 69 towns, Cecchi Gori had 67 screens concentrated in Rome and Florence, and Cinema 5 (Berluconi's film exhibition arm) owned 75 screens in eleven towns (*Il settore cinematografico italiano* 1998, p. 116). Interestingly, Cinema 5 does not privilege Medusa's films in its own exhibition circuit. In 1996, no major players operated in the South of Italy, where the number of tickets sold per capita was below one. At present in the Italian peninsula, there are 83 multiplex structures operating 859 screens (ANICA, 2004). Cinetel, the agency that collects daily admissions and box office on 70 per cent of the Italian screens, distinguishes between multiplexes – structures with at least eight screens - and multicinemas - which are structures with five to seven screens. In 2004, together they covered 53 per cent of the market with a return of 30 per cent more than the national average. The result is that Hollywood films, which are heavily promoted and distributed with many prints,[14] are the films saturating multiplexes in their first run, and the international market is a crucial factor in their profit. Because multiplexes are managed by American companies, the multiplication of screens has only produced the multiplication of projections of the same film.

In 2004, the top twenty films at the international box office were American, or some kind of co-production arrangement between the US and two or more European countries.[15] For eighteen films out of twenty, revenues from the international market were higher than the US takings. Hollywood majors recover production and marketing costs from their domestic market, so that the revenues from the international circuit have already been amortised. Even films considered a flop by Hollywood's moguls, such as *Troy* (Wolfgang Peterson, 2004), which made 'only' US$133 million domestically, thus did not recover its production budget of US$150 million, to which must be added US$45 million for prints and advertising. However, the film made a profit as it took US$364 million internationally. To aid pan-European distribution and exhibition against the Hollywood tsunami, the European Union has developed the network Europa Cinemas, part of the MEDIA program, which provides financial support to cinemas that show European films, partly redressing the balance. In 2007, there were more than 1,800 screens in the network showing European films as 61 per cent of their annual output.

One important factor in Italian distribution is its seasonal trend. Traditionally, Italian first runs concentrate during Spring and Autumn, with an increase in December (with the Christmas film, usually a comedy). Looking at data (*Il mercato cinematografico italiano*, 2004–06), it emerges that during Summer there is a concentration of non-Italian first runs, but it also emerges that there is a progressive adjustment from Hollywood to the Italian film season.

Data on distribution in multiplexes and the rise of their favour with the Italian public contradict a study commissioned by MEDIA Salles to the Italian university Bocconi about the rise or fall in audiences and audience behaviour (*European Cinema Journal - MEDIA Salles*, 2003, p. 2), which points to the methodological difficulty of pinpointing audience tastes. The researchers found out that the 15- to 34-year-old demographic in the various European territories is the sector of the public that tends to favour the multiplex formula, but there is great variation in the composition of population by age from country to country. In Italy, the 15–35 age range represents only 28 per cent of the total population, and is likely to drop further because of the fall in the birth rate. The researchers suggested that it would be wise in Italy not to invest in youth-oriented forms of exhibition, and to instead take into account the territory in terms of cultural and urban characteristics. Thus the exhibition system should be more diversified, with networks of smaller cinemas offering broader choices in terms of film genres. Further research conducted in 1996 on audiences' behaviour (*Il settore cinematografico italiano*, 1998) reported that 54 per cent of the Italian population does not go to the movies, and those who go a few times a year represent 21 per cent. People who go to the cinema between one and three times a year represent 20 per cent of the population, and a small core of movie buffs who go to the movies once a week corresponds to 4 per cent of the sample. A film is chosen not because of the theatre, but because it makes the headlines - which means an increasingly small number of films are getting a correspondingly larger slice of the box-office receipts.

What can be inferred from the discrepancies between the recent data about exhibition is the recent consolidation of a capitalist mode of distribution, often controlled by large conglomerates, including the Italian Medusa Film,[16] which squeeze out national quality films from the market. Table 1.5 exemplifies the control of the Italian box office by Hollywood conglomerates, which affects directly the circulation of Italian films in their own market. Only a small number of Italian films are distributed by US majors' affiliates in Italy.

From the data, it emerges that Berlusconi's Medusa Film is also a leading player, exercising effective control over film distribution. In fact, Medusa is an international distributor and its performance is due to the fact that it distributes European as well as American films. In 2006, among many other films, it distributed Woody Allen's *Match Point* and Martin Scorsese's *The Departed*, which were both among the top 10 box office hits for the year. In turn, two Italian films , *Il mio miglior nemico* (2006, Carlo Verdone), a comedy with Carlo Verdone, and *Natale a New York* (2006, Neri Parenti), another comedy with Christian De Sica, came fourth and fifth respectively. Typically, films featuring Carlo Verdone or other popular comedians are released around Christmas to cash in on the festive season – hence the derogative definition of 'Christmas films'. Also Filmauro, owned by Luigi and Aurelio De Laurentiis, specialises in the production and distribution of popular comedies. Another hit produced and distributed by Filmauro was *Manuale d'amore*, released in 2005, with its sequel, *Manuale d'amore – 2* released in 2007, both directed by Giovanni Veronesi.

Two other interesting observations that emerge from the data are that Sacher continues to be one of the best performers in terms of ratio between the number of films distributed and revenues, while on the other hand we

TABLE 1.5 TOP 20 DISTRIBUTION COMPANIES (REVENUES) IN 2006

Company	No. of films distributed	Revenues (€)	Percentage on total revenues
UIP — United Int. Pictures	46	71,419,257.46	13.07
Medusa Film Spa	86	70,946,743.92	12.98
Buena Vista Int. Italia Srl	59	65,727,581.85	12.03
20th Century Fox Italia	43	64,310,462.22	11.77
01 Distribution	61	51,841,017.24	9.49
Sony Pict. Italia Srl	45	50,523,675.83	9.25
Filmauro	10	44,694.039.25	8.18
Warner Bros Italia Spa	62	40,688,713.24	7.45
Eagle Pictures Spa	40	32,900,030.78	6.02
Bim Distrib. Srl	48	13,033,063.60	2.39
Sacher Distrib. Srl	6	6,903,044.70	1.26
Moviemax Srl	14	5,941,262,30	1.09
Mikado Films Spa	94	5,480,726.95	1.00
Lucky Red Distrib.	55	4,573,773.05	0.84
Mediafilm Spa	14	3,981,828.95	0.73
Nexo Spa	9	3,502,524.75	0.64
Fandango Srl	32	2,478,529.90	0.45
Dnc Distrib. Spa	7	1,887,333.54	0.35
Ist. Luce Spa	57	1,211,871.40	0.22
Teodora Film Srl	15	967,562.30	0.18

Source: Ufficio Studi/CED ANICA.

must register the total failure of Istituto Luce, the government distributor and promoter of Italian art films.

In the case of co-productions, despite specific national regulations, on a general level a production company owns 100 per cent of the distribution rights in its own country, but the rights in other countries are shared in proportion to the monetary contribution. Thus, for example, if Italy co-produces a film with France and the company participates with 20 per cent of the budget, the exploitation rights in other territories will be shared on a 20:80 basis. Also, there is the case of television channels participating in the co-production; in that case the television network would receive all the revenues from television exploitation, but in exchange would not share the revenues from other modes of exhibition.

As a way to sum up production, distribution and cinema attendance, Table 1.6 compares the most important European film industries with the US, Japanese and Australian film industries. The most interesting data are related to the number of screens operating in Italy, which represents the lowest percentage in relation to the number of inhabitants among industrialised countries. Frequency is the lowest if we exclude Japan, where tickets prices are the highest. It is thus clear that in terms of film attendance, if this is a valid element of a national film industry, Italy is still facing one of the worst crises in its history

HOME VIDEO

To complete the analysis of the Italian film industry a brief mention of the home video market is necessary. The life of a film continues well after it is withdrawn from theatres into the DVD market, then cable television, then commercial or public television, with further exploitation potential when the passage to high-definition television and the relative multi-channelling will be completed. The home video market has increased more than exponentially in seven years, thanks to the drop in prices of DVD players.[17] Revenues from DVD and video rentals and sales went from virtually nothing in 1999 to 900 million Euros in 2006, of which 272 million Euros were for DVD rentals. This figure was a slight decrease compared to 2004 and 2005, which the Unione Italiana Editoria Audiovisiva explained as being linked to the distraction caused by many high-profile sports events in 2006 (such as the FIFA Soccer World Cup and the Winter Olympics) (*Rapporto sullo stato dell'editoria audiovisiva in Italia*, 2006).

People also preferred cheaper rentals from catalogues (older than thirteen weeks from the date of release). Surprisingly, DVD sales were

TABLE 1.6: COMPARISON OF EUROPEAN, US, JAPANESE AND AUSTRALIAN FILM INDUSTRIES

	USA	JP	EU 15	EU 25	AUST	GB	FRA	ITA	SPA	GER
Film produced	611	310	689	764	23	133	203	138	133	121
Average ticket Price (in €)	5.15	9.4	6.12	5.71	6.12	7.02	5.82	5.68	5.14	6.13
No. of screens	36,594	2,825	26,531	29,400	1,909	3,342	5,302	3,171	4,390	4,870
Total popn*	295,734	127,417	382,306	457,030	20,090	60,441	60,656	58,103	40,341	82,431
Screens/popn ratio (100,000 inhabitants)	12.37	2.22	6.94	6.43	9.5	5.53	8.74	5.46	10.88	5.91
Attendance (total)	1,536,000	170,092	34,000	1,005,000	92,000	171,300	194,800	116,342	143,900	156,700
Frequency (%)	5.19	1.33	2.44	2.20	4.58	2.83	3.21	2.00	3.57	1.90

* In thousand

Source: Il mercato cinematografico Italiano, 2000–2004.

almost double, with 428 million Euros, confirming the preference that has emerged also in other advanced European countries to buy DVDs in order to build personal video libraries. In Italy, this practice goes back to the 1980s, when the distribution via rentals and sales of videos was de facto entrusted to newspapers and weekly magazines because of the lack of proper infrastructures and practices. In that period, there was a weekly supplement war among newspapers publishers which instituted a process of *settimanalizzazione* of newspapers with the distribution of glossy magazines during the week. *L'Unità*, the official organ of the former Communist Party, started to distribute video cassettes in conjunction with the newspaper. *L'Unità* was soon followed by *Corriere della Sera*, *la Repubblica*, *Panorama* and *l'Espresso*. This practice was not only a marketing strategy to gain a larger readership, though reaching beyond an élite readership was obviously a fundamental element in these practices. The deployment of new strategies to sell more daily papers can better be explained within a context of shifting audiences. The 1980s was the decade in which Italian spectators retreated in their cosier domestic spaces thanks to commercial networks, which could provide ongoing, up-to-date, accessible information. The new strategies to sell newspapers effectively established a new habitus of buying the newspaper along with the enclosed magazines, books, CDs and video cassettes. The distribution of different items with newspapers was also meaningful in spatial terms, as in Italy the *edicola* (news-stand) is the distribution point that reaches virtually all national territory, including small localities.

Video cassettes started to be distributed with specific offers: retrospectives of *auteur* cinema (especially the French New Wave, Wim Wenders, Hitchcock), genres (comedies, Westerns, cartoons), Italian classics and blockbusters. Videos became thus objects of appropriation, which were accumulated in home video-libraries. Their materiality did not stop at watching the movie, but it had a symbolic function as cultural capital.

However, the Associazione nazionale videonoleggiatori italiani (National Association of Video Renters) took the *Corriere della Sera* to court in Milan with a case of unfair competition, as the newspaper was selling films which still had a market in the video rentals sector. In 1996, the tribunal handed down a decision which prohibited the sale of the newspaper with the regular enclosure of video cassettes. However, this practice still continues with the transferral of films from video cassettes to the digital format, extending the exploitation of old films, and is linked to the acquisition of libraries and copyrights by newspapers' publishers. Selling DVDs through the *edicola* continues to be a staple practice, as there is an average four Euros difference in price between normal trade and the *edicola*. Through this outlet, in 2006 sales amounted to 221 million Euros, nearly a quarter of the total revenues.

Consumption is higher in the home video market than at the box office, confirming that Italians do watch films, but in the more comfortable domestic setting. The level of education and age are also important factors in the consumption of DVDs or the use of VCRs. For example people with a university degree or high school diploma prefer to go to the cinema, while lower classes watch more television. People between fourteen and 44 years of age constitute the higher percentage of owners of DVD players (*Rapporto sullo stato dell'editoria audiovisiva in Italia*, 2006, p. 8).

There is, of course, a burning question here: what DVDs do Italians buy? Policy in broadcasting regulations, as we saw earlier, has had a significant impact in bringing back Italian fiction in television prime time, but in the sale of DVDs, Italian consumers turn to Hollywood blockbusters (see Table 1.7). This reflects the fact that there are still difficulties in the distribution of Italian films in the home video market. Still, in 2000 it was difficult to find video cassettes of films made in the mid-1990s because the transfer of a film on a VHS and its commercialisation were linked to the film's performance in theatres. Therefore, if an Italian film did not encounter the favour of the public in the home box office, the production company did not release distribution rights for the home video market.

In conclusion, it is evident that the major problem faced by the Italian film industry is the effect of internal structural problems that include fragmentation in production and distribution, and a system of subsidies that privileges the financing of single films, rather than supporting companies on a structural level. Standardisation induced by globalisation has been fought in the media, with the substitution of imported series with local fiction, but this in turn is extremely local and parochial, and not exportable. Conversely, data related to the home video market clearly show the hegemony of Hollywood's conglomerates. Moreover, because distribution rights *per se* do not ensure high returns on films, US majors are also committed to co-produce European films, so that they can multiply their revenues. Italian film box office hits occur from time to time, and these are picked up by US distributors – for example, Miramax –

TABLE 1.7 TOP 10 DVDS SOLD IN ITALY IN 2004

	Title	Distributor
1	*Finding Nemo*	Buena Vista
2	*The Lord of the Rings: The Return of the King*	Medusa
3	*Pirates of the Caribbean: The Curse of the Black Pearl*	Buena Vista
4	*Harry Potter and the Prisoner of Azkaban*	Warner
5	*Spider Man 2*	Columbia Tristar
6	*The Passion of the Christ*	Eagle Pictures
7	*Brother Bear*	Buena Vista
8	*Troy*	Warner
9	*The Last Samurai*	Warner
10	*Home on the Range*	Buena Vista

Source: Il mercato cinematografico italiano, 2000-2004

but this is too occasional and cannot guarantee steady returns to the industry.

NOTES

1. See the debate between Italian and French academics collected in Ilvo Diamanti and Marc Lazar's *Stanchi di miracoli: Il sistema politico italiano in cerca di normalità* (1997).

2. The Italian Institute of Statistics (ISTAT) predicts a yearly increase of immigrants of 110,000, taking the incidence of 4 per cent on the whole population in 2010.

3. Thirteen per cent against an average 18 per cent in the European Union. Data are from ISTAT (http://istat.it).

4. Interview with the author, Rome, May 2000.

5. There is another factor worth considering. In the same period in which Hollywood left the shores of the Tiber, a kind of esoteric cinema, which initially interested only a small number of film buffs, started to emerge from Germany. By 1975, New German Cinema had replaced the interest toward

Italian and French cinema in the United States, gaining enormous exposure in New York and constant presence on American screens. See Rentschler (1984).

6. *Programma MEDIA dell'unione europea*, Antenna MEDIA (1997), Turin, p. 9.

7. Davide Ferrario interview in *Dopo Mezzanotte* DVD Features.

8. Data from Siae, UPA, Rai, Univideo, AFI, Bilancio dello stato.

9. In Italy, fiction refers specifically to television series and mini-series.

10. As a comparison, Miller et al (2000) report that in 1997, the average cost of an American film was US$53 million.

11. Interview with Gabriele Salvatores, Brisbane, November 2006.

12. In 1993, the Australian and Italian governments signed a co-production agreement. In this way, as a co-partner, Australia can indirectly benefit from European and Italian subsidies.

13. In 1998, Warner Bros opened three multiplexes in the province of Vicenza and Verona (Veneto) and Bari (Apulia) in a joint venture with Village Roadshow, with a total of 26 screens.

14. Miller et al. (2001) estimate that the cost of prints is often 50 per cent of the total production cost of a US film.

15. New Zealand was present in two films, *Lord of the Rings: Return of the King* and *The Last Samurai.*

16. Berlusconi's Mediaset is the only company listed on the stockmarket.

17. In 2007 it was possible to buy a DVD player for 30 Euros. Between 2002 and 2004, the number of DVD players sold has grown four times over, from 742,000 to 3,076,000. DVD recorders have registered the biggest increase, from 7,000 to 127,000, and also the combination DVD+VCR has grown from 171,000 to 595,000 (*Source:* Univideo).

2. THE GLOBAL CONTEXT

Discussions about Italian cinema in the postwar period are framed according to a narrative that sees the national cinema emerging from the destruction of World War II and performing strongly in the difficult circumstances created by the Cold War and American cultural hegemony. The history of Cinecittà and that of Italian cinema are bound in the way the ups and downs of the first reflect on the performance of the second. In the period between 1945 and the middle of the 1960s, the operations of Hollywood in the eternal city transformed Cinecittà from a national film studio to an international production epicentre. Likewise, Italian cinema flourished and, for a short period, rivalled the Hollywood studios. Conversely, from the middle of the 1970s, at the onset of a profound crisis in the Italian film industry – mostly caused by the withdrawal of the majors from Italy – the history of the national cinema is characterised by a celebratory narrative of the accomplishments of Italian filmmakers, cinematographers and other above-the-line professionals in Hollywood. These triumphs are measured by the number of nominations at the Oscar Academy Award as the ultimate goal, erasing any effort to turn the local industry into a profitable national venture that is able to talk to, and represent, the national imaginary at the end of the century.

It is thus useful to trace a brief chronological history of Cinecittà, in order to understand how the past has shaped present Italian cinema. Because Cinecittà and the Italian film industry are part of the global audiovisual production economy, is driven by Hollywood's dispersal of feature film production, first we must look at the dynamics of international film production according to the 'New International Division of Cultural Labour' (see Miller 1996; Miller et al. 2005). A section on Italian co-productions within the European audiovisual framework concludes this chapter about Italian cinema in the global context.

THE NEW INTERNATIONAL DIVISION OF CULTURAL LABOUR

Capitalism has a tendency to divide production into a growing number of separate and smaller tasks to increase its efficiency and to maximise profit. Encouraged by Adam Smith's idea of free trade, the division of labour is a key to efficiency, based on claims that countries should not make what can be made cheaper in other countries. Capital mobility, internationalisation of trade and the reorganisation of production on an integrated global scale have profoundly changed labour demand and the division of labour (Sassen 1988). The development of the offshore manufacturing sector in the Third World, through direct foreign investment has created a transnational space for the circulation of capital and labour. Today, the global spatial division of labour not only defines skill differences inside a firm, but also identifies sector differences outside a firm, fragmenting production to regions and countries that can offer labour and services at the lowest market price. The global spatial division of labour, otherwise known as the New International Division of Labour (NIDL) (Fröbel et al. 1980), is based on peripheral developing countries producing for world markets, and is best understood through the concept of regional political economy (Moulaert and Wilson Salinas 1983).

International capital takes advantage of low wages and a de-unionised workforce to source offshore production. The NIDL is about both maximising profit and minimising costs; it is underpinned by free trade agreements and it relies on global cities that service the global economy. In the cultural field, the idea of labour specialisation is translated into fragmented intellectual and creative skills. In Hollywood's ever-expanding global empire, the NIDL is applied to a concept of differentiation and internationalisation of cultural labour, with the same economic advantages. The New International Division of Cultural Labour (NICL) (Miller et al. 2005, esp. pp. 111–72) is functional to Hollywood's constant reinvention, direct foreign investment, takeover of new markets and exploitation of local talent in specific sectors. In this regard, it must be understood that Hollywood's offshore production is often based also on specific local skills, validating the claim that the NICL must be viewed as the division of production (localisation of manufacturing), in addition to the division of labour (manufacturing processes). Films can be likened to 'world goods' which are products that in whole or part 'are grown, processed, manufactured, recorded, filmed or staged in a multiplicity of locations' (Cohen and Kennedy 2000, p. 16).

Several elements are fundamental to the NICL in the film industry: flexible specialisation, the packager concept (project-by-project production) and vertical disintegration of production processes replaced by independent firms linked by transaction in markets (Storper 1989). In this, the driving element is Hollywood's distinction of 'above-the-line' talent and 'below-the-line' crews (Coe 2000, p. 84). The first indicates the key sector of budgets and includes decision-making roles (writers, producers, stars and directors), while the second comprises technical and camera crews (also carpenters and electricians), logistical (health and safety, and catering, for example), extras, professionals and technical workers in creative roles (makeup artists, set and costume designers, and recently sound and visual effects experts), who work in non-decision-making roles. The above-the-line workers are able to negotiate high salaries and move easily to other countries for short periods of time where they work with the below-the-line workforce, which is hired at lower costs than in the United States. This is the variable that enables the cost to be contained (Miller et al. 2005, p. 119).

There are two reasons for Hollywood outsourcing production. The first is creative and is linked to the localisation of manufacturing – specific skills or specific geographic locations – while the second is economic, connected to the manufacturing process – cheaper labour for geographically non-specific films. The latter is increasingly becoming the driving force behind runaway productions (Miller et al. 2005); however, we will see that the case of Cinecittà is more complex, as Cinecittà is now investing in studios in cheaper foreign locations in order to direct certain film genres while continuing to service Hollywood.

Migrating film production is connected to large-budget international features which, along with spatial disaggregation, are based on specialisation of production (Goldsmith and O'Regan 2003, p. 9). Thus large-budget films can have multiple sites of production related to particular skills required in the production and cost-cutting concerns. The relocation of production outside Hollywood for economic reasons – tax incentives and subsidies, less unionised labour force and various local benefits – is not always the only element driving film production outside Los Angeles. Taking into account the localisation and fragmentation of manufacturing, a historical film requiring elaborate costumes could necessitate some services that Rome can offer, where firms such as Tirelli Costumi can guarantee manufacturing excellence.[1] Often, flexible specialisation and globalisation of the workforce also means that top-level individuals, such as costume and set designers, cinematographers and makeup artists, become a highly paid commuter workforce, as they travel to global locations to work on specific projects. Many Italian professionals and crew members pioneered this trend. Just to name a few, Carlo Rambaldi (special effects), Vittorio Storaro (cinematography) and Milena Canonero (costume designer) worked in Hollywood from the early 1970s when production in Cinecittà started to decrease dramatically. It is a fact that European costume designers, for example, have really won fame and acknowledgment only when they have worked for American studios or American directors (Engelmeier and Engelmeier 1997, p. 25). However, this kind of labour migration is only limited to top professionals, as unions in the United States prevent foreign technicians from working in the United States.

Animation films, special effects and some post-production are typically outsourced to Asian countries. India is, for example, the latest country to attract Hollywood's capital, as the immense IT manpower, technical expertise and studio infrastructure at low cost – often a quarter of that charged by US companies – is seen as the new ideal destination for Hollywood's runaway productions: motion pictures, TV serials and commercials (Srivastava 2004). Studios scattered around the world — from

Toronto in Canada to the Gold Coast in Australia, passing through Germany's Babelsberg and Prague, to cite a few – constantly invest in updating their infrastructure (special effects, digital sound, water tanks[2] and so on) in a bid to attract Hollywood's money. The obvious conclusion is that, through this spatialisation and stratification of labour, Hollywood maintains ownership of the means of production, while other countries compete among themselves as mere providers of labour or specialised skills. Hamid Mowlana notes that: 'The impact of growing competition on the incomes of Americans is a "winner-take-all" economy which is widening the gap between rich and poor and concentrating income and wealth in fewer hands.' (Mowlana 1997, p. 17)

ITALY'S POSITION IN THE NICL

Hollywood's film production in Italy in the postwar period can be attributed to two key elements. The first had to do with US internal problems, namely the rise of domestic underdeveloped entertainment technologies – television, gramophones and record players – which were taking away audiences, and the second with the end of the vertically integrated studio system. Also, a new consumer culture that emerged in the 1950s and in the 1960s led, according to NIDL proponents, to a new expansion and accumulation of capital (Schaeffer and Mack 1996). The most labour-intensive operations were relocated to developing countries, with a gradual shift to more adaptable smaller enterprises. This move created a single market for labour and a world market of industrial sites. Hollywood's runaway productions in Italy in the same period can easily be framed within this development of capitalism, and an early form of NICL must be traced back to the postwar period. This early example of globalisation of cultural labour sustained art cinema as a Euro-American genre internationally distributed, but these films also opened up avenues for more popular films, such as the Italian comedy, to be distributed and appreciated internationally – for example, *Matrimonio all'italiana* (Vittorio De Sica, 1964).

From its position as a provider of skilled labour or locations, Italy is

now turning to other countries as suppliers of
locations. Today, Italy is an industrialised
compete in terms of costs with emerging coun
Europe. Italy's position in the NICL as la
explained through an alternative perspective
efforts of public–private entrepreneurship
engaging in updating and replacing existing infrastructures, while
maintaining high manufacturing skills. In the second instance, in a trickle-
down pattern, Italy uses emerging countries, including India and China, by
striking co-production agreements to broaden the market base, to find
locations and cheaper labour, to access incentives and funding normally
available to the partner country, and to facilitate temporary immigration
and importation of equipment. For example, Amelio's latest film *La stella
che non c'è* (2006) was shot in China, while Francesca Archibugi shot
Lezioni di volo (2005) in India, a co-production involving France, Italy, the
United Kingdom and India. The opening to Eastern European countries is
a response to Europe's Eastern Enlargement policy (Marin 2005, p. 1),
which advantages Western European countries' relocation of production
to Eastern European countries in order to save on their labour costs which
are now too high. The logic of film co-productions with regard to Italy
will be discussed in the final section of this chapter.

FROM RUBBLE TO STARS TO RUBBLE

One point of connection between the internationalisation of labour and
global integration of the film industry on the one hand, and the need for
local industries to attract foreign capital to sustain local production and
development on the other, is the reorganisation and restructuring of film
studios. For its extraordinary success in the 1950s and 1960s, Cinecittà
represents one of the key case studies in the history of national film studios
turned international to lure Hollywood's runaway productions. The case
of Cinecittà is emblematic because it details the ups and downs of the
Italian film industry in the postwar period. In particular, the fortunes of

l film industry – performance of local films at the domestic and
ional box offices – have depended on Hollywood's offshore
duction in Italy. Indeed, the history of Italian postwar cinema *vis-à-vis*
Hollywood is one that intersects, diverges and intersects again as it follows
the vagaries of international film capital to different locations.

Cinecittà's history is usually told from the point of view of the Cold
War (Muscio 2000, p. 116; Wagstaff 1995).[3] More specifically, the
relationship between Italy and the United States is written according to a
dominant left-wing narrative of cultural imperialism. This is, of course,
because the United States emerged as militarily, economically and
politically hegemonic after World War II. The participation of the United
States in the war ended the country's pre-war isolationism and totally self-
sufficient film production. Conversely, the Italian Communist Party
emerged as the force behind the Resistance against Fascism and Nazism,
and Togliatti's political and cultural strategies were naturally aligned with
the Soviet Union. Therefore much of Italy's postwar political history is
framed within the Cold War narrative and the country's dependence on
economic aid from the United States, which in turn informs the United
States–Italy economic, cultural and political relationship.

However, things are more complex because, on the one hand if
Hollywood's presence in Italy in the 1950s and 1960s can easily be
categorised as one of cultural domination and economic exploitation, on
the other, the return of the majors to Italy meant that massive capital was
injected into the local industry and the labour force. In fact, the Italian film
industry flourished in the decade between the end of the 1950s and the
1960s, coinciding with the most prolific period of Hollywood's investment
in Italy.

Cinecittà's history starts with the destruction of Italy's biggest
production company, Cines, that occurred in 1935. The new *città del
cinema* (cinema city) was built to replace Cines' studio, but also to satisfy
Mussolini's ambitious dreams to create a replica of Hollywood near Rome.
Like the idea that moved American film production from the East Coast to
Los Angeles, the site was chosen for its low real estate value and for its

landscape, which enabled the production of different genres. Mussolini had already put in place a state subsidy system in order to encourage film production, inaugurated the Venice Film Festival in 1932 and opened the Centro Sperimentale di Cinematografia in 1935. Here, Roberto Rossellini, Alessandro Blasetti, Federico Fellini, Vittorio De Sica and others worked under the patronage of Mussolini and the Fascist regime until the fall of Fascism in September 1943. Other studios were located in Turin, Venice and Leghorn, and operated as alternative sets by the same companies that owned part of the studios in Cinecittà, Tirrenia Company and Scalera Company. Rome was without doubt the centre of film production.

In the mid-1930s, it therefore appeared that the Italian film industry was on its way to a partial recovery, although it was never in the position to represent serious competition, and the technological gap – the introduction of sound – between Hollywood and Rome persisted. When the Vatican launched a campaign against the modern, cosmopolitan images that promoted a decadent life and values that came from Hollywood's films, Mussolini acted in the name of national cultural identity. Specifically, he acted in the name of a national film industry under the control of the state, and thus of Fascism. In 1938 he enforced Law no. 379, which cancelled all the previous arrangements regulating the presence of foreign films in Italy. Law 379 partially stopped the importation of American movies. The majors withdrew from the market, but films made by small, independent producers continued to flow into the Italian market. Mussolini's concerted plan that included censorship, import restrictions and public funding to films was only partially able to contain Hollywood's dumping strategy. When the American troops disembarked in Sicily in 1943, in Palermo:

> Native audiences were watching American movies ... before the island was entirely clear of Germans. To many liberated peoples, the return of Hollywood movies meant escape from war weariness. In Italy, after a few months of Allied occupation, more people were going to the movies than before the war ... (Jowett 1975, p. 324)

Under the Nazi occupation of Rome between 8 September 1943 and June 1944, when Rome was liberated, Cinecittà was looted by the German troops. During the same period, American bombs destroyed seven of the twelve studios, and as the American troops entered Rome, Cinecittà became a refugee camp (Brunetta 1998, pp. 3–4). Liberated Italy offered a picture of a country thrown into chaos and misery, deprived of even basic necessities of life. In the view of Hollywood's producer representatives, the first priority was to restore the cinema, in order to nourish – as the usual Hollywood narrative of universal appeal claims – an audience craving its favourite American stars who had been banned from the country by Mussolini in 1938.

Thus, according to a Cold War perspective, the United States had to eliminate restrictions on international trade to contain Soviet power, to suffocate the left in those countries that showed signs of a possible shift in that direction (and Italy was one of those countries) and to strengthen private enterprise economies, eliminating on the way any possible germ of Nazism and Fascism in Germany and Italy. Hollywood treated film as an economic commodity (Guback 1969, p. 7), while the US government considered the cinema industry to be more like a cultural item 'subject to exceptional treatment' (Jarvie 1994, p. 156).[4] Hollywood's strategies were to seek government help to ensure first that the film business was conducted under conditions of free trade, and second that interference by foreign governments was minimised. Although the US government had tried to break vertically integrated companies since 1939, 'Hollywood was able to count on the services of the State Department and its diplomatic posts on the ground' to regain its lost markets in Europe (Brunetta 1994, p. 145). Thus the American Embassy and the Psychological Warfare Board (PWB) carried out the development of American feature films in Italy from 1944 onwards. As the PWB authorised the reopening of all picture theatres in liberated territories, it provided for the control of all films circulating in Italy, distributing both propaganda films and narrative genres.

In October 1945, Decree no. 678 from the provisional Italian government revoked the protectionist law and the cinema industry entered the free market regime. In 1946, only 62 national feature films were produced, while 850 films were imported, of which 600 were American. By 1954, a total of 5,368 US films circulated in Italy (Guback 1969, p. 39; Brunetta 1982, p. 170). The Italian government passed decrees placing limits on imports, but in practice it never enforced them. Hollywood producers had two goals on their mind: to enjoy the new takeover of a lost market, and to present a mental picture of America and its values which was entirely and exclusively positive. Hollywood's films depicting prosperity, full employment, democracy and happiness were particularly welcomed by the Italian government led by the Christian Democrats. Masses of movie-goers flocked to the picture theatres to see images of the 'America' described in thousands of Italian migrants' letters.

The economic and political hegemony of the United States after World War II clearly contributed to the nation setting the terms of debate and the agenda of priorities. The US State Department helped to break artificial barriers to the expansion of private US news agencies, magazines and motion pictures. The Motion Picture Export Association was created to provide for certain exemptions from antitrust laws for cartels established only to engage in foreign trade. Once the US had re-conquered the Italian market, American producers – MGM in the first instance in 1949 (Nowell-Smith 1996, p. 5) – saw advantages in co-producing films in Italy as a way to utilise frozen money left from before the war and take advantage of tax incentives and subsidies from the state to Italian cinema producers. In 1947, Luciano Emmer and Enrico Gras wrote in *Hollywood Quarterly* that the proceeds from the distribution of American films were very large by Italian standards and that there were suggestions that 'American interests might consider investing [the] funds through participation in Italian film production on a fifty-fifty basis' (Emmer and Gras 1947, p. 357). The funding system of a 10 per cent bonus on films' takings that was put in place by Mussolini remained unchanged after the war. The neorealist directors and the Italian Communist Party strongly criticised this form of subsidy, as it only rewarded big box office productions. This system *de facto* inhibited the production of neorealist cinema, but it was fully exploited by Hollywood and Italian producers in co-production ventures. Other advantages for Hollywood were the favourable exchange rate and the fact that Italian labour costs were 85 per cent lower than in the United States.

Hollywood returned to spectacular productions in a bid to contrast the challenge of television in the United States, thus Cinecittà, with its cultural tradition of lavish big-budget historical films and skilled expertise in costume and set design, became the ideal place to shoot big productions with hundreds of extras and grandiose sets. Between 1950 and 1965, Hollywood produced 27 films in Cinecittà (Bono 1995). Heavy marketing, the exploitation of glamorous images of stars – who at this point were flocking to Rome to enjoy the 'sweet life' – and high production value ensured that Hollywood's films had the best exposure and distribution. However, simultaneously Italian cinema flourished. The injection of US capital into the studios increased the financial base of Italian producers, with companies such as Titanus producing and distributing both high- and low-end features for a differentiated market.

THE PRODUCERS

The history of Cinecittà cannot be told without considering three major production companies: Titanus, Carlo Ponti and Dino De Laurentiis. The history of their rise and demise from the immediate postwar period to the 1970s is emblematic if we try to read the relationship between Hollywood and Italy as a problematic one, instead of a simplistic approach that casts one in a position of cultural domination and one as subservient partner.[5] Naturally, the success of the Italian film industry in the decade between the mid-1950s and the 1960s cannot be attributed only to these three producers, but it is important to recognise that, through their operations inside and outside the Italian territory and the many international awards and recognitions their films received, they served as a driving force for many other producers. Overall, the three producers' diversification of genres and budgets enabled them to pay for high-quality productions with box-office returns from popular films (such as Totò's films or the comedies directed by Steno).

Goffredo Lombardo inherited Titanus from his father Gustavo after his death in 1951. Gustavo started in the film business in 1908, representing Film Italiana in Naples, a company based in Turin.[6] Slowly, he acquired distribution rights for the Italian market for the French companies Gaumont and Le Film d'Art, the American Edison, and other major Italian production companies, extending his business across the peninsula. In 1928, Gustavo Lombardo founded his production arm, Titanus, oriented toward popular, low-cost productions. Between 1938 and 1944, Titanus produced only two low-quality films a year, catering for the more popular end of the market, especially the southern market with Totò's films. After the war, Titanus survived distributing American films, as there was a steady and reliable supply coming with some pre-sold pricing advantages. Between 1949 and 1952, Titanus made a fortune with Matarazzo's trio of films *Catene* (1949), *Tormento* (1950) and *I figli di nessuno* (1951), a series of family melodramas with low production values. In the meantime, the US backlog slowly started to vanish, thus from 1952 Titanus increased production. The company produced Italian comedies (*Poveri ma belli* and the trilogy of *Pane amore e ...*), spaghetti Westerns, noir and detective films, documentaries, dramas and adventure films, effectively becoming the initiator of the so-called *neorealismo rosa* (pink neorealism). However, Titanus also opened up spaces for art cinema – for example, producing Visconti's *Rocco e i suoi fratelli* (1960) and *Il gattopardo* (1962), and producing and distributing *La ciociara* (Vittorio De Sica, 1960). Along with working with Italian directors such as Vittorio De Seta, Giuseppe De Santis, Luigi Comencini, Luchino Visconti and Pier Paolo Pasolini, Titanus continued to import and distribute foreign films, especially by French directors Claude Chabrol and Jean Luc Godard. In the early 1960s, two big-budget productions almost sent the company broke: *Il gattopardo* and Robert Aldrich's *Sodoma e Gomorrah* (1962), both produced with the backing of Hollywood distribution. The company survived and had another brief successful period in the 1970s with *Anonimo Veneziano* (Enrico Maria Salerno, 1970), *L'uccello dalle piume di cristallo* (Dario

Argento, 1970) and *Casanova* (Federico Fellini, 1976), but eventually in the 1980s and 1990s it had to succumb to television production, specialising in popular drama in the form of serials and film for television.

Carlo Ponti started his career as a film producer with his first success, *Piccolo mondo antico* (Mario Soldati, 1940). After the war, Ponti worked at Lux Films, producing up to fifteen films a year. Carlo Ponti and Dino De Laurentis formed the Ponti-De Laurentiis company, which produced major films such as Rossellini's *Europa '51* (1952), Robert Rossen's *Mambo* (1954), *La strada* (Federico Fellini, 1954), King Vidor's *War and Peace* (1955) and *Le notti di Cabiria* (Federico Fellini, 1957), which was the company's last film to be released. From 1955, Ponti decided to continue by himself working in both Italy and Europe. He specialised in *auteur* films for the international market, producing *Doctor Zhivago* (David Lean, 1965) and co-producing big budget films such as Michelangelo Antonioni's *Blowup* (1966), *Zabriskie Point* (1970) and *Professione: reporter* (1975). The growth and diversification of Carlo Ponti's film production is similar to that of Titanus, and in some respect to that of Dino De Laurentiis, although the latter took a decisive turn in thematic orientation when he relocated to the United States. Carlo Ponti always aimed at making big-budget films with big stars and high production values because his goals were high-quality films and high box office returns.

The history of Dino De Laurentiis' participation in the film industry is reminiscent of the film moguls during Hollywood's studio period. He was a pioneer in the economics of international co-productions, and his career trajectory is very similar to that of Goffredo Lombardo and Carlo Ponti, but with a final twist which saw him relocating in the United States in 1970. Here he produced some quality films, *Serpico* (Sydney Lumet, 1973) and *Three Days of the Condor* (Sydney Pollack, 1975). The remake of *King Kong* in 1976 (John Guillermin) was an extraordinary global box office success, but many other ambitious films with big budgets that he produced throughout the 1980s and 1990s were notorious box office flops.

In the early 1980s, De Laurentiis diversified his operations with the opening of two food stores called DDL Food Show, one in New York

City and one in Beverly Hills. At the same time, following his dream of owning a large production studio, he built a large complex in Wilmington, North Carolina, which functioned according to Hollywood standards. After enthusiastically taking the oath of American citizenship and buying his own distribution company, Embassy Pictures, from Coca-Cola to secure his films' ancillary rights, De Laurentiis set his eyes on Australia, constructing a US$10 million studio on the Pacific Highway (Coomera on the Gold Coast) in Queensland, thanks to a low-interest loan from the Queensland government. However, in 1988, after many box-office flops, the De Laurentiis Entertainment Group collapsed and Dino was forced to file for bankruptcy, selling the Gold Coast studio and Wilmington (Associated Press 1983; Sheraton 1983; Bice 1987; Jones and Whyte 1987; *Irish Times* 2007).

After a 45-year absence, in 2000 De Laurentiis returned to Cinecittà's historical Studio 5 to shoot a United States–France-financed production, the submarine blockbuster *U-571* (Jonathan Mostow), and the following year he shot parts of *Hannibal* (Ridley Scott, 2001), the sequel to *The Silence of the Lambs* (Jonathan Demme, 1991). In 2005, the indefatigable Dino, now over 80 years old, collaborated with Cinecittà to build the Cla Studios in Ouarzazate, Morocco. Today, Dino De Laurentiis is a shareholder of Cinecittà Studios, which has been completely privatised.

A DIFFICULT LIFE

The reasons for the abrupt withdrawal of US financing in Italy, starting from the middle of the 1960s, are various and well known. First, in the 1960s Italy was no longer a war-torn economy and industrialisation had pushed wages and workers' benefits up. After the law on cinema that was passed in 1965, the Italian film industry started to show signs of a deep crisis. According to De Laurentiis, who abandoned Italy in 1970, the 1965 law was too rigid in its pursuit of protecting national cinema and national identity.[7] The law imposed restrictions on the nationality of key figures, such as key actors, professionals, screenwriters, producers and directors, making it difficult to export internationally. Italian producers and directors were forced to work on low-budget projects of dubious quality which failed to even find favour with Italian audiences.

A few films were made in Cinecittà in the 1980s, with the help once again of limited US investments. *C'era una volta in America/Once Upon a Time in America* (Sergio Leone, 1983), *L'ultimo imperatore/The Last Emperor* (Bernardo Bertolucci, 1987) and *Il nome della rosa/The name of the rose* (Jean-Jacques Annaud, 1986) are the tip of the iceberg, and signal unproductive times for domestic cinema. Despite the fact that in 1980 the Roman film studio complex was still considered the most modern, inflation and high workforce costs – a permanent crew of 600 technicians and master craftsmen was no longer tenable in post-Fordist times – limited Cinecittà's strong role in the local and international film industry.

In the mid-1990s, a policy of development and reorganisation of the Italian film industry and public–private entrepreneurship introduced by the Treasury Department transformed Cinecittà into a joint-stock company, becoming in 1998 Cinecittà Holding S.p.A. Cinecittà Studios S.p.A. had already been privatised in 1997. This privatisation must be seen within the context of the economic recession that hit Italy in 1992–93. The deficit of the Istituto per la Ricostruzione Industriale (IRI)[8] had soared; thus the leading state companies were turned into joint stock companies. The old firms, like Cinecittà Studios, that were too inefficient to compete with the pressures from the international market were put up for sale. The restructuring of Cinecittà was not a straightforward and easy affair. It was plagued by infighting within the holding group that controlled the studio, Ente Cinema. In 1994, a plan by the Ente Cinema S.p.A., fully controlled by the Treasury, through its operating companies, Cinecittà, Istituto Luce and Cinecittà International, proposed to open the public film sector to private investors. The plan recommended that land, property and Istituto Luce remained under state control, while infrastructures – including a twelve-screen cinema – would be built through private investments. The reorganisation of Cinecittà involved the creation of a public holding company, with control of land and facilities. Cinecittà Servizi was created to manage the facilities. All the parties involved agreed that the state would maintain land ownership.[9]

Following these directions, the initial restructuring plan had selected in 1996, among some twenty companies, the Italian public broadcaster RAI, Mediaset Television network (owned by Silvio Berlusconi) and Britain's Rank Group, owner of London's Pinewood Studios, which were each to own a 20 per cent stake. The holding company of the Cecchi Gori Group (one of Italy's main film production and distribution companies at the time), Fin.Ma.Vi., and a group of small Italian production companies, Consorzio Produttori Indipendenti, would acquire the remaining shares. However, this decision drew criticism and also complaints from Cinecittà's unions, as they feared that they would have less security with private investors. The Italian Treasury rejected the pool of proposed entities. At the time of the negotiations, the government was headed by the Partito Democratico della Sinistra (PDS, ex-Italian Communist Party), with Massimo D'Alema as prime minister and a centre-left coalition in the parliament. State intervention in the cultural industry and the opposition to foreign influence in cultural matters have always been a staple of the Italian Communist Party's cultural policy. This may partly account for the exclusion of Britain's Rank Group, while preventing the involvement of Berlusconi's company aimed to avoid concentration in media and infrastructure's ownership.

Reorganisation and recovery of efficiency were therefore the key priorities of Cinecittà's restructuring. Finally, in 1998, Cinecittà was transformed in a joint-stock company, becoming Cinecittà Holding S.p.A. Cinecittà Studios had already been privatised in 1997. The Department for Arts and Cultural Activity controlled Cinecittà Holding, which in turn controls Cinecittà Studios with 17.5 per cent of the shares. The Istituto Luce S.p.A., a state-owned structure that operates in the production, distribution and exhibition sectors and is the main national film archive, owned 7.5 per cent of the shares in Cinecittà Studios, taking the facto state control of Cinecittà Studios to 25 per cent. Private shareholders were Aurelio De Laurentiis, through his production company Filmmauro Srl, with 15 per cent of shares; Vittorio Merloni, head of the third European company in the production of appliances, Diego Della Valle, a leader in leather production and design, and Vittorio Cecchi Gori, with 11.25 per cent of shares each; and finally Robert Haggiag, a film producer and distributor, and Efibanca, each with 7.5 per cent of shares (Vivarelli 1999).

With Cinecittà's privatisation, in 1999 the studios turned a profit of 2.5 billion lira from a former loss of 6 billion lira. A number of Italian films were made at the time: *Il pesce innamorato* (Leonardo Pieraccioni, 1999), *Trasgredire* (Tinto Brass, 2000), *La carbonara* (Luigi Magni, 2000) and *Liberate i pesci* (Cristina Comencini, 2000), while English language production that used the studios facilities included Anthony Minghella's *The Talented Mr Ripley* (1999), Michael Hoffman's *William Shakespeare's A Midsummer Night's Dream* (1999), Philip Haas's *Up at the Villa* (2000), Julie Taymor's *Titus Andronicus* (1999) and the already mentioned *U-571* by Jonathan Mostow. Two English language films by local directors that were made in Cinecittà during this period are Giuseppe Tornatore's *The Legend of 1900/La leggenda del pianista sull'oceano* (1998) and Zeffirelli's *Tea with Mussolini* (1999).

Following the exceptional international success of Benigni's film *Life is Beautiful* (1997), Jack Valenti, chief of the Motion Picture Association of America, along with the Italian cinema community, laid the foundations for initiatives aimed at getting more Italian cinema on US screens. In reality, US directors and studio chiefs had their eyes set once again on Rome, lured back by Cinecittà's upgraded post-production facilities. The strong dollar, Italy's offer of diverse scenic locations, excellent set and costume design, rising costs at Shepperton Studios from 1997, and especially the favourable production conditions offered by Cinecittà Studios were fundamental elements for Hollywood's return to Cinecittà. In fact, the studio's facilities can be hired on an 'as needed' basis.[10] The system can be compared to that of a hotel, as producers and directors can rent stages, sound editing rooms, sets and editing rooms for the whole production or just for parts of it. Two hundred people work full-time in Cinecittà, and this includes some technicians, carpenters and set designers.

Personnel can thus be hired on a needs basis, but individual directors can decide to work with their own professionals. The program with the most attractive incentive is the offer by the studios to build sets for a fraction of the cost. In return, Cinecittà retains the right to keep the sets as part of a permanent backlot. This adds to the already existing permanent sets (the swimming pool used in Fellini's *Amarcord*, three ancient Roman sets and the submarine set from *U-571*). An example of this arrangement is the set built by Dante Ferretti for Ettore Scola's *Concorrenza Sleale* (2001) that was transformed into mid-nineteenth century New York for Scorsese's $100 million *Gangs of New York*.

Hollywood's return to Cinecittà in 2000 was also generated by a relatively good performance of the Italian film industry at the box office in the previous years. In 2000, Silvio Soldini's film *Pane e tulipani*, the story of a unhappily married woman who travels to Venice and finds true love, grossed 10 billion lira at the box office, leaving behind American films *Boys Don't Cry* and *The Cider House Rules*. Other Italian films also performed well: *Lacapagira* (Andrea Piva, 2000), a low-budget dark comedy with strong dialect dialogue set in Bari (Apulia) that depicts the drug dealings of the local mafia; Marco Tullio Giordana's film *I cento passi* (2000), inspired by the real story of Peppino Impastato, a Mafia boss's nephew who is killed for his public anti-Mafia standing; Guido Chiesa's *Il partigano Johnny* (2000), inspired to Beppe Fenoglio's classic novel on the Resistance; Pasquale Scimeca's *Placido Rizzotto* (2000), a film about a 1940s union organiser who resisted and fought against the Corleone Mafia, and finally Roberta Torre's latest musical, *Sud Side Story* (2000) all received critical and public recognition.

Hollywood's investments in Italy created a phenomenon called 'Miramaxizzazione' (Coletti 2000), whereby the involvement of the company was not only limited to distributing Italian films in the United States (a venture that proved extraordinarily successful in the 1990s with *Il postino* and *La vita è bella*), but went so far as to nurture Italian projects in Italy (Giuseppe Tornatore's *Malena*) or contract Italian directors to work in the United States (two examples are Gabriele Muccino and Davide

Ferrario).

Miramax's patronage has not only affected the economy of work at Cinecittà, but also the content of some Italian films. Italian cultural historians Carlo Ginzburg and Adriano Prosperi have demonstrated in their analysis of Renaissance painting that intellectual activity cannot be separated from material activity because technical and economic factors are not exogenous phenomena to the artistic cultural phenomena (Ginzburg and Prosperi 1975). Put simply, there are various relationships that come into play in the production of any cultural and artistic artefact. Just as in the Renaissance context of art patronage, the commissioning body can be read in the text – which is, in our case, the film. In 2000 Miramax became more involved in Italian co-production, setting up its only division outside the United States in Rome, investing in Italian films and promoting the Italian brand insofar as this appealed to the American and international public. In fact, the American distributor and producer would only invest in films that pleased American taste – that is, stereotypical films depicting nostalgia, melancholia and beautiful women. Tornatore's films *Malena,* featuring the overwhelming sensuality of Monica Bellucci, and *Leggenda del pianista sull'oceano*, are good examples of the influence of US-backed production. Director Pasquale Scimeca commented that: 'If the Americans come with their stereotypes of what Italy is – all shoot-em up, mafia all the time, we are through.' (quoted in Coletti 2000)

Between 2003 and 2005, Cinecittà increased its operational infrastructure. Increasing competition in Hollywood's global dispersion of economic activity, especially toward Eastern European countries outside of the Euro dollar area, and renewed incentives in US states and cities to put a stop to runaway productions,[11] have forced Cinecittà to create a critical mass of studios which are able to offer an even more diversified set of pre- and post-production services and locations. Cinecittà now controls studios in via Pontina (the ex-Dinocittà), those created by Roberto Benigni in Papigno near Terni, and Ouarzazate in Morocco. This complex, bigger that any other studio in Hollywood or Europe, has two large sets of 1,800 square metres each. The Ouarzazate studios rely on a large desert area with scenic backdrops that have been depicted in classic blockbusters such as *Lawrence of Arabia* (David Lean, 1962), *Cleopatra* (Joseph L. Mankiewicz, 1963) and most recently *Gladiator* (Ridley Scott, 2000), *Alexander* (Oliver Stone, 2004) and Ridley Scott's *Kingdom of Heaven* (2005). Production costs in Ouarzazate are between 20 and 30 per cent lower than the already cheap locations in Eastern Europe; the studios also offer a skilled workforce of technicians and costume designers, which means that large productions are able to migrate to Morocco without transporting infrastructures and technicians. This allows further cost-cutting in the below-the-line budget, enabling greater expenditure in the above-the-line slice of the budget (Coletti 2000; Sharrock 2005; Karam 2005).

The objectives of Cinecittà's expansion outside Rome are twofold: on the one hand, there is the necessity to have all the sets working at full pace; on the other, there is a need to have enough set capacity to ensure constant turnover. For example, in 2004 HBO chose Cinecittà to produce the series *Rome*, occupying six theatres. The production of the second series occurred between March and November 2006, while the first series was being broadcast. *Rome* flopped in Italy, but had some success in England and the United States. Meanwhile, the cost of production skyrocketed and HBO halted production. The third series is thus in jeopardy, and there are fears in the industry that the third part will go to another location, perhaps Ouarzazate.

Cinecittà Studios is now operating through multiple studios (national and international) and cross-border financial operations. Saskia Sassen predicted that global capital mobility would lead to a different form of capital–labour relations and new requirements for centralised management and control (Sassen 2001, p. 36). It is possible to see this development of centralisation and establishment of hierarchical relationships between the various studios that now form 'Cinecittà Holding'. On the occasion of the seventieth anniversary of Cinecittà's foundation, the Department of Cultural Goods and Activities and the Treasury elaborated a plan for the fourteen companies that are part of the Holding to be reduced to only four by the end of 2007: Istituto Luce and Film Italia, controlled at 100 per cent;

Circuito Cinema and Cinecittà Studios, controlled respectively with 27 and 25 per cent shares. Some of the companies acquired along the way had already been sold (Mediaport, a multiplex cinema, and Cinesud, a company founded for the promotion of cinema in South Italy), while Cinefund (the private equity fund that should have financed between five and six films a year) will be liquidated as soon as the Treasury decides between closing the company down or selling it (Nido 2007). Cinecittà's operations will concentrate on promotion of the studios as a brand, with a view to obtaining from the Italian government a norm that will refund 15 per cent of IVA, the equivalent of British VAT and American sales tax, to productions. Labour-intensive and technology-intensive productions will be dispersed to different studios according to specific requirements. Given this geographical dispersal of the studio's activities, professionals and technicians (the below-the-line workforce) will increasingly face employment uncertainty. Some of the top professionals are able to travel to other countries (for example, Silvia Guidoni, first assistant costume designer who worked in Romania for *Cold Mountain* and in Prague, and is hired on a regular basis by Italian costume designers Gabriella Pascucci and Carlo Poggioli),[12] but carpenters and electricians, for example, are the expendable below-the-line workforce, as they can easily be replaced by locals.

As we have seen, an increased globalised, integrated, hypermobile and consolidated system of international film production has sparked the emergence of film production centres that depend upon Hollywood capital for their economic viability. Single national film industries had to adjust to this new environment, implementing fundamental technological and policy changes. Much of the changes have occurred in the technology of digital special effects in production and post-production phases, and in film and infrastructure co-financing. In the last decade, Cinecittà's major operating effort has been to update its infrastructures, especially its digital facilities, to be able to offer competitive services on the national and international market, in terms of costs and quality of services. However, similar to what happened in the 1960s, Cinecittà's operations have once again become too dependent on Hollywood's investments. As labour costs have increased further, especially after the adoption of the Euro as currency, Cinecittà has been forced to find a solution through the geographical dispersion of its activities and centralisation of management. There is now limited local film production in via Tuscolana's studios, as it is now too expensive to film there within the limited budgets available to Italian directors. Despite the fact that post-production is mostly carried out in Cinecittà, Italian low-budget film production is now dispersed throughout the peninsula, taking advantage of incentive offered by regional film commissions.

ITALIAN CO-PRODUCTIONS IN CONTEXT

From the 1992 Maastricht treaty, which anticipated the European Economic Union, film co-productions have become a staple mode of production because European filmmakers have faced two major problems: funding and distribution. Despite concerns of national identity, European independent producers have, by necessity, taken on cooperative strategies, putting aside the paradigm of national tradition, cultural specificity and artistic integrity.

The Museum of Broadcast Communication defines international co-productions as a 'generic term that covers a variety of production arrangements between two or more companies undertaking a television (or film or other video) project' (Museum of Broadcast Communications 2005). International co-production means that co-producers are from different countries. In general terms, film co-productions cover different arrangements, from the simplest deal between a company providing capital and another foreign firm providing actual production, to companies co-producing a film with joint creative control. Simple international co-productions include organisations that provide funding in return for distribution rights, but do not own the constitutive elements of the production. Co-productions between multiple partners increase funding two- or three-fold, raising the production value of the film. Also, co-production treaties allow film productions, especially those from well-established national companies, to be considered as 'national audiovisual work' ('film of national interest', in the Italian case), thereby qualifying for different forms of government support. In the case of European co-productions, the agreements and treaties between European countries constitute a legal framework within which producers from these countries may work together.

The strengthening of European co-productions underpinned by both bilateral agreements between single countries and European audiovisual policy is a response and an adaptation to American hegemony in global film distribution. Creative and cultural integrity aside, arguments both for and against co-productions – in our case, pan-European productions – are fraught with ideological tensions between nationalism and internationalism. Much of post-1950s Anglo-American film studies was marked by a nationalist predicament of the discipline (Betz 2001, p. 35). National cinemas existed in a self-conceptualised and self-defined concept against Hollywood by establishing boundaries between high (European) culture and low or popular (American) culture. Throughout the 1950s and 1960s, this continuing process of cultural legitimacy was also identified with cultural and national identity. Whereas Hollywood cinema was indicated as a transnational cinema, with universal appeal because of its narrative transparency and continuity storytelling (in reality, because of its universal presence given the nation's international economic power), national cinemas – typically European – were invested with intellectual and artistic claims that addressed national identity, expressivity and individuality.

Hollywood and national cinemas presented textual and institutional differences, where national cinemas' textual differences dealt with form and political critical commentary, while institutionally they presented different modes of production and circulation than Hollywood. One mode of circulation was, for example, the label 'European art cinema' as a genre depicting more sexually explicit material and directly linked with French, Italian and Swedish film production in the 1950s and 1960s. As the argument goes, national cinemas were the indicator of national cultural integrity, while today co-productions must be 'less specialist' (Hill 1994, p. 61) in order to secure wider distribution in other countries. In one word, European films must now resemble Hollywood films. The reality is that, since the end of World War II, co-productions have coexisted along with films produced 100 per cent with national capital.

The argument here is that very few inroads into the understanding of co-productions can be made if we look at the specificity of films and how much of national or local culture pan-European films are able to address and represent, or if we persist in analysing the contradictions inherent in producers' and directors' effort of combining commercial elements with aesthetic and artistic intentions. Europe today has a population of 380 million people, against 280 million people in the United States. It is clear that the enlargement of the distribution pipelines is what really matters beyond national cultural boundaries. What needs to be addressed is how successful the European audiovisual policy is in its strategy to address common economic needs of European nations through mobilising transnational resources that can support national and regional cinemas. In fact, European and single state subsidies are strictly related: securing support from one of the funds available at European level qualifies a film for national subsidies, and vice versa.

As for the distribution rights and promotion, there is no pan-European distributor for European films, as distributors are tied to local markets, their different values and different copyright laws. Also, distributors and exhibitors operate mostly within their national boundaries. Thus the low level of films distributed outside their market is the most important structural problem, despite the efforts of the program MEDIA that supports distributors taking their chance in distributing European films.

Naturally, the idea of European co-productions muddles further if we take into account the fact that, with Hollywood's dispersion of capital and financial investments, and the presence of the majors on the European continent with their national affiliates, often a European co-production involves multiple partnerships between European countries and the United States. An example is the most successful European co-production of the

1980s, *The Name of the Rose* (1986), directed by French Jean-Jacques Annaud and starring Sean Connery, with a $30 million budget funded by Germany, Italy and France. Luckily the story, adapted from Umberto Eco's best-seller, required monks from many parts of Europe, thus making it possible for British, French and Italian actors to work in their own language, turning the film into a truly European production. The difficulty to find money for the film was overcome after the German producer Neue Constantin struck a deal with Twentieth Century Fox for North American theatrical and television rights, as well as worldwide video rights. The film made $116 million worldwide, but only $7.2 million in the United States (Finney 1996, p. 251), confirming American gatekeeping practices against films imported into the national territory.

European co-production is a practice Italian directors and producers have been exploiting as a method to broaden their financial base, ensure the circulation of Italian films in other markets and spread investment risks. Countries with which Italy has struck co-production agreements in the last twenty years are as far away as New Zealand, Australia, China and India. Table 2.1 shows the geographic dispersal of Italian bilateral co-production agreements to 2006.

Italian co-production agreements stretch over four continents and it is clear that issues of national identity and cultural specificity become irrelevant. Therefore Italian dispersion of production must be seen in the context of international economic investment (with the model of a pan-European film industry in mind, rather than a pan-European cinema), with emphasis on co-financing as opposed to creative/financial co-production, and bilateral agreements that came in response to the failure of the WTO after Seattle, and as a result of the NICL. Thus co-production agreements are in reality economic investments whose returns gravitates around sales at international film festivals, short theatrical releases for niche markets within the countries involved in the production, DVD sales and other ancillary rights.

The demand for co-productions by independent European producers has clearly increased. In 1987, co-productions constituted 12 per cent of

TABLE 2.1 GEOGRAPHIC DISPERSAL OF ITALIAN BILATERAL CO-PRODUCTION AGREEMENTS
TO 2006

Europe and Eastern Europe	American continent	Asia-Pacific
Albania, Austria, Belgium, Belgian French Community, Bulgaria Czech Republic, Slovak Republic, France, Germany, Great Britain*, Hungary, Yugoslavia, Macedonia, Portugal, Romania, Russia, Slovakia, Spain, Sweden	Argentina, Brazil, Canada, Chile, Cuba, Mexico, Venezuela, Uruguay,	Australia, China, India, Japan, New Zealand
	Middle East Israel, Turkey	**Africa** Algeria, Morocco, Tunisia, South Africa

The co-production agreement with Great Britain was signed in 1998 and ceased in 2006.

Source: Ministero per i Beni e le Attività Culturali, 'Accordi di coproduzione internazionale'.

the total films produced in Europe, while in 1993 this number increased to 37 per cent (Finney 1996, p. 92). Table 2.2 reflects these data in the Italian context, showing that co-productions are clearly a vital part of the national film industry.

In 2004, co-productions amounted to 29 per cent of the total film output. In other words, there was slightly less than one co-production for every two films funded with 100 per cent Italian capital. Between 2000 and 2004 the co-productions trend was positive, but in 2005 Italian film production suffered a reduction of 40 films in total output. This significant reduction was the direct result of the decrease in films produced with state subsidies. The diminished public funding available to filmmakers also reflected on the number of co-productions. Overall, between 2000 and 2004 Italy signed 218 contracts of co-production, with nearly a third (67) negotiated with France alone.

TABLE 2.2 CO-PRODUCTIONS AS A PERCENTAGE OF TOTAL FILMS PRODUCED IN EUROPE

Year	Italian capital 100%	Co-productions	Majority co-productions	Minority co-productions	Total
2000	87	16	7	9	103
2001	71	32	21	11	103
2002	97	33	16	17	130
2003	97	20	13	7	117
2004	97	41	18	23	138
2005	70	28	13	15	98

Source: Osservatorio Italiano Audiovisivo (2006).

If we zoom in on the number of co-productions in 2004 and 2005 with European states (see Tables 2.3 and 2.4), we can see that Italy privileges European countries with which there are already consolidated partnerships – France, the United Kingdom, Spain and Germany – while co-productions with smaller or distant countries constitute only a small percentage.

The European cross-cultural initiatives in the 1980s produced an increase in film co-productions between European countries, leading to the implementation in 1988 of the pioneering fund, Eurimages, via the Council of Europe. In 1990, the Council of Ministers of the European Union designed the program MEDIA which, on the basis of five-year blocks, has injected 815 million Euros in audiovisual production between 1990 and 2006. After nearly twenty years of European audiovisual policy, it is possible now to say that Eurimages has been a far more successful program than MEDIA, because it allows co-productions with a greater diversity of countries compared with MEDIA. Eurimages is in fact a flexible program that contributes with interest-free loans to any one co-production up to a maximum of 20 per cent of the budget, and allows co-productions between at least three independent producers from the fund's member states. Loans can then be repaid from producers' net revenues.

TABLE 2.3 CO-PRODUCTIONS WITH EUROPEAN STATES

Country	2004	2005
United Kingdom	15	13
France	17	11
Spain	14	8
Germany	3	2
United States	1	2
South Africa	0	2
Switzerland	3	1

Source: Osservatorio Italiano Audiovisivo (2006).

TABLE 2.4 TOTAL FILMS PRODUCED IN 2005 THROUGH CO-PRODUCTION AGREEMENTS (%)

Country	%
United Kingdom	25
France	22
Czech Republic	2
Hungary	2
South Africa	4
Romania	2
Morocco	2
Iceland	2
Greece	2
Japan	2
Denmark	2
Belgium	2
Austria	2
Luxemburg	2
United States	4
Russia	5
Switzerland	4
Germany	4
Spain	16

Source: Osservatorio Audiovisivo Italiano (2006).

Eurimages also supports documentary, cinema exhibition, and distribution and marketing. In the 1990s, Italy has made a large use of Eurimages, with a peak of co-productions under the Eurimages umbrella in 1996, when 21 films out of 22 co-productions were funded through this program (see Table 4.2). Eurimages has had its detractors. Some critics maintained that the program was a framework hard-pressed by France's motivation to co-produce with European partners (Finney 1996, p. 109), but in reality the fund proved successful on a number of occasions in helping new talent to take over.

The following section explores Italian–French co-productions as an emblematic case study of Italian film partnerships in Europe. In the case of Italian–French co-productions, they made up a third of the Italian entire national filmic output (Jäckel 2003; Betz 2001, p. 22).[13]

ITALIAN AND FRENCH CO-PRODUCTION STRATEGIES

Italy signed the first dual production agreement with France in 1946, followed by the first official co-production agreement in 1949. By 1950, Italy had already widened her field of intervention by signing bilateral agreements with Spain, the United Kingdom, the United States and Austria, and by 1960 Italy had extended her partnerships to West Germany, Yugoslavia, Turkey, Japan, Argentina and Venezuela. However, it was with France that Italy had the most prolific filmic output, both in economic and artistic terms.

During the silent movies period, Italy depended on France's technical equipment, professionals and money; in the 1920s, Italian and French film companies (along with Scandinavian, British and German) were already cooperating in order to combat Hollywood's economic and cultural power. However, only after World War II did the two countries intensify their collaboration with different levels of monetary involvement and with sharing professionals and technicians. From the 1950s to the 1970s, Italian–French partnership helped both countries increase their film production, employment and screen quota, sharing both markets and launching new stars (Jäckel 2003). In fact, after the end of the war, film co-productions greatly contributed to rebuilding both countries' film industries. Despite some criticism from the left and the unions in both

TABLE 4.2 EURIMAGES-SUPPORTED AND TOTAL CO-PRODUCTIONS, 1990–2005

Year	Italian co-productions with the support of the Eurimages fund	Total co-productions
1990	1	21
1991	1	18
1992	2	13
1993	6	20
1994	4	24
1995	11	15
1996	21	22
1997	10	16
1998	10	13
1999	13	N/A
2000	12	16
2001	11	32
2002	12	33
2003	13	20
2004	13	41
2005	7	28

Sources: European Audiovisual Observatory and ANICA.

nations, cross-cultural fertilisation did not threaten national specificity. The two countries' cultural affinity, similarity of film funding schemes and size of markets allowed a rich collaboration between the two 'cousins' on either side of the Alps (Jäckel 1996, p. 87). Among some melodramas that copied Hollywood linear plots and conventions, there was also a high proportion of genuine artistic output that received international critical acclaim and success (Jäckel 2003). In the 1960s, much of art cinema in both countries was made through co-productions: Visconti's *Rocco e i suoi fratelli* (1960), which established the popularity of Alain Delon, and Antonioni's first four films, *L'avventura* (1960), *La notte* (1961), *L'eclisse* (1962) and *Deserto Rosso* (1964), were all Italian–French co-productions. Popular cinema, such as the series *Don Camillo and Peppone* (1952, 1955, 1972), was able to address some sharp criticism to Italian society. The

1960s can in fact be defined the 'golden age' of Italian–French co-production, which reached an average of 100 films per year. From the middle of the 1970s, film partnerships between Italy and France took a plunge, falling an average of 20 per year. This number decreased steadily during the 1980s, which reached a threshold of eight films per year on average.

During the 1990s, Italian and French co-productions started to increase again, thanks to Eurimages; the program proved successful in supporting quality films by known directors or first features, and greatly contributed to the discovery of new talent. Ferzan Ozpetek's first feature film *Hamam – Il bagno turco* (1997) was in fact an Italian–French–Turkish co-production. Other Italian–French co-productions, often with a third minority partner, realised in the 1990s through the Eurimages program by known directors who had theatrical distribution and, in some cases, exceptional performance at the box office or prestigious awards, were Gianni Amelio's *Le chiavi di casa* (2004, It/Fr/De), *Lamerica* (1994, It/Fr/Ch), *Il ladro di bambini* (1992, It/Fr/Ch); Francesco Rosi's adaptation of Primo Levi's book *La tregua* (1996, It/Fr/Ch/De); Roberto Faenza's *Marianna Ucria* (1996, It/Fr/Pt); Cristina Comencini's adaptation of Susanna Tamaro's *Va dove ti porta il cuore* (1996, It/Fr/De); Wim Wenders and Michelangelo Antonioni's *Al di là delle nuvole* (1995, Fr/It/De); Francesca Archibugi's *Con gli occhi chiusi* (1995, It/Fr/Es) and *Il grande cocomero* (1993, It/Fr/Nl); Paolo and Vittorio Taviani's *Fiorile* (1993, It/Fr/De); and Marco Bellocchio's *La condanna* (1990, Fr/It/Ch). Amelio's *Le chiavi di casa* and Rosi's *La tregua* are set in different countries, reflecting the presence of different producers, but the other films depict stories that, on first analysis, one could call *specifically* Italian. In reality, all the films engage with universal themes that have to do with culture, heritage and history (*Marianna Ucria, Fiorile*, but also *La tregua*), or with inter-generational clashes, social realism and contemporary politics. Their storylines open possibilities for transnational communities to engage with contemporary national traumas, replacing national concerns with the intersubjective openness to universal feelings of angst in the last decade of the millennium.

Nanni Moretti has produced all his films with France, starting from *Palombella Rossa* (1989), except for the political documentary about the split of the Italian Communist Party in 1989, *La cosa* (1990). Moretti's success with critics in France is evidenced in the number of times he was nominated at the Cannes Film Festival and the number of awards he received in France. Both *Caro Diario* (1992, Best Director) and *La stanza del figlio* (2000, Golden Palm) received prestigious awards at Cannes, while *Aprile* (1998) was nominated for the Golden Palm, but lost to Benigni's *La vita è bella*. France's appreciation of Nanni Moretti is addressed in *April* with a French critic interviewing Nanni Moretti about his cinema and the state of Italian politics following the election of Silvio Berlusconi as prime minister in 1994.

As the contemporary Italian film industry struggles between subsidies and attempts to turn the industry into a profitable venture with private investments, France has put into place several policies in support of cinema. The Centre Nationale de la Cinématographie (CNC), which was created in 1946, supports the film industry through three taxes: a tax (11 per cent) on the ticket price, irrespective of the nationality of films, which is entirely distributed to the film sector for both national films and co-productions (in 2005, this tax alone provided 113 million Euros) (European Audiovisual Observatory 2006, p. 52); a tax of 5.5 per cent on television's revenues from advertising, licence fees and subscriptions, which is distributed to both television and cinema production; and finally, a tax of 4 per cent on home video and DVD rentals, which is again distributed to film production. In 2005 alone, this mechanism produced 255 million Euros for French cinema. Other bank and tax incentives – for example, support from the regions, and the support from Canal + (which has contributed with 130 million Euros in 2005) – must be added to the film finance scheme. This system has led to an increase in film production from 146 films in 1990 to 240 in 2005, with an increase in the total money invested in the sector from 501 million Euros in 1990 to 1,286 million Euros in 2005. Tickets sales have also increased from 120 million in 1990 to

174 million in 2005, maintaining the French cinema market share at 37 per cent on average.

French mechanisms of film finance are therefore linked to the performance of the sector, contrarily to the Italian finance framework, which is linked to the performance of the national economy. For Italian producers and directors, co-producing with France means that they can take advantage of many incentives destined to French cinema, including a direct support to distribution and exhibition of co-productions (with minority and majority capital investment).

As a consequence of the healthier performance of French cinema, Italy renewed a bilateral agreement with France in 2000, which was enforced in 2003. This agreement is one of the most flexible frameworks in the world, similar to the bilateral agreements between France and Great Britain and Spain. The accord allows Italian and French producers to profit from their national funding; it allows purely financial co-productions (thus without any creative control from one of the partners)[14] and a contribution of capital as low as 10 per cent of the budget.

The commitment of both France and Italy to increase their partnership to reach the 1960s levels of co-production, in order to again strengthen their respective film industries, was also pursued by the Lazio Film Commission (Regione Lazio) and the Commission du Film d'Ile-de-France. In 2005, the two regions signed an agreement to collaborate on the establishment of a common database with projects and screenplays. The most important element is that producers from both nations will be able to access film funding from their regions for films shot in the two locations. The French fund is quite large, as it amounts to 15 million Euros per year. The Regione Lazio will contribute to 30 per cent of the budget, which will be recouped from ticket sales, television rights and DVD sales. Furthermore, after the successful negotiation with Ile-de-France, the Regione Lazio activated consultations with Madrid and Berlin for similar agreements, in order to create a creative, industrial and financial pool between the four largest continental European cities, where locations shooting will become a means to differentiate stories. This indicates further that filmmaking today is understood more as an industrial/financial enterprise that bypasses concerns of national culture and identity, shifting the focus of film production to a world economy based on the rise of global cities, each with its distinctive cultural allure and industrial competence, which takes us back to the new international division of cultural labour discussed in the first part of this chapter.

NOTES

1. Tirelli Costumi has made costumes for more than 60 films: *The Age of Innocence*, *The English Patient*, *Amistad*, *Titanic* and *Moulin Rouge* are among the most recent and famous.
2. Recently Warner Bros built the largest water tank in the Southern Hemisphere for underwater scenes for the film *Fool's Gold*. The water tank was built at the Warner Bros theme park Movieworld on the Gold Coast, Queensland, and will now remain as permanent infrastructure for future productions. In exchange, the US production enjoyed A$800,000 in subsidies from Queensland Pacific Film and Television Commission. Warner Bros also inaugurated a new way to deal with location permits and fees by donating A$35,000 to the Queensland Parks and Wildlife Service as a contribution to rebuild the region around Innisfail devastated by Cyclone Larry.
3. Later, Christopher Wagstaff corrected his own evaluation by showing Italy's film export figures from soon after the war to demonstrate a worldwide appreciation of Italian cinema (Wagstaff 1998).
4. See also Jarvie's account of how film personnel were embedded in the United States armed forces (1998, p. 37).
5. A collection of essays edited by Vito Zagarrio (1988) recounts this interesting period of Italian film history, taking as a case study the growth and crisis of Titanus in the period 1945–75.
6. For a comprehensive historical analysis of the Italian early cinema industry, see Bernardini (1978).
7. *la Repubblica interview*, 2005, internet video; Friendly (1970, p. 36).
8. IRI is a state holding company. It was founded in 1933 to hold the industrial and commercial companies acquired by the state in order to resell them after a restructuring of the company. In this way, the state could capitalise as

much as possible on the initial outlay.

9. 'Ente Cinema's three-year plan proposes creation of communications centre in Rome', *Il Sole 24 Ore*, 7 December 1994, p. 9.

10. Interview with Carole André-Smith, International Marketing Director, Rome, April 2002.

11. For example, Los Angeles, New York and Louisiana have reintroduced incentives. In 2004, the value of film production in Los Angeles increased 19 per cent compared with 2003 (Mele 2005).

12. Interview with Silvia Guidoni, Rome, 10 May 2007.

13. In the case of France, in the decade 1960, co-productions surpassed national productions.

14. The co-production agreement between Italy and New Zealand, signed in 2004 by New Zealand Prime Minister Helen Clark and Italy's Minister of Culture, Giuliano Urbani, was expanded so it could allow finance-only co-productions, including new audiovisual formats, production technologies and distribution media.

3. THE CREATIVE CITY AND FILM: TURIN

This chapter concludes the section on spaces of production by providing a case study of an emerging city in the Italian constellation of film production. From the mid-1990s, and in a more prominent way in the new millennium, Turin has emerged slowly as an alternative place to Rome for audiovisual production. This book emphasises film as a cultural industry, and Turin provides one of the best examples of the connection between tradition and innovation in cultural policy and industrial and institutional frameworks. However, many other cities in Italy could lend themselves to the same kind of analysis, as they have too become the centre of production for a handful of local directors, providing different cultural allure and aesthetics, as well as different sociological universes.

The chapter discusses how the combination of tradition and innovation in cultural policy and in the industrial and institutional framework has enabled the renaissance of filmmaking in Turin. I will also discuss different and contrasting ways to represent Turin in four films, *Così ridevano* (Gianni Amelio, 1998), *Figli di Annibale* (Davide Ferrario, 1998), *Preferisco il rumore del mare* (Mimmo Calopresti, 2000), *Dopo Mezzanotte* (Davide Ferrario, 2004). The discussion will highlight how the city becomes a prominent feature in the films, with the external shots providing connotative meanings to the narrative. My discussion can be framed within an emerging way of thinking about cinematic representations of the city and their intersection with the geography of production (see Clarke 1997; Shiel and Fitzmaurice 2001; also Baudrillard 1988). This body of research highlights that is becoming increasingly difficult to separate the cinematic representation on the screen from the city itself.

LOCATING FILM IN THE CREATIVE CITY

There is an inextricable relationship between one of the most important cultural forms of the twentieth century – cinema – and the most important form of social organisation – the city. Indeed, since the end of the nineteenth century, urbanisation and the development of cinema as an industry as we know it today enjoyed a direct correlation. Both cinema and the city have been able to address this correlation between mobility, images, mass consumption, urbanisation, tourism and culture.

A tradition of filmmaking is a key element in the development of a competitive industry. During the silent era, Turin was at the forefront of Italian cinema, but after World War I, the Italian film industry sharply declined, with obvious repercussions on the studios in Turin. Turin, the place where the high aristocratic and military ranks lived, soon developed as the centre of film production: by 1908, Turin was producing about 60 per cent of the national film output, and between 1910 and 1915 the city was still producing half of all Italian films. *Cabiria*, the most successful film of the period, premiered in 1914 in Turin. The success of Italian historical epics was such that in 1914 George Klein, an independent American distributor, invested in the purchase of two large villas in Turin to be converted into film studios, but his project failed at the onset of World War I.

Turin's geographical location close to France, and Piedmont's cultural, political and historical ties with France, were also important factors in the city's central role in the film industry. At the turn of the century in Italy, there were far less economic resources than in England, France and Germany. Thus the early cinema industry had to rely on French production and technology, Pathé's projectors and programs, and French experts and technicians.

Turin was also the most prominent city in the technological experimentation of closed-circuit television broadcasting and then short-wave transmission. In 1952, the television station at via Montebello transmitted one of the first plays on short wave to the corso Sempione's station in Milan. Subsequently, television stations opened in the larger regional capitals, but the official Radio Televisione Italiana's (RAI) headquarters, which had to do with legal matters, were in Turin.

The medium was then in its infancy, and the metal industry economy prevailed over television. During the economic miracle of the late 1950s and 1960s, Turin was the centre of massive migrations from the south, with around 60,000 people a year arriving to work in the large Fiat factories at Lingotto, Mirafiori and Le Vallette. In the same period, large suburbs with high-rise housing such as La Falchera were built in the outskirts of Turin to accommodate the migrants coming from the south. They are now home to the new proletarians, composed of the legal and illegal migrants from Africa and East Europe, the Italian working class, including the youth working class, the unemployed and people with short-term jobs.

Turin attracted national attention during the late 1960s and throughout the 1970s, with the turbulent years of union and student demonstrations against the giant car manufacturer Fiat. The city has only recently bounced on to the world stage, attracting global media attention as the host of the 2006 Winter Olympic Games, helping it to become an international tourist destination. In this, Turin's geographical location was an important element – as was the case in its nineteenth century industrial development. Turin was – and still is – one of the poles of the so-called industrial triangle (Milan–Turin–Genoa), with access to many important highways: leading to Milan to the east, Genoa to the south and France to the west.

During the 1970s, Turin's population started to diminish. Economic recession in the mid-1970s, industrial restructuring and decentralisation in the metal sector caused a drop in industrial employment, with a subsequent economic crisis. In October 1980, the notorious 'march of the 40,000', in which skilled managerial blue-collar workers demonstrated against a long period of collective bargaining and strikes, marked at the same time the union's debacle at Fiat and a slow decline of Fiat's own centrality in the country's economy (Sheldon, Thornthwaite and Ferrero-Regis 1997).

From the 1980s, Turin has been at the centre of industrial restructure, bearing the consequences of the passage from a Fordist to a post-Fordist form of production. Nevertheless, two decades of enlightened cultural policy, urban renewal, the opening in 2000 of the National Museum of Cinema and securing the city as host of the 2006 Winter Olympics rebranded the city, shaking off its industrial past and promoting it as a cultural hub. In fact, well before the publication of Richard Florida's (2002) book *The Rise of the Creative Class*, Turin's council employed strategies promoting aspects of the city that appeared antithetical to the city's identity. Turin's place in the national imaginary was as the centre of Italian industrial development and home to the national metal industry with the Fiat factory, but the economic crisis in the 1980s forced Turin to a strategic reorientation of its economy. The first municipal interventions aimed at shifting the perception of Turin as an industrial city towards branding culture and creativity through an aesthetic restructuring of the city. The Communist mayor Diego Novelli, in office between 1975 and 1985, was pivotal in the change of this perception. For example, the 1920s Fiat factory Lingotto was restructured in 1983 by architect Renzo Piano (famous for his 1970s project Beauburg in Paris).

This conversion of function was coherent with the role that Lingotto had in the 1920s: from guiding the city in her industrial development, it then became a multi-purpose exhibition space, leading the city towards the economic development of the service sector and of cultural economy. This redevelopment and rebranding of Turin reflected the theory of economic development of small regions, called Sistemi Locali Territoriali (local territorial systems), or SLoT (Ires Piemonte 2004). The concept of SLoT in turn reflects a complex system of local history, folklore, religion, culture and economy that in Italy has its premise in the Renaissance's processes of valorisation of sustainable economy (small, highly skilled companies), social cohesion and quality of life. The concept of *territorio*, and especially that of *interventi sul territorio* (intervention on the territory), goes back to the 1970s, when the PCI elaborated ways to intervene locally by influencing regional public policy. Areas of interest in the sector of creative economy are those around Biella and between Turin and Alessandria (textiles, tied to the fashion industry), Valenza (goldsmithing) and cultural industries (Turin), while other areas of recent economic development had to do with servicing the 2006 Winter Olympics.

From the 1980s, Turin's council funded projects directed at increasing public spaces, pedestrian malls, displays of public art, venues for cultural activities and so on.[1] In the mid-1990s, the council continued this process, devising an urban renewal plan which took Barcelona and Lyon as examples of good urban and cultural planning. Further urban restructuring included a program of cultural intervention – especially in the heart of the city – and transport improvement.

The first Urban Renewal Plan was implemented in 1999 and lasted for five years. It ran along three lines. It was aimed first at encouraging access to international markets and second at specifically assisting in local enterprise and provision of television production incentives. In this process, the plan required local community involvement in the care of the city. Workers' unions were involved in consultation and active participation; other elements were private (banks, mainly) and public enterprises and institutions. This program of public–private funding proved to be successful, especially because it was part of a larger framework of economic and cultural intervention. In this regard, van der Burg, Dolfsma and Wilderom (2004) offer some insight into the positive role that private investments can play, especially for museums and art investments. In particular, banks (the Compagnia di San Paolo and the Cassa di Risparmio di Torino) were very active with a donation in 2000 of 85 per cent of their entire funds to the arts given to the Piedmont region (Piedmont Cultural Monitoring System, *2001 Annual Report*, p. 7). The third goal of the Urban Renewal Plan aimed at the international promotion and branding of the city, including conferences, publishing, cultural and sporting activities, of which the recent Winter Olympics have been a successful outcome.

Despite a disastrous national box office in 2000, during 2001 the overall demand for cinema in Turin increased 1.6 per cent over 2000. This was due to the increase in screens in the regional capital; however, this revival of

TABLE 3.1 THE CULTURAL INDUSTRY IN TURIN — RESOURCES IN 2000

Sector	Investment (millions of Euros)
Public funding (state, region, province and municipalities)	246
Bank-backed foundations and councils for the evaluations of artistic and cultural heritage	60

TABLE 3.2 THE CULTURAL INDUSTRY IN TURIN – CONSUMPTION IN 2000

Sector	Sales (in million of Euros)
Live performance, cinema and ticket sales for exhibitions and museums	75
Publishing industry sales	878
Audiovisual and multimedia sales	165

Source: Adapted from data in the Piedmont Cultural Monitoring System, 2001 Annual Report, p. 7.

cinema culture and the promotion of the National Museum of Cinema have to do with the larger concerted plan of city renewal and planning, and are the result of different strategies which took place at the same time. The function of the National Museum is not limited to collecting cinematic relics, reels, books, props and ephemera, or screening films; rather, it is also actively involved in the cultural economy of the cinema – production – at the local level. In fact, the museum works in synergy with the Piedmont Film Commission, which is hosted in its premises, and the Turin International Film Festival.

The commission has a website that promotes filming in Turin and the region, featuring 6,300 photos of locations. This marketing strategy resulted, between January and September 2001, in attracting twenty productions – ten feature films, four films for television, two soap operas, three documentaries and one short film – with an investment of about 30 billion old liras (15 million and half Euros), giving employment to 200 actors, over 300 technicians and 4,000 extras. In that period, the audiovisual industry in Turin registered the largest increase in the creative workforce, with an increase of 38 per cent in the number of employees and 45 per cent in revenue (Piedmont Cultural Monitoring System, *2001 Annual Report*, p. 9).

Approximately 2.4 per cent of the national workforce is employed in the cultural sector, meaning that 42,000 people are employed in Turin in this sector. This figure includes professionals working in the arts (painters, sculptures, writers, photographers, graphic artists, directors, musicians, dancers); intermediate professions in creative service industries (journalists, translators, TV announcers, and cinema, radio and TV technicians); the cultural industry, including publishing houses, music publishers and recorded media printing companies; libraries, museums and archives and arts-related education.

As Table 3.3 shows, in the five years since the implementation of the Film Commission, investments have been steady, with a slight drop in the number of features produced but an overall raise in productions due to the increase in shorts, documentaries and commercials, and music videos. The

TABLE 3.3 PRODUCTION ACTIVITY IN PIEDMONT BETWEEN 2005 AND 2001

	2005	2004	2003	Total 2001–05
No. productions	36	31	27	145
No. films	8	6	12	56
No. fiction TV shows	6	13	5	32
No. soap operas	2	2	1	9
No. shorts/documentaries	15	10	9	48
Worked weeks for production	172.0	198.5	181.0	880.5
Worked weeks for pre-production	36	56	38	180
Local technical personnel	605	580	480	2,835
Local actors	169	204	332	1,304
Extras	12,459	14,151	5,820	43,700
Commercials and music videos	11 3	5	*	
Investments in Piedmont (€)	29,350,105	30,012, 770	27,115,275	142,256,255.00

*There are no available data for the period 2001–02.
Source: Adapted from the Annual Report of the Film Commission Torino Piemonte (2005).

total number of production is higher than that of the Film Commission Lombardia (107), which has a higher number of television productions. Also, many producers have returned to Turin in the last few years, despite close competition from the Film Commissions in Campania and Friuli-Venezia Giulia. From an analysis of the films made in 2005 in Turin, it is possible to see that the majority of production companies are based in Rome or Milan. The main reason for choosing Piedmont and Turin lies in the fact that the Region Piedmont offers a program of funding called *pre-finanziamento* (pre-financing), which is secured by Finpiemonte and covers the period between the beginning of production and the first instalments of subsidies and funding from the government or from television networks.

In 2004, the region was present at specialised markets and festivals in Europe, presenting a promotional documentary on Turin's locations with a soundtrack by the internationally renowned musician Paolo Conte. In 2005, a new documentary, *Torino Piemonte Production Facilities*, was again circulated and presented in London along with the screening of Davide Ferrario's film *Dopo Mezzanotte.* Also, in the decentralisation of the European Community's services and infrastructure, Turin secured one element of the European MEDIA program, Antenna Media, which promotes European cinema, offers support, consultancy and training, and receives applications to the MEDIA funding system.

The geographically uneven development of the international film industry, with the demise of art houses and independent distribution circuits, has led generally to a flourishing of national, regional and local film festivals. In 1999 in Italy alone, there were more than 60 film festivals with national focus and interest. The establishment of the Turin Film Festival, dedicated to independent filmmaking, in its twenty-third year in 2007, played a key role in the convergence between cultural policy and cultural production, and helped in the rejuvenation of the city's cultural heritage.

Because of close competition from other international film festivals, Nanni Moretti was appointed at the beginning of 2007 as festival director.

The hope was that the director's favour in Europe, and especially France, could contribute to raise the profile of the Turin Film Festival as an international festival. An ancillary economy of film festivals and cultural industries is in fact tourism; however, despite the festival, up to 2001 Turin had a weak tourism-based economy, thus cinema and live entertainment were attended predominantly by local patrons. Strategic planning in the last five years, the organisation of the Winter Olympics and the presence of European audiovisual infrastructures have now started to produce changes in this sense. For example, in 2006, the National Museum of Cinema was visited by over one million patrons, overtaking the famous Egyptian Museum.

HISTORY AS CITY EXPERIENCE: *COSÌ RIDEVANO* AND *DOPO MEZZANOTTE*

In this chapter, I argue that combined interventions by private corporate and public institutions in the economy and culture of the place have put Turin back on the map of filmmaking. This is reflected in an emerging way of thinking about cinema that is not related exclusively to textual representation and content, but also to the geography of production (see Clarke 1997; Shiel and Fitzmaurice 2001). An interdisciplinary approach can help explain how the culture of place blends with local economy; thus this section deals with the intersection between locality and representation in film.

Numerous feature films with good domestic reception and some international resonance have been set in Turin. From 1995, films such as *La seconda volta* (Mimmo Calopresti, 1995), *Tutti giù per terra* (Davide Ferrario 1997), *Figli di Annibale* (Davide Ferrario, 1998), *Così ridevano* (Gianni Amelio, 1998), *Preferisco il rumore del mare* (Mimmo Calopresti, 2000), parts of the six-hour epic about the generation of 1968, *La meglio gioventù* (Marco Tullio Giordana, 2003) and *Dopo mezzanotte* (Davide Ferrario, 2004) were produced and set in Turin, presenting an alternative cityscape to Rome and Milan.

The town's several architectural, and thus historical, layers offer many possibilities for filmmaking. From Roman vestiges to medieval castles, through to Baroque, modernist, Fascist and industrial architecture, the town's architectural styles are more than a colourful background. Gianni Amelio remarked that Turin in fact is 'a town that oozes with history, not the traditional one, but history as life experience, on the streets, on people's faces, in the colours: it has put a mark on everything, an extraordinary thing for those who make cinema' (Gianni Amelio, in Prono 1999, p. 16).[2] In *Dopo mezzanotte*, for example, the relationship between physical geography and cinema history becomes a powerful element in the protagonist's identity and engagement with reality.

During the industrial expansion of the early twentieth century, Turin hosted one of the most active workers' movements in Italy. A fragment of this history is displayed in Monicelli's film *I compagni* (1963), an Italian–French co-production with Marcello Mastroianni, set in the early 1900s. The film shows the period of strikes in Turin and the historical process of nation-building in the genre of the *commedia all'italiana*, with Marcello Mastroianni as the accidental hero typically caught between the two opposed factions: strikers and scabs. The film was released in 1963, one year after the workers' battles with the police in Piazza Statuto, and during the intense period of political unrest and strikes caused by the deal of the Tambroni government with the extreme right-wing party Movimento Sociale Italiano (MSI). *I compagni* was one of the films presented in June 2006 by the National Museum of Cinema in Bruxelles within a retrospective of films made in Turin that aimed at promoting Italian cinema.[3]

Unlike *I compagni*, Gianni Amelio's film *Così ridevano* (1998) takes a pessimistic view about individual consciousness. Hinting at Visconti's *Rocco e i suoi fratelli* (1960), the film tells the story of two brothers' migration to Turin during the economic miracle, between the end of the 1950s and 1963. Their identity dislocation, personal alienation, displacement and the obsessive and perverse relationship between the brothers are the themes played in a hostile, cold and rainy city. In this film, all the characters – whether they are Piedmontese or southern migrants – are depicted as losers and hopeless in front of the rapid process of industrialisation, as they are deceived by the false illusion of progress.

Gianni Amelio presents a city painstakingly similar to Turin in the early 1960s. In this film, the reconstruction of the decaying slums of the city centre where the migrants lived during the economic miracle is flawless: the narrow, damp and sunless via Santa Chiara and via della Consolata delimit a space which – despite its physical centrality – is marginalised. Despite the renewal of the city and the restructuring of many buildings, unlike the outskirts, the centre of Turin has changed very little in the last 40 years. The streets have remained narrow, the facades are still the same, the tram tracks are in the same place. The film's interiors were set in an abandoned building in via Milano, not far from the depicted via Santa Chiara and via della Consolata. Here corridors are dark and claustrophobic, the walls seem to squeeze the eldest brother Giovanni, while the external shots show us a city with a leaden sky, heavy rain and fog, despite the clear sky and sunny days during filming. Amelio wanted to avoid postcard shots, as much as he did in *Lamerica*, in which the beautiful and dramatic Albanian landscape is craftily blurred by his cinematographer Luca Bigazzi.[4] In *Così ridevano*, the beauty of the Baroque city centre is thus blurred and many of the medium shots show us the characters compressed between narrow walls. The continuous open arcades of the markets in Porta Palazzo – expression of the Hellenistic agora, masterpieces of modern town planning and aesthetic delight of the Mediterranean city (Mumford 1961) – are shot during a rainy night; the large square is full of rubbish from the daily market which Giovanni collects as his first job in Turin. This shot fully expresses Amelio's pessimistic view of history, particularly the illusion that rationalism and modernity would deliver individual and social critical consciousness.

The marginalisation, angst and sense of abandonment of the characters can only be expressed through a cold, hostile city in which the claustrophobic streets create a labyrinth difficult to negotiate, especially for the migrants coming from the south. The sense of both geographical and historical displacement reveals Amelio's pessimistic vision of history and is exemplified in the scene in which Giovanni (Enrico Lo Verso) wanders in a maze of empty streets after being released from prison. A Communist demonstration in the background remains far from him, and the red flags in the distance are merely a blurred red stain. In *Così ridevano*, the spire of the Mole Antonelliana appears suddenly in all its grandiosity to a family of migrants from Sicily who mistaken it for the 'Duomo di Milano', revealing once more the complete geographic dislocation of the film's characters.

A completely different view is taken by Davide Ferrario's *Dopo mezzanotte*, in which the reassuring walls of the National Museum of Cinema in the Mole Antonelliana are Martino and Amanda's refuge. Here their dreams become reality, as their lives are affected and transformed by the cinema history that oozes trough the walls of the Museum. Ferrario's economy of work makes *Dopo mezzanotte* a small budget film, shot with a small cast of young actors and with a digital camera, which allows cost cutting with night shooting. Ferrario wanted young and unknown actors (a part from Martino) to maintain a naturalistic approach to the film. One of the film's narrator's remarks is in fact directed at how early cinema was reconceptualised from a cinema of attraction (places, technological wonders, curiosities, anthropology) to one of spectacle with the establishment of the star system and the use of grandiose sets, thus losing the original – although idealistic – idea of naturalistic cinema. *Dopo mezzanotte* addresses this less known history of Italian silent cinema by splicing early films' footage into the main story. Martino, the main character, is interested in the original meaning of film, when it was perceived as the *objective* portrayal of reality. The mechanical representation of reality, and cinema's modernist perception as objective and impartial, is emphasised in *Dopo mezzanotte*'s positivist approach to history through footage of the city's late 1800 and early 1900 urban landscapes and the people who inhabit it.

The film tells the story of three characters: Martino, the Museo Nazionale del Cinema's caretaker; Amanda, a young girl who works the night shift in a fast food shop in the city, but lives in the outer suburb La

Falchera; and Angelo, Amanda's boyfriend and a petty crook who dreams about owning a Jaguar. Amanda's rebellion against the exploitative boss brings the characters together, with the situation resolving itself in Angelo's accidental death and Martino and Amanda's happy relationship.

The incident between Amanda and her boss is caused by a dispute about the shop's closing time. Amanda needs to clean up the shop at five minutes to midnight so that she will not miss the bus home to La Falchera. On the surface, the scene addresses issues that have to do with de-unionised labour and the 'McDonaldisation' of working relationships and consumption. Connotatively, Amanda's problem rests on the alienation of low-paid, temporary workers who live in the outskirts of cities and spend a lot of their time travelling. The relationship between space and the time in the distance between home and the workplace is important in determining labour exploitation in a capitalist economy. The suburb La Falchera features consistently in Davide Ferrario's *Tutti giù per terra*, *Figli di Annibale* and *Dopo mezzanotte* as a place of alienation and marginalisation, opposite to the city centre, now restored and gentrified. His main characters live in La Falchera; thus they have to travel long distances to reach the centre. Ferrario casts his gaze on the spatial distribution of Turin urban centre on the basis of the social division of labour.

Dopo mezzanotte is modelled also on the opposition between the inside and outside of the Mole, top and bottom, respectively – the highest point in the Mole's spire from which Martino looks at the city, and the streets between the Mole and the river Po. The top of the Mole is not a space of daily routine, but a conceptualised space, of 'scientists, planners, urbanists, technocratic subdividers and social engineers', in Lefebvre's (1991, p. 38) words, which highlights Turin's architectural rationalisation during the Renaissance. Turin's large boulevards that criss-cross the city from east to west and north to south, and that can be seen from the top of the Mole, are reminders of the original Roman military camp, Augusta Taurinorum, on which Turin was built and then perfected by sixteenth and seventeenth century architects.

Martino, like Walter in *Tutti giù per terra*, is a modern *flaneur* who engages with the shadows of film history and also with the reality of the city, the sense of place that the film conjures and the history of the city's urban development and planning. Martino's *flaneurism* continues the great obsession of the nineteenth century that was history. In *Dopo mezzanotte*, the city's history is juxtaposed with that of cinema. Martino territorialises his knowledge about the past as he is concerned about how film practices have occurred from and through Turin, how cinema in the city engaged with the environment and social relations, and how it organised this environment in the frame. The film is also concerned with a historicist approach to cinema: short early films are shown and compared with similar contemporary situations, places and people to highlight a continuum between the past and the present. In one word, the film combines the external history of cinema and its connection to the city with the internal, discrete history of cinema, through reels, short films, early cinema's technology and the museum itself. In its claims about the past, the film is concerned with the loss of a positivist view of the world, loss of common sense, social practice and political power that in the period of Modernism were reunited in both everyday discourse and abstract thought (Lefebvre 1991, p. 25).

However, the figure of the *flaneur* tells us more than just the ludic peregrinations of Davide Ferrario's characters. Amanda and Martino are contrasted in terms of the fact that while Amanda wastes her time on public transport, Martino embraces the modern city, removed from constrictions that prevent him from living the city's aesthetic and social proximity. Similarly, Walter in *Tutti giù per terra* shuns every responsibility, such as working or finding a job or attending university. In his refusal to become like everybody else, with an unsatisfying job, a mortgage and trapped in a dysfunctional relationship, Walter criss-crosses Turin, being completely absorbed in his own life and space. The film was criticised for Ferrario's use of framing in the beginning of the film that reminds the aesthetic of publicity spots. On the contrary, through Walter Turin, the city centre – with its upmarket shops, billboards, graffiti and people's faces – reminds us of the 'convergence of urban space, technologies and symbolic functions of images and products' (Crary 1990, p. 20).

BOREDOM, MELANCHOLY, *ENNUI*

Boredom is a symptom of excessive consumerism and affluence. In *Figli di Annibale* and *Preferisco il rumore del mare* the main characters show the signs of what Kuhn calls 'sociological boredom', or the ill-effects of industrialised labour and leisure (Reinhard Kuhn in Petro 1996, p. 191). Both films present the south as the existential solution to superficial relationships, unemployment and corruption.

The two films are set in contemporary Italy. In *Figli di Annibale*, Domenico (Silvio Orlando) is a migrant from Naples, now unemployed, who lives in Turin. For ten years, he has been in *Cassa Integrazione*, the redundancy fund, from the car factory Fiat. The allusion is to the crisis of 1980, when Fiat put 24,000 workers on Cassa Integrazione, and then announced the immediate dismissal of 14,000 workers (Ginsborg 1990, p. 403). During the film, we come to know that Domenico is a survivor of the *reparto verniciatura* (the paint assembly line), historically the strongest unit in union activism. Turin is only visible in the opening shot of a graffiti-reading Falchera, the working-class suburb that features in all Ferrario's films. Despite the fact that Domenico has been offered a job as builder, he is disillusioned and still lives in the nostalgic and melancholic memory of his job as a metalworker, which gave him class pride. Domenico plans to rob a bank and escape to Switzerland. The following scene features Domenico travelling to Como, where he in fact robs a bank, taking as hostage Tommaso (Diego Abatantuono). It becomes immediately evident that Tommaso is a very collaborative hostage; in fact, he jumps at the opportunity to leave a loathsome wife and the risk of bankruptcy behind. Tommaso takes over and convinces Domenico that they must travel south to catch a boat to Egypt, and live off the stolen money. The film becomes a trip throughout the Italian peninsula until they arrive in Otranto, Apulia, where Tommaso has a love affair with a policeman.

Preferisco il rumore del mare features Silvio Orlando in an opposite role to *Figli di Annibale*. In *Preferisco il rumore del mare*, he plays Luigi, a man from Calabria who migrated supposedly during the economic boom. Luigi directs a large factory, which is owned by the father of his ex-wife. During a summer holiday in Calabria, Luigi meets Rosario, whose father is in prison and whose mother has been killed during a shooting between opposite factions of the local *'ndrangheta* (the Calabrian equivalent of the Mafia). Luigi brings Rosario to Turin, in a community funded by Don Lorenzo (played by Mimmo Calopresti). Luigi wants to help Rosario to study and change his life, but secretly he also hopes that Rosario, a religious, reserved, hard-working young man, will have a positive influence on his son, Matteo. He endures paternal authority, which Luigi administers hoping to instil good values in his son, only causing in return Matteo's transgression of the father's rules and values, although without carrying his wrongdoings to the end. Slowly the two boys become friends, but a misunderstanding drives them apart, as Luigi thinks that Rosario stole some money from his home. Rosario returns to his village in Calabria.

Luigi lives in a villa on the hills, while Rosario lives in the community in the outskirts of Turin. Through Rosario we can catch a glimpse of dysfunctional types, unemployed, ex-drug addicts, the silent multitude who seldom appear in Italian films. Luigi is separated from Matteo's mother, who is depressed and bored and lives in a villa in the countryside, spending her time painting. However, he is incapable of cutting emotional ties with his wife, with the excuse that she is Matteo's mother, and thus is unable to manage his sentimental relationship with Serena, his lover of many years.

Both films expose the corruption of present society through the characters of Tommaso and Luigi, and both films present the south as an innocent alternative to something gone wrong with modernity and modernisation. Despite the bullets of the *'ndrangheta*, for Rosario the sound of the southern sea is preferable to the relationships that he had in Turin.

Tommaso and Domenico in *Figli di Annibale* arrive in Egypt only to discover that it was not like what they had dreamed. In a postscript they reveal that modernisation has also arrived in Egypt and that everything is so expensive that soon they will run out of the money from the robbery. *Preferisco il rumore del mare* does not provide solutions or answers for Luigi's existential ennui and inability to establish empathy with the people surrounding him.

Chapter 8 addresses the ways in which the south has been rethought in the light of *pensiero meridiano* (meridian thought). Here it is sufficient to say that the fracture between modernism and postmodernism rests in the language of topography: the north is symbolically obsolete – Domenico's redundancy from Fiat, Tommaso's escape from family and bankruptcy, Luigi's solitude despite his wealth – while the authenticity of the south is an illusion. The two discourses of boredom and postmodernism are thus connected through a language of exhaustion and decline.

NOTES

1. From the early 1980s, the municipality of Turin was also the first institution to implement local policies to mobilise and coordinate services for increasing immigration from the Philippines, Somali, Eritrea, Morocco and Central Africa to Italy. See Caponio, Nielsen and Ribas Mateos (2000).
2. The book collects interviews and screenplay from the film.
3. Other films in the series were *Le amiche* (Michelangelo Antonioni, 1955) and *La donna della domenica* (Luigi Comencini, 1975).
4. Interview with Luca Bigazzi, Milan, December 1997.

PART II

CONFLICT AND CHANGE:
CULTURAL AND POLITICAL
SCREEN CONTEXTS

4. ITALIAN FILM CRITICISM: A BRIEF HISTORY

Along with geographic redistribution of production practices and financing, and the emergence of different topographies in film, Italian cultural and political screen contexts in the period 1980–2000 are in need of an historical re-mapping. This chapter is concerned with the hegemony of a specific ideological discourse in the Italian postwar intellectual milieu, which explains a specific stance by Italian critics towards the domestic cinema that emerged in the 1980s and 1990s.

From the end of World War II, the cultural policy of the Italian Communist Party (PCI) included intellectuals in representing the reality of rural and proletarian life. The philosophy behind the PCI's cultural intervention was to establish a counter-hegemony to the political, economic and religious forces that dominated in Italy in the aftermath of the war. Neorealism in literature and in cinema was the cultural expression of this philosophy, while Gramsci's writings on literature, opera, theatre, serial fiction, aesthetics and, in a limited way, cinema influenced the entire Italian progressive intellectual milieu, and in particular filmmakers and film critics. A cinema of spectacle and entertainment was associated with Hollywood, while a politically engaged cinema that talked about a new reality – the Resistance, hunger, poverty – was considered innovative in both content and expression.

During the 1950s, the officialdom of Italian film criticism did not elaborate a theory of film, as it clung to defending neorealism's sociological aspect and ideological project against bourgeois criticism. Therefore it denied the emergence of a cinema of imagination, from Rossellini's *Viaggio in Italia* (1954) to Visconti's historical realism, especially in *Senso* (1954) and later *Il Gattopardo* (1963). Things became complicated when, during a conference held in Perugia in 1971, a new generation of critics started to question the validity of categories that contrasted art with commercial film. Some critics identified the need to reconceptualise film criticism and the role of the critic with a more open approach to popular or commercial motion pictures, with the intent of breaking with a tradition of realist and politically engaged texts.

A similar second rethinking of Italian cinema's style and content occurred in Pesaro in 1988, during a special section on Italian cinema within the International Film Festival of New Cinema. Initially, a new reflection on the theme of 'new' Italian cinema signalled more the need by some critics to recognise and adapt to changes and transformations of screen culture and in film production and distribution than the need to conceptualise a real theoretical renewal. However, some influential 'official' film critics, Lino Miccichè and Goffredo Fofi to name a few, continued to judge the 'new' Italian cinema from a negative stance. From the middle of the 1990s, there has been an effort – especially by Mario Sesti and Vittorio Zagarrio – to collect essays that explore Italian cinema from many different angles, thus re-composing the fragmented image of the industry.

This chapter traces three moments in the formation of the Italian film critical discourse from the postwar era to the 1990s which attempted to make sense of a changing industrial, cultural and economic landscape. The chapter concludes with a brief discussion of the *auteur* theory and its recent renegotiations. It will consider how, in Italy in the late 1980s, the *auteur* concept persisted for economic reasons, but a more flexible assessment of films through *leitmotifs*, or generic grouping of films that presented common characteristics, emerged.

IDEOLOGY AND FILM CRITICISM

Between 1945 and 1947, as part of a strategy increasing the organisation of propaganda, the *Fronte Nuovo delle Arti* (New Front of the Arts) advocated a new realism in the arts. It strongly opposed market forces, and supported the revival of the historical artistic avant-garde. The intellectual preoccupation of the late 1940s in defining film as an art form took place in a specific way in Italy. Neorealism was functional to the creation of a paradigm of art cinema, with its refusal of extreme stylisation and spectacle and its emphasis, in turn, on realism, humanism and everyday life. Critics, writers and directors involved in the neorealist movement worked with the Centro Sperimentale di Cinematografia, founded by Mussolini in 1932, and later in Cinecittà, which opened in 1937, also founded by Mussolini. During the 1930s, the new generation of critics shared an interest in Pudovkin's and Ejzenstejn's essays and theories (Brunetta 1998, p. 374). The Fascist regime took much inspiration from the Soviet regime practices in the arts, as they were functional to the regime. Mussolini himself saw in the Leninist revolution a useful parallel with the Fascist revolution and admired its autochthonous cinema, which would then shape the establishment of the National Film School in Rome and then the centralisation of film production with the creation of Cinecittà (Garofalo 2002, p. 231). The early connection between critics, directors and writers at the Centro Sperimentale di Cinematografia continued in the postwar period, when the idea of the integration of cinema with a larger intellectual and philosophical project became fruitful thanks to the particular political situation of alliance of all anti-Fascist forces.

The renewed theoretical debate in the journals *Bianco e Nero* and *Cinema* was heavily influenced by Umberto Barbaro, cinema critic for the Communist newspaper *L'Unità*, who insisted on a civic and political engagement of the arts with a larger revolutionary project. In particular, Barbaro was anxious to establish a connection with his work from the 1930s. In this way, he carried his ideological approach into the 1940s and 1950s, increasingly defending Soviet film theory (Brunetta 1998, p. 381). *Filmcritica* also published influential articles on theory and practice in cinema spanning the decades from 1950 to 1970. Galvano Della Volpe, Umberto Barbaro, Roberto Rossellini, Luchino Visconti, Pier Paolo Pasolini and the Communist art historian Giulio Carlo Argan were regular contributors to *Filmcritica* and other journals (Della Volpe et al. 1972). Critics also debated economic reforms of the film industry, such as the introduction of the notorious quality award (*premio di qualità*). After

1945, the Italian state continued to support the cinema industry with subsidies, in accordance with a *dirigiste*[1] economic model, which has been the backbone of the Italian film industry to date. In the late 1940s, state film subsidies were financed through a fund of tax paid by distributors on imported films – it was called the 'dubbing certificate' (Jäckel 2003, p. 241). The quality award was then distributed to domestic films which had performed well at the box office. Rossellini was against this mechanism. He maintained that a quality award needed to be paid at the completion of the film, independently from its performance at the box office. Rossellini advocated a similar model to the new French measures introduced in 1953, whereby the quality award was meant to finance small-budget films by emergent filmmakers, which in turn introduced new tastes and appreciation for domestic films. Rossellini attributed the failure of Italian cinema to produce a substantial renewal after the neorealist season ended to the state's *economic* censorship (Rossellini 1972, p. 57).

The PCI continued to theorise the social and cultural integration of all social classes initiated by Fascism, but with a different ideological colour. In the postwar period, a specific intellectual discourse linked to PCI politics was hegemonic and remained dominant, especially in film criticism, for 40 years. In the 1940s, the initial quarrel among intellectuals saw the opposition between political activism and participation on the one hand and anti-activism and political disengagement of intellectuals on the other. This position reflected the ideological interpretation of culture as it was debated under the ambit of the cultural policy of the PCI after World War II. For the Communist Party, postwar debates on realism focused on the necessity of a contact between intellectuals and proletarian masses, and on the continuous exchange between intellectual knowledge and popular knowledge. Within this debate, as early as 1945, a demand for the recognition of cinema within a broader cultural front also emerged. In this, the role of the critic was that of widening the popular knowledge of cinema and sanctioning the political and militant function of cinema.

After the exclusion of the PCI from government with the 1947 elections, the party adopted a rigid political and ideological position in the relationship between party and intellectuals. At this point in time, state policies were aimed at changing the register of Italian films from neorealism to a more commercial and socially disengaged orientation. The preoccupation of the Italian government and the Catholic press was directed at undermining Italian neorealism through the advocacy of tradition and family value. The aforementioned mechanism that governed the distribution of the quality award was one of the government's strategies to control film production, with a pro-capitalist and anti-communist goal in mind. The PCI initially battled for freedom of expression, in favour of neorealism and for state subsidies to aid cultural production. Thus directions in the PCI's cultural policy were also influenced by disputes between the PCI and the Italian government in postwar Italy in regard to the drawing and implementation of policies for the cultural industry, and in particular the film industry.

FILMMAKERS AND FILM CRITICS AS ORGANIC INTELLECTUALS

Film content and film criticism were indissolubly bound together. Gramsci's writings, published for the first time between 1947 and 1949,[2] strongly influenced the PCI's position on the role of intellectuals, and the De Sanctis-Croce-Gramsci line succeeded, confirming neorealism and populism in cinema and literature, while it banned every evasion into intimate explorations in cinema and the hermetic trend in literature. Giovanni Verga's *I Malavoglia*, which constituted the basis for Visconti's *La terra trema* (1948) and later for *Rocco e i suoi fratelli* (1960), was considered the prototype for the new expression of realism in literature and cinema. Subsequent debates about neorealism against the emergence of a new cinema also reflected different ways to think about the political and ideological engagement of filmmakers and film critics.

It is important to note that in 1945 anti-Fascism constituted a common ground of identification for communist militants and for intellectuals who firmly believed that after the war there were the exhilarant possibility and the conditions for building a different society (Binetti 1997, p. 365). The PCI's ideological pluralism, a sort of 'universal Marxism' (Binetti 1997, p. 363) which was aimed at including the heterogeneous Italian intelligentsia, was the result of the Salerno's turn in 1944 (*la svolta di Salerno*). In that historical congress, Togliatti's strategic politics of inclusion prevailed, with their political-ideological articulations – including the party's cultural policy, inspired by the Soviet model of socialism. The cultural policy of the PCI followed a trajectory that started from the inclusion of intellectuals in the reality of rural and proletarian life to a Zdhanovist model in culture and art at the beginning of the Cold War (Misler 1973). However, the PCI's position in relation to the role of intellectuals was criticised by some intellectuals.

One of the first intellectuals alienated from the PCI was Elio Vittorini, one of the most outstanding representatives of Italian culture of the second postwar period. Vittorini fought against Fascism from within the Resistance movement and then became a PCI member after the war. In 1945 he founded *Il Politecnico*, one of the most influential journals of the postwar years, but in 1947 the journal ceased publication when Vittorini left the PCI after a polemic with Mario Alicata and Palmiro Togliatti. At the base of the *querelle* between Vittorini and Togliatti was the necessity to define the function of the left-wing intellectual, which Vittorini saw as politically independent from the party. Also, from the beginning of their career, both Luchino Visconti and Pier Paolo Pasolini entertained a conflictual relationship with the PCI, caused by the directors' homosexuality and by their departure from neorealism in content and form. Likewise, Giuseppe De Santis clashed with the PCI, as he attempted to address difficult issues like women's sexuality (in *Riso amaro* 1949) and also to make films with a more commercial appeal.[3] From the 1950s on, the aspect of cultural engagement of intellectuals with the Communist Party continued within the officialdom of the PCI. The debate was polarised between Galvano Della Volpe and Umberto Barbaro, who represented a more traditional left-wing film criticism. Some other critics – Pasolini, for example – labelled this ideological stance as a critical distortion which privileged a socio-political discourse of cinema over a film theory approach (see Edoardo 1972; Misler 1973). In 1959, during a round table published in *Filmcritica*, with the title *Esiste un nuovo cinema italiano?* (*Does a new Italian cinema exist?*), Pasolini argued against the trivialisation of social themes as in Monicelli's, Loy's and Lizzani's films. These film directors were deemed conformist, making a plot-driven cinema that continued neorealism in a conventional form (Bruno 1972, pp. vi–viii). Eventually, this debate sealed the definite turn of the new Italian cinema away from neorealism. Pasolini advocated a research on a new way to represent reality with a shift from representing 'what has happened' to 'what could happen'. Eventually, the Zdhanovist orientation of the PCI in cultural matters, the invasion of Hungary in 1956 and the public revelation of Stalin's crimes provoked tensions in the cultural milieu which led to a fracture between the PCI and many more intellectuals.

THE DECADES 1960 TO 1980

As we have seen, concerns for ways to see and represent reality in cinema have been recurring regularly among Italian film critics and filmmakers. The break of the Italian filmmakers of the 1960s and early 1970s away from neorealism must be seen in the context of the evolution of what John Orr calls neo-modernist cinema.[4] In the 1960s, the presence of melodrama in neorealist films was thought as an impediment to the spectator's awareness of the construction of cinematic language, while the image power was to question political orthodoxies and society. A static cinema was replaced by camera's mobility, fluid panning, medium-long shots with swift zooms in and out, pastiche, irony and constant self-reflection. These features, wrongly attributed to 'post'-modern cinema, are, according to Orr, essential features of 'the cinema's continuing encounter with modernity' (Orr 1993, p. 2). Despite owing to Italian neorealism, neomodernist cinema of the 1960s ran parallel to the technical advancements of the image and its inherent ambiguity.

Accordingly, Italian cinema became a cinema of ambiguity.

Michelangelo Antonioni made films on the failure of the bourgeoisie to create new values that matched those destroyed by modernisation and technology, challenging older values of patriarchy with his portrayal of the modern female persona through his preferred actress, Monica Vitti. In Antonioni's films, narration is subverted, the tension is nullified, and the process of cause and effect is altered. Bernardo Bertolucci (*Il conformista* 1970), Liliana Cavani (*Il portiere di notte*, 1974) and Pier Paolo Pasolini (*Salò*, 1975) began the retro movement with films on the disturbing link between Fascism and its erotic attraction, highlighting the uncertainties of knowledge and questioning social, psychological and political continuities between the present and the past.

Film criticism remained hegemonic within the institutional left. But the youth revolts in 1968–72 called for a re-evaluation of cultural life in opposition to the PCI. During a conference held in Perugia in 1971, organised by the National Union of Cinema Critics, a new generation of film critics – Adelio Ferrero, Sergio Frosali, Ernesto G. Laura, Italo Moscati and Giorgio Tinazzi, all born in the 1930s – debated the role of the film critic and criticism outside the rank and files of the PCI. Adelio Ferrero, film critic at *Mondo Nuovo*, stated that the preoccupation of the PCI with the continuity of cultural tradition resulted in the repression of consciousness and of the will of disruption (Ferrero 1972). According to Ferrero, the PCI pursuit of the myth of respectability in the postwar period resulted in an attempt to capture the support of the middle class (the 'universal Marxism' to which Binetti refers) (Ferrero 1972, p. 14). Ultimately, the PCI policy of *grandi alleanze* (grand alliances) resulted in the abandonment of a progressive political and organisational cultural policy.

It is useful to recall that, in the postwar period, the construction of the clash between a political and engaged cinema with artistic intentions on the one hand and commercial – and thus disengaged – cinema on the other resulted in the formulation of a theoretical and critical framework that put neorealism at the centre of social, ideological and aesthetic analysis. For Italian postwar filmmakers and critics, the aesthetics of realism, the social engagement of the directors and intentionality were thus the inseparable pillars of left-wing criticism. The break away from neorealism by directors such as Federico Fellini, Luchino Visconti and Michelangelo Antonioni was consequently considered a departure from engagement with reality according to a leftist reading.

Conversely, at the Perugia Conference, some Italian film critics started to question the theoretical categories of art/commercial film and the nature of the relationship between the film critic and the filmmaker. In the early 1970s, the reaction against neorealism was so profound that films such as *Paisà*, *Umberto D* and *La terra trema* were considered 'failures' because of their melodramatic populism and petit bourgeois limitations. Similarly, film criticism was considered elitist and too compromised with party ideology. In this regard, Ferrero wrote that 'while the critic is obstinately busy in confirming or denying the quantity of realism in Visconti's latest film, the public runs to see *Pane, amore e fantasia*' (Ferrero 1972, p. 11). The intent, then, was to open a critical discourse to works such as popular films that were not considered worthy of critical analysis because of their appeal to popular audiences. The audience success of *Pane, amore e fantasia* (Luigi Comencini, 1953) kicked off the trilogy of a popularised form of neorealism crossed with comedy, with its two sequels *Pane, amore e gelosia* (Luigi Comencini, 1954) and *Pane, amore e ...* (Dino Risi, 1955) depicting life in marginalised rural villages in a context of massive migration to the cities.

This advocacy of commercial or popular cinema aimed at a better understanding of how commercial cinema as a product organises its own consumption and fruition, and it resulted in the emergence of issues such as the spectator's position, pleasure and consumption. The attack against the officialdom of left-wing film criticism and its failure to understand mass communication mirrored the observations that Gianni Bosio made in 1965 about the coincidence between the crisis of leftist cultural renewal and the success of television (Ferrero 1972, 14). Essentially, the PCI failed to understand the connection between the growth of mass consumption and production, television, youth counterculture, pleasure and the emergence of neomodernist currents in art and cinema (Gundle 2000). The party's high-brow position against television stalled 30 years of creative and constructive criticism of mass media, causing a delay in the formulation of serious policy analysis and legislation in broadcasting regulations. Umberto Eco remarked that this high-brow position was 'an indication of the cultural underdevelopment of civilised people at a time when a historical and anthropological mutation was taking place in Italy' (Eco 1983, p. 113).

At the Perugia conference, Ernesto G. Laura, former director of the Venice Film Festival and director of the journal *Filmstoria*, looked at the crisis in film criticism from a different perspective. He attributed the demise of the film critic, of cinema journals and the increased communication gap between film critics and audience to the 1960s and early 1970s film distribution system. Laura lamented that the film critic wrote for the acculturated public of the *prime visioni* (first-run theatres). First-run theatres were more expensive and equipped with the latest technologies — Panavision screens and stereo sound systems — while cinemas in the outer suburbs could not afford technological conversion. Some films would only be distributed for first-run circuits, establishing in this way the production of B-grade films exclusively for distribution in second- and third-run theatres. These films would neither reach the first-run circuit nor the international market, and consequently would never undergo a formal content and aesthetic analysis by film critics. This situation consolidated the establishment of two different tiers of public, with different taste and no communication between them (Laura 1971, pp. 33–34). Popular cinema analysis remained largely underwritten until the early 1990s, when Paolo Pillitteri started to re-evaluate the Italian comedy as an indicator of popular mentalities and the expression of social dynamics that intersected with political and cultural conflicts of the time (Pillitteri 1992, p. 20). It is therefore important to distinguish between how Italian film critics perceived popular films at the time of the Perugia conference — the spaghetti Western, the soft-porn genre, the Italian comedy and the *giallo*,[5] all considered as inferior genres – and how these genres are now undergoing a process of re-evaluation and revision because of the postmodern reconsideration of the relationship between mass culture and high-brow culture (see especially Jameson 1979; Huyssen 1986).

Despite the sharp criticism directed to the official film critique, at the Perugia conference the function of the film critic in the 1970s was still intended as *impegnato* (politically engaged), as a translator and filter for a non-educated audience, in the sense of the Gramscian organic intellectual. Film reading remained style-centred, and content and stylistic qualities of films were expected to deliver social and political awareness and consequently social and political transformation. Retrospectively, it is possible to say that neo-modernism was concerned with shifts in cinematic language, but the role of the filmmaker and the function of the film remained understood as inherently political, with pedagogic and ideological functions.

Lino Miccichè was an authoritative figure in Italian cinema culture. He was born in the 1930s, and for about 30 years he was in charge of the film column in the Italian Socialist Party (PSI) newspaper *L'Avanti*, until he gave up his membership of the PSI in 1989. A prolific writer, Miccichè published books on Italian cinema, especially about Luchino Visconti and the period 1960–80, up until two years before his death in 2004. With his involvement in film policy as an administrative advisor to Italnoleggio and the Ente Autonomo di Gestione per il Cinema, and his academic position as a teacher of film history and film criticism, Miccichè was the incarnation of the convergence between film criticism and the academy so lamented by the critics at the Perugia conference. Lino Miccichè can be considered the most representative film critic speaking from within the officialdom of left-wing politics. In 1965, he founded the Mostra Internazionale del Nuovo Cinema held in Pesaro (International Festival of New Cinema), which he directed until 1987. Quite interestingly, Miccichè left the direction of the Pesaro Festival the year before the festival was dedicated, under the direction of Franco Montini, to the exploration of the emergent Italian cinema. The two events are more than a mere coincidence, because

Miccichè was very critical of the cinema which emerged in the 1970s and continued well into the 1980s. For Miccichè, the uprising of 1968 produced a break with previous generations but ultimately 'confused attempts and various tendencies, odd movements that the yearly worsening of the crisis has entangled in an almost inextricable knot', producing undesired effects on cinema and its ideological function (in Brunetta 1998, p. 426; Miccichè 1975, 1995).

Italian cinema struggled to find a new direction until the end of the 1980s. Despite Miccichè's openness to new directions and theories in film in the 1960s, he also failed to understand historical shifts in mass culture, maintaining a high-brow position and helping to carry through, with another influential film critic, Goffredo Fofi, the disdain for the new directors of the 1980s. During this time, critics found it difficult to classify the extremely variegated aesthetics of the films that were produced; the concept of the director as engaged intellectual continued to influence Italian film criticism until well into the 1990s. Moreover, following a style-centred textual reading film, critics lamented the disconnection of the young Italian directors from social reality. Goffredo Fofi judged Gabriele Salvatores as an 'author of pseudo-1968 repatriates, and with *Sud*, of a little didactic-rebellious theatre which is superficial and conventional, very Northern for its peculiar political hypocrisy that belonged to the Left-wing culture of Milan' (Fofi 1994b, p. 596). Fofi's remark denotes this predisposition to overlook and disregard, for instance, the films that addressed the past, such as *Cinema Paradiso* (Giuseppe Tornatore, 1988), *Mediterraneo* (Gabriele Salvatores, 1991) and *Domani accadrà* (Daniele Luchetti, 1988). In 1997, he continued his tirade against Italian cinema, identifying it as conformist, mediocre, petit bourgeois and rhetorical (Fofi 1997, p. 150).

In some other instances, the impossibility of finding common characteristics that would classify the New Italian Cinema as a movement contributed to identify it as a 'fragmented cinema' (Bo 1996, p. 28). Nevertheless, fragmentation became one of the New Italian Cinema's identifying characteristics, and from the beginnings of the 1990s, some

Italian critics like Mario Sesti and Vito Zagarrio deployed different strategies in the interpretation and understanding of the Italian filmic output (see Sesti and Zagarrio 1998).

DEATH OF THE *AUTEUR*? REASSESSING CONTEMPORARY ITALIAN CINEMA

Most of the problems that the Italian critics encountered in approaching the cinema produced between 1987 and the mid-1990s were concerned with the fact that the films escaped the traditional paradigms of film theory. These films could not be legitimised because they did not lend themselves to an authorial reading following an aesthetic paradigm. This paradigm was formulated with Italian neorealism as a precursor of art cinema and then modernist cinema, and remained dominant in film criticism and in the academy. Thus judgments passed in the name of the fathers of Italian cinema and of the aesthetics of the *auteur* film denounce the absence of a readable film form. The high degree of difficulty in seeing the cinematic output of this period through different methodologies reveal the institutional and contextual constraints that accompany all cultural production.

The emergence of French film criticism at the end of the 1940s, the theorisation and legitimisation of the director as *auteur* and the influence of *Cahiers du Cinéma* contributed to the construction of the antinomy between two clusters of concepts: the political engagement of the intellectual/realist/art film versus the disengaged/entertainment-oriented Hollywood film. European art cinema defined itself in opposition to Hollywood's narrative and aesthetic conventions, privileging the interrelation of content and form, with its emphasis on their unity, originality, newness of creative composition and processes emerging from the film. These qualities were found in directors such as Renoir and Fritz Lang, and some American directors such as Orson Welles and John Ford, and contributed to the separation of superior films from the main run of commercial products. The decline in film audiences in the 1950s partly produced the growth of the French New Wave, which in turn contributed to the rebuilding of the French national film industry under the provision of state subsidies which recognised film as an industry as well as an art form (Neale 1981, p. 27). Through the legitimisation of French directors as artists, the concept of the *auteur* became the rationale for the diversity of European film, but also the unity of the films produced by certain *auteurs* during the 1950s and 1960s. The *politique des auteurs* was functional to establishing the role of the film critic as the interpreter of the 'traces', the signs, the footprints that the author leaves behind. Without detracting from the intentionality and subjectivity of art cinema and its aesthetic, it is important to remember that it is not possible to separate European art cinema from the European–American trade in motion pictures, US capital investment, film culture journals of the early 1960s and the academy that bolstered art films (Guback 1969; Allen and Gomery 1985). In the 1950s, America's movie audience diminished due to a series of problems, one of them the rise of television. Hollywood thus had to generate a new kind of audience with new kinds of films.

As we saw in Chapter 3, intensified American economic involvement in Europe after World War II helped create an economic base for art film in Italy. Also, Italian neorealist films produced after the war by Rossellini, De Sica, Visconti and De Santis had already been exported to the United States, and they proved crucial at the end of the war in constructing an American taste for European cinema. With the cross-fertilisation between Italian and American cinema, the boundary between American films made in Italy and Italian films became blurred: American film producers employed Italians in their big-budget films; Italians made their own large-scale films with American stars; Italians even started to make their own successful spaghetti Westerns, which were then exported to America and to the rest of the world.

To exemplify the intertwined relationship between American and Italian cinema, it is sufficient to mention Federico Fellini, whose career certainly took off with Hollywood's involvement in his films, and the growing reputation of Cinecittà internationally and nationally with

American majors bankrolling Italian language films for European and American audiences. As discussed in Chapter 2, thanks to Hollywood's capital, in the 1960s the Italian film industry was thriving, with 65 per cent of the box office taken by domestic films. Meantime, Fellini's fame grew in the United States, with writers and critics publishing work about him, and the American Film Institute and United Artists putting Fellini's films on constant display. According to Burke (1996), the trajectory of Fellini's career paralleled the trajectory of the *auteur* theory and American involvement in the Italian film industry. It rose at the same time as Truffaut's article about art cinema, in 1954, with *La strada* and started declining in the mid-1960s, in conjunction with Roland Barthes' 1968 article 'The death of the author'. By the 1970s, Fellini had become increasingly frustrated with the production machinery, requests by producers and distributors, the dubbing into other languages, and the advertising and marketing campaigns. Fellini at some point said that he had naïvely thought that by becoming the legend 'Fellini' he would find it easier to work as a director (Burke 1996). Interestingly, Fellini's self-professed inability to express himself as an *auteur*, and the increasing fragmentation of the subject, became the very distinctive elements of Fellini's appraisal as an *auteur*.

This period coincided with Italy's own crisis in the film industry, and the decline of Cinecittà and of the European art film. By the end of the 1960s, Hollywood was finding it increasingly costly to produce in Italy, the national complex tax system and bureaucracy discouraged American producers, and internal problems with security and terrorism drove the majors away (Goldsmith and O'Regan 2003). Not only was the subject-matter fragmented, but film production became very irregular and inconsistent, and budgets needed to be put together with many small packages. Fellini eventually had to surrender to make films with television backing.

Effectively, from the 1970s, authorship has become a commercial and critical strategy, a function to circulate certain texts, a device to attract funding from different sources, and an element to establish the relationship between certain texts and audiences, which was exploited by Hollywood itself to establish directors such as Martin Scorsese in the 1970s. Within an accelerated commodification of culture, distribution and marketing have become powerful and global elements in the circulation of films. The author-name (Foucault 1977) has thus become a significant marketing label, and the concept of the author reappeared in the 1980s and 1990s 'as a commercial performance of the business of being an *auteur*' (Corrigan 1991, p. 104). All in all, *auteur* theory is the most persistent and enduring way to make sense of cinema, and for this reason Italian film critics and academics have refused to give up the concept of authorship.

In the early 1980s, with the crisis of grand ideologies and political systems, and the rupture of the ideological-political-cultural front, political films, modernist film theories and grand theories were no longer relevant. The new Italian directors themselves also refused authorship as a category of classification of their films.[6] The new *auteur* became the filmmaker, hinting at the name of the film exhibition founded in 1982 in Milan. The *auteur* concept was replaced by a more flexible paradigm that assessed films based more on observations, statements and fragments of dialogues taken from banal daily routine. Common to films by many directors were a new minimalist language and shrinking budgets. It was at this time that the Italian philosopher Gianni Vattimo forged his philosophical concept of *pensiero debole* (weak thought) (Vattimo and Rovatti 1983). The concept came forth as a reaction to the intellectual and teleological crises that emerged with debates about modernism and post-modernism; it expressed the need for a pause from Cartesian rationalism and was in polemic with a model of strong rationality that offered totalising interpretations of the world.

Weak thought was very much a public affair, given the strength of historicist thought and classical culture in Italy. The relationship that weak thought advocated with history was one of liberation from fragments and ruins of the past, promoting critiques of modernity and its symptoms. Much of this critique emerged in the films produced from the early 1980s to the 1990s by new directors who shared with Vattimo a generational sensibility for cultural critique. In these films, there are no immediately evident references to previous cinema movements. There is, instead, an intention to avoid 'framing' or searching for the director's gaze, the *régard* or *lo sguardo*, that was so central to the *auteur* theory. Stories unfold inside apartments where everyday-life objects define what Cristiana Paternò called 'the aesthetic of the coffee machine on the stove'.[7] Francesca Archibugi's debut feature film (her early films were shorts), *Mignon è partita* (1988), presents a simple use of the camera that avoids sophisticated framing. Narratives look at simple stories of everyday life, where one is a hero for simply doing his or her civic duty: 'Out there, there is nothing, or there is little, and it is very tiring to go and look for it. And anyway, we no longer have enough strength to do it,' said Sandro Petraglia in an article in *il manifesto* in 1991. This profound disillusionment with the 1980s political and cultural reality indicates the profound connection that exists between the generation of counter-cultural discourses within society itself, and artistic and cultural production. The severed relationship between critics, directors, academia and the slow disappearance of reviews of Italian films in major magazines and newspapers was in fact a symptom of the collapse of a strong counter-cultural discourse.

The cinema of the 1990s thus emerged from a discrete, weak cinema, paraphrasing Vattimo's philosophical concept of weak thought – and in fact Galimberti called the cinema of the 1980s 'the unaware son' of the weak thought (Galimberti 1996, p. 367). Lack of funding produced the pauperism of the cinema of this decade, with filmmakers happy enough to be able to make a feature with very little aspirations. These films, such as those by the raising star Silvio Soldini, were works in progress, never-finished works that could be developed further if the filmmaker could find more money. Soldini said, in fact, that: 'Our films are little, which does not mean mediocre, but they are produced with a minimum of means, and are only able to tell a few images at a time.' (in Serenellini 1985, p. 117)

In the 1990s, the *auteur* returned as a useful and strategic category for film criticism, interpretation, production and marketing. Films by Gabriele Salvatores, Daniele Luchetti, Mimmo Calopresti, Nanni Moretti, Giuseppe

Tornatore, Enzo Monteleone and Marco Tullio Giordana – and one could include also Maurizio Nichetti, Francesca Archibugi, Wilma Labate, Sergio Rubini, Edoardo Winspeare, Cristina Comencini, Guido Chiesa, Mario Martone and more – can neither be categorised as avant-garde or modernist cinema, nor as mainstream films, but they increasingly were reviewed under the rubric of the *auteur* concept. These films belong to the middle-quality level, or popular art film, with circulation at international film festivals, and occasional box-office success nationally and internationally. A valid question can be raised about how to account for this filmic output. Italian critics attempted definitions such as *neo-neorealismo, minimalista* (minimalist) and *carino* (cute, nice) (Quaresima 1991), which were neither explanatory nor comprehensive of the many styles and themes developed. Early critical accounts highlighted minimalist aspects of this cinema, or micro-realism of the films, referring to the absence of heroes and grand narratives (Quaresima 1991, p. 39). This early assessment of the New Italian cinema by Italian critics reflected a difficulty in abandoning the traditional paradigms of film theory.

Notes

1. Toby Miller (2005, 2006) defines a *dirigiste* film industry one in which the state controls subvention of training and production, with minimal or no support for distribution and exhibition. Other features have to do with content: a *dirigiste* film industry is characteristically preoccupied with the ideology of nation, rather than pleasure. These features have to coexist. Typical *dirigiste* film industries are the Western European, while Hollywood, Bollywood and Hong Kong adhere to a model of *laissez-faire*.

2. *Letters from prison* and the first volume of *Prison notebooks* were published in 1947.

3. For an interesting insight into the relationship between De Santis, the PCI and the making of *Riso amaro*, see the documentary by Martini *De Santis and Moretti: Citizens and Filmmakers* (1995).

4. John Orr deals mainly with the films produced in the period 1958–78 which

that gave rise to art cinema and American independent filmmaking. Rodowick takes a further step in commenting radical political and avant-garde filmmaking (counter-cinema) in his detailed historical and theoretical account of what has increasingly been defined 'political modernism' in recent history of film theory (1988). A commonality is the authors' attempts to link the film practice of the two decades 1950–70 to modernism.

5.   Literally, yellow. The definition originated from the series of detective stories published by Mondadori, whose covers had a yellow background.

6.   My interview with Kiko Stella, Milan, May 2000, and Enzo Monteleone, Rome, May 2000.

7.   My interview with Cristiana Paternò, Rome, April 2000.

5. RETURNING HOME TO HISTORY

The first three chapters of this book were concerned with the modes and models of production of the Italian film industry in the national, global and local contexts. They outlined processes in place to secure funding from many sources, conditions of production that have to do with processes of centralisation or decentralisation, and distribution. Chapter 4, dedicated to an analysis of the heavy influence of postwar Italian film theory and criticism on contemporary domestic cinema, investigated historical factors determining current confusion of Italian film critics in the face of a cinema that has been difficult to classify according to traditional paradigms in film theory.

This chapter is the first concerned with the mapping of themes and issues in contemporary Italian cinema, shifting the attention to Italy itself, and to the political, economic and cultural changes which occurred throughout the 1980s and which surfaced in the films produced in the period. The chapter offers an account of how, in the late 1980s, after a period of economic recovery from the 1970s oil crises and restoration of a new social and political conservatism, the Resistance and the Holocaust emerged as strong themes in an attempt to return to strong stories. The problem that surfaced in the films was that in the late 1980s and 1990s the political struggle over the interpretation of national history had entered a new and confused stage. New images of the national past addressed this confusion by presenting profound fractures in Italian society and culture in history films. The conclusion is that, in a period of economic expansion, conservative backlash and restoration, looking back was an attempt to retrieve collective memories.

ECONOMIC PROSPERITY, POLITICAL DEBACLE

After the oil crises of mid-1970s, there were signs in Europe of economic growth and recovery from the recession. From the beginning of the 1980s, Northern Italy embarked on a period of a rapid economic recovery. The renewed prosperity of the region was mainly due to four combined factors. First, commodity prices fell, especially the price of oil, enabling Italy to import raw materials and export its manufactured goods under the new brand of 'Made in Italy'. Second, labour militancy received a historical blow with the October 1980 strike at Fiat, when 40 thousand workers marched against the trade unions. From that date, a hard-line anti-collectivism characterised industrial relations for a decade. The third factor is directly linked to the second, as it measures the weakening of the unions. In the early 1980s, the system of automatic indexed wages was slowed down, and in 1985 a referendum confirmed its reduction (Clark 1996, p. 395). The effects were measured in the increase in business confidence in investment. Fourth, industrial restructuring embarked on by employers from the mid-1970s led to falling rates in industrial employment. Over a million industrial jobs were lost between 1981 and 1991. At Fiat alone, the number of blue-collar workers went from 110,049 in 1980 to 60,180 in 1987 (Sheldon et al. 1997, p. 90). On the other hand, new skilled jobs were to be found in service industries, or in small and medium firms in Northern and Central Italy, which became the base of a markedly diversified economy. Figures show that in the first five years of the 1980s the indices of employment by economic sector increased by 70 per cent in the tertiary sector, while it decreased dramatically in agriculture and 10 per cent in industry. By contrast, unemployment was at its height (see tables in Ginsborg 1990, pp. 449–50), showing that workers losing their jobs in the industrial and agriculture sectors were not absorbed into the new economy, where jobs were obviously filled by a new generation of professionals, namely the first generation of Italians to have entered the system of mass education after the 1962 reform.

This industrial reorganisation was based on technological restructuring, flexible specialisation and high-quality manufacturing for export. By the end of the 1980s, Italy had become the fifth largest industrial nation in the world. In addition, this startling economic recovery – a 'second economic miracle' as Ginsborg (1990, p. 409) defined it – could not have taken effect without a significant domestic increase in mass consumption and relative political stability with Bettino Craxi's government.

Let me mention a few contextual elements that played a fundamental role in the social and economic changes of the 1980s. The Craxi-led coalitions between Christian Democrats and the Socialist Party, which lasted from 1983 to 1987, was the first government led by a Socialist prime minister, and also the longest continuously serving government since World War II. It is important to note that the re-launch of the Socialist Party in 1980 by Bettino Craxi with a group of journalists and academics was done under a platform of recovery of national values and identity in a political and economic context (Mason 1986, p. 22). Ginsborg notes how, after the collectivistic ideals of the 1970s and the political *riflusso* (flowing back) of the 1980s, the 'enterprise culture' – a new ethos – seemed to have 'found its natural home in Italy' (Ginsborg 1990, p. 408). Laura Laurenzi summarised this ethos well when she wrote in 1987 that:

> Yes, Italy is becoming a country of rich people in which the dedication to luxury is an end that is spreading more and more and that is capricious … Until recently, we were ashamed to be rich, now Italy is pervaded by a febrile desire of capitalism. A nice wish, a hot desire for entrepreneurship and profit. The ethics of dignified poverty has been swept away, it has drowned in the mourning grey of the 1970s. Now money, according to paradigms that once belonged only to protestant cultures, is a divine grace: those who are rich are elected by God. (Laurenzi in Cappellieri 2007, p. 41)

Rhetorical and patriotic speeches, as well as political campaigning by the Socialist Party,[1] aimed at boosting Italian exports under the slogan of 'Made in Italy'. The 'Made in Italy' concept was a clever revival from the 1950s, when it first appeared in Florence and Rome with high couture and design. However, in the 1950s Italy continued to suffer from France's supremacy in fashion, and design production was a very elitist phenomenon (Cappellieri 2007, p. 33). The immense social, political and cultural changes brought about by the 1960s and 1970s irreversibly modified relationships between genders, races, political power and social base, and classes. By the end of the 1970s, fashion, design, architecture and art broke definitely with modernism, drawing freely from a decontextualised use of history. Milan, Bettino Craxi's home town, became the capital of fashion and design, the magnet of post-modern creativity; design studios and brands such as Alchimia and Memphis were pivotal in the establishment of the new ethos of content=image=market. The success of the 'Made in Italy' brand in the 1980s was also based on intangible factors, conjured up by the aesthetic and cultural inheritance of Italian Renaissance. Thanks to this inheritance, the 'Made in Italy' brand was able to combine 'high culture' with craftsmanship in its claims of quality and excellence in materials and execution. Some Italian regions, within an economy of flexible specialisation, and thanks to traditions of craftsmanship linked to the territory, were able to innovate and convert their traditional production into a logic of specialisation on a local scale. As in the nineteenth century, in which the textile sector heavily contributed to the expansion of the Italian industry, fashion replaced Italian art film as the most important international ambassador for the country in this period.

The 1980s were thus the years dedicated to the material world, marked by an obsession with fitness, career, the launch of pop stars, the rapid rise of fashion stylists and brands. In 1982, Giorgio Armani made the cover of *Time*, which opened up the American market to Italian fashion and the brand 'Made in Italy'. This wind of innovation and opportunities was also felt in film production in Milan. With the crisis of Cinecittà, young filmmakers in Milan made a bet that the city would become the city of cinema – in a similar way to what happened to New York in the early 1970s, during the Hollywood crisis. Milan was dubbed the East Coast of Italian cinema, in opposition to the now 'archeological' Cinecittà (Serenellini 1985, p. 115). Maurizio Nichetti had just made *Ratataplan*

(1979), which had considerable success in the niche market of Milanese leftist intelligentsia.[2] With the deregulation of the broadcasting system at the local level in 1976, by 1982 there were 1,594 local television stations, creating economic opportunities for the stations' owners and for local advertising. Thus advertising agencies mushroomed, and with them came not only an explosion of sector magazines selling space to promote brands, but also market research, opinion polling, audience ratings, consulting, design, graphics and marketing, and, finally, commercial 'free' television which offered various opportunities to young filmmakers to train in the audiovisual industry. With the lowering costs of technology, the integration between film, television and records (once separated sectors) increased (Pilati 1992).

In 1981, a structure gathering independent and experimental filmmakers, called Filmmaker, was founded in Milan with the support of the Provincia di Milano. The group included directors Bruno Bigoni, Silvio Soldini, Kiko Stella and Giancarlo Soldi, and cinematographer Luca Bigazzi (who worked with Gianni Amelio in the 1990s). The working environment was favourable, as the economy was propelled by advertising and commercial television. Many directors formed cooperatives in which the figure of the director-producer (or the triangulation director-producer-writer) became a fundamental feature of a new production mode. A structure collecting four of these small companies, Cooperativa Indigena, headed by Minnie Ferrara, provided a framework for alternative distribution and networking with other small companies in other parts of Italy.[3] The cooperative closed in 1989.

In addition to the increased consumption of superfluous goods, an enormous outburst of national pride followed the occasion of Italy's victory in the 1982 World Cup soccer competition, which recalled the memorable 1970 match between the two nations. The final match of the 1970 competition is the pro-filmic event in the film *Italia-Germania 4 a 3* (Andrea Barzini, 1990), which provides a gloomy analysis of the bewilderment and disillusion of the generation of 1968 in 1990. Footage of the match and the voice of the journalist commenting on Italy's heroic victory metaphorically recall better times, but as the match comes to its victorious end, the relationships between the protagonists, enclosed in a villa, are shattered by the impossibility to communicate; their retreat in self-commiseration over their failures marks the disintegration of love relationships and political commitment. As the New German Cinema greatly influenced the imaginary of new Italian filmmakers in the 1980s,[4] with Margarethe von Trotta's film *Die Bleierne Zeit* (*Anni di piombo*, 1981), Wim Wenders' *De Americanische Freund* (*The American Friend*, 1977) and Fassbinder's work finding large audiences in Italy, it is worth to recall here the final segment in Fassbinder's *Die Ehe der Maria Braun* (*The Marriage of Maria Braun*, 1979). In this film, the last seven minutes of the World Cup championship soccer match between Germany and Hungary in 1954 comment on the difficult reunion between Maria Braun and her husband Hermann. Those final minutes also mark the restoration of the German nation and the economic miracle of the 1950s. In *Italia-Germania 4 a 3*, the soccer match also works more than a chronological authentication. It is in fact the signifier of 1980s restoration of national pride and unity through a sports event staged in a period of thoughtless prosperity, instead of the utopian values of the 1970s. Self-commiseration, the claustrophobia of the villa's interiors and the intimate recounting of the characters' experiences epitomise the phenomenon of repentance, which is discussed later in this chapter.

A crucial factor for the restoration of a new political and social conservatism in the 1980s was thus an economic revival just after one of the most sensitive periods in Italian history – that is, the years of terrorism. This economic development was promoted with *The Italian Economy Between the Wars 1919–1939*, a large exhibition of Fascist economy and industrial expansion that was held at the Colosseum in September–November 1984. Tim Mason (1986) provides a pivotal analysis of the disturbing political implications that the exhibition encapsulated. The theme of the show, as Mason defined the exhibition, was the establishment of the continuity between the economic achievements of the country in the inter-war period and those of the 1980s. Overall, it was a statement of the continuity of modernisation as an almost natural process.

The political sponsorship of the exhibition came from the Socialist Party. It was produced by IPSOA (the Post-graduate Institute for Business Studies and Organisation), Italy's leading school of business management. A group of historians who were part of Renzo De Felice's school provided historical consultancy and wrote essays in the massive catalogue of the exhibition. Also, some bureaucrats from the Christian Democrats at government level were involved to provide permission to use the Colosseum. Mason's conclusive argument about the massive spectacle offered by the exhibition was that it reflected:

> the general and vital fact that the political struggle over the interpretation of national history in Italy seems to have entered a new and confused stage, a stage in which old fixed points of reference (progressive/reaction; authority/ democracy; nationalism/internationalism) are being eroded (Mason 1986, p. 20).

Fascism and anti-fascism no longer seemed to be able to provide a fixed and reliable framework for interpretation and debate, as nationalism was being re-evaluated and dissociated from Fascism. This battle over interpretations of the past pointed to a state of uncertainty in which new images about the national past were proposed by improbable combinations of media managers, politicians, intellectuals, historians and philosophers.

The exhibition thus projected itself as 'an apolitically inclusive, reconciliatory and celebratory act of national self-documentation' (Mason 1986, p. 20) at the same time as the Socialist Party was trying to separate its left-wing political and ethical origins from conservative economic manoeuvres. The PSI's design aimed at undermining the unity of the three official workers' unions, CGIL (Confederazione Generale Italiana del Lavoro), CISL (Confederazione Italiana Sindacati Liberi) and UIL (Unione Italiana Lavoratori), stopping collective bargaining and strikes, and implementing the abolition of wage indexation. The overall picture of economic vitality and growth that Italy was spreading at that time with its export of the 'Made in Italy' brand through fashion, food,[5] manufacturing and design was very much part of a plan of patriotic reconciliation through unproblematic history. By separating the politics of Fascism from the economic achievements, Craxi's era in fact aimed at constructing an unproblematic history of Fascism which would lead in the following years to the deep questioning of the values and validity of the Resistance. A portrait of the legacy of the Craxian era and its political class emerges in the cynicism of Botero, a politician played by Nanni Moretti in Daniele Luchetti *Il portaborse* (1990). Botero is a chameleon who plays with other people's lives and moral integrity, and gradually becomes the corrupt Italy himself.

A preoccupation with history pervaded the cinema of those years. Some of this preoccupation was non-conciliatory. In this sense, the films of Gabriele Salvatores, Gianni Amelio, Daniele Luchetti, Mimmo Calopresti and Nanni Moretti can be regrouped according to how they address moral values and moral judgments in history. Their films are unforgiving, they present profound fractures in Italian society and culture, exposing the new hedonistic culture. On the contrary, films like *Cinema Paradiso* and *Il postino* project nostalgic images of the postwar period as innocent. In these films, cinema self-reflexivity substitutes for history, which thus becomes a history of images. Spectators consume history in the same nostalgic, unproblematic way in which the images of *The Italian Economy Between the Wars 1919–1939* were consumed: a heap of fragmented film images in which bits can be picked up or rejected without having to know the full story of those images.

As discussed previously, the New Italian Cinema is a discourse in which other discourses such as film criticism, politics, economy, culture and philosophy intersect. Unfortunately, the economic development of the country in the 1980s did not produce an economic expansion in the film industry. Independent directors/producers had very few financial resources in their hands, and they mostly relied on television production or on limited state subsidies. Hollywood's strengthening in the 1980s in

Europe and in the global market, thanks to its practice of local investments, provoked changes in the global economy of film – particularly in regard to production and distribution – while the Italian film industry was unable to address a series of strategies to maintain a solid base in its domestic market. The economic crisis in the film industry produced minimalist films whose main theme was the confusion arising from shifting historical and cultural paradigms. This confusion took the form of angst, anxiety and repentance, as represented in *Italia-Germania 4 a 3*.

HISTORICAL REVISIONISM

With the demise of union power and the progressive disillusion with politics, a dramatic decline of commitment in the public arena followed. From the 1980s, many historians initiated a critical revision of the ideals that marked the first half of the twentieth century. The common theme was the constant exclusion of the anti-Fascist ideal, its revolutionary tension and its ideological components. On the contrary, historical Fascism was the object of a re-evaluation that found the best example in the work of Renzo De Felice and his collaborators, who were gathered around the series 'I fatti della storia', by the publisher Bonacci. This reinterpretation avoided and eliminated historical and political responsibilities of Fascism, minimising its conservative and anti-democratic nature, and equated the totalitarian Fascist regime with other authoritarian regimes. The Resistance, whose European dimension was voluntarily ignored, was seen only in the Italian perspective, as a cruel civil war where both sides are put on the same level. Also, De Felice, speaking about his most recent book, published in 1995, in the context of right-wing nostalgia after the victory of the first centre-right coalition led by Berlusconi in 1994, attacked the notion that both the Resistance and the Republic of Salò were mass movements. For De Felice, they were both marginal fronts in the context of national culture, which was, on the contrary dominated by a 'grey zone' of *attendisti* (waiting to see what happens) (in Folli 1995)

The close critique of the anti-Fascist paradigm was played on the media. State television network RAI maintained a high level of history programs dedicated to the Resistance. In the decade 1985–95, the total number of programs broadcast about the Resistance and anti-Fascism was 109, second only to another prolific period of historical inquire, the decade 1965–75, when this number amounted to 120 (Winterhalter 1996). The process of revisionism comprised the critique of paradigms that were commonly accepted as founding features of the democratic republic (the Resistance as the liberation war, and anti-Fascism) through themes that were explored for the first time. The treatment on television of topics such as the Italian population's collaboration with Fascism, the detention of Italian prisoners in German concentration camps, or soldiers who fought on the Russian front and never returned attempted to rewrite Italy's own understanding and repositioning of the notion of war victims. The emergence of these topics must be seen in the broader context of international politics. Germany's own *Historikerstreit* exploded in 1986, in the context of a German neo-nationalist resurgence. As the *Historikerstreit* attempted to deal with the problem of German identity from a conservative point of view, it extended this process of normalisation of German history to a process of normalisation of the history of World War II in the major European countries (Bosworth 1993, p. 74; La Capra 1994, p. 43).

As a result of public debate about the Resistance, monolithic accounts of history and the status of professional historians were being undermined. The public and authoritative function of the academic historian as the only legitimate storyteller of the past was being questioned. The mass media had appropriated the role of the historian as the oracle of the nation. Fears were expressed that the media were replacing impartial accounts of history based on factual evidence with a partial, subjective and popularised version of history. Also, biography, oral history and local narratives were recognised as fundamental components of the process of construction of a common memory. They became novel structural components of a new direction in what history was and how it was told. This process had started in the 1970s, with the pivotal work of Italian historians Alessandro Portelli, Luisa Passerini and also Carlo Ginzburg in oral history and cultural memory. They opened different possibilities of historical narration, repositioning the categories 'history' and 'memory'. This approach reflected on much cultural production in the 1980s and 1990s. Cinema responded to this growth of personal stories with the production of many films adapted from autobiographies or biography – to quote a few, *I piccoli maestri* (Daniele Luchetti, 1997), *Ormai è fatta* (Enzo Monteleone, 1999), *La tregua* (Francesco Rosi, 1997), *Tea with Mussolini* (Franco Zeffirelli, 1999), *La vita è bella*, which is loosely inspired by Benigni's father's memories as a war prisoner in Germany, *Jona che visse nella balena* (Roberto Faenza, 1993), adapted from the autobiography of Jona Oberski *Anni d'infanzia*, *Placido Rizzotto* (Pasquale Scimeca, 2000), *I cento passi* (Marco Tullio Giordana, 2000) and *El-Alamein* (Enzo Monteleone, 2002), the factual content of which derives from oral accounts and diaries of the survivors from the famous battle in 1942 which represented the most important defeat of the Italian-German troops in the North African campaign. Thus the war, the Resistance, the Holocaust and 1968 – so-called 'grand events' – returned in the Italian cinema of the 1990s narrated in the form of memory in an effort to return to strong stories and realism. By using autobiography and actual facts narrated in the form of mnemonic recollection, the New Italian Cinema tried to combine history with experience, history with memory.

In 1989, contingently with the fall of the Berlin Wall, after a decade of diminishing membership and the subsequent painful revision of its role in Italy and in Europe, the PCI separated into two smaller parties (Rifondazione Comunista and Partito Democratico di Sinistra). The PCI crisis reopened old wounds. The question that emerged then concerned the Resistance and the actions of the partisans. Specifically, it was debated whether the guilt for Nazi reprisals against civilians[6] must be attributed to the Germans and the Fascists, who materially carried out the executions, or must instead shift on to the partisans who, with their actions, provoked them. A book published in 1991 by Left-wing historian Claudio Pavone (1998), *Una Guerra civile: Saggio storico sulla moralità nella Resistenza*, tried to come to terms with this question and with the equation of whether Fascism equals Communism – similar to the equation that emerged in Europe between Nazism and Stalinism, and between the Holocaust and the Gulag.

Pavone's book was published against the backdrop of the fall of Communism, the dismantling of the Western and Eastern European blocs, the 1989 PCI split and a distrust of the institutions which culminated with the *Tangentopoli* inquiry on corruption. These events and the previous process of historical decontextualisation of Fascism crystallised in a profound process of revisionism of the ideal and political positions about the Resistance that were formed in the aftermath of World War II. For the right, the Resistance was equal to civil war. In this way, the right charged the formula negatively and cast the responsibility for the massacres of civilians on the left, trying to subvert the historical and collective memory of the Fascist massacres and the responsibilities of Fascism in the alliance with Nazi Germany after 8 September 1943. The notion of the Resistance as a civil war was an interpretative category that was boldly refused by the Left. This position was, of course, very much in line with the construction of the Resistance as liberation war and the myth of unity that emerged with Togliatti's line of political unity against Fascism (Sassoon 1981). This myth handed down by the institutional Left suppressed an alternative view of the Resistance that focused immediately on the partisan war as a civil war. Fenoglio's first account of his participation in the Resistance was contained in his first collection of short stories, *Racconti della guerra civile*, which Einaudi refused to publish in 1949. Elio Vittorini, editor at Einaudi, also embargoed Fenoglio's following novel, *La paga del sabato*. An iron curtain was drawn on divisions among the partisans, which only resurfaced in later decades.

Pavone boldly argued that the left must accept the definition of Resistance as civil war. In fact, for Pavone, there is no better occasion than a civil war, where the two parts are irremediably diverse and divided, to show truly the motivations behind the parts involved. Pavone reaffirmed that after 8 September there was much more at stake than the liberation of Italy from the Germans. In fact, behind the Resistance was the fundamental notion of identity and the idea of Italy as a democratic republic that needed to be restored (Pavone 1998, p. xvi). Hence the Resistance as civil war determined historically a clear separation between left and right. The Communists, who aimed at constructing a democratic national identity that was disjointed from that of Fascism, must be legitimated in their violent acts against Fascism. Pavone defended the actions of the partisans by defending their self-management of violence against the regularly instituted violence of the state, and denouncing that the exorbitant violence practised by millions of people during the war could not be charged on to a few thousand citizens whose practice of violence was their own choice (Pavone 1998, p. 415).

Many historians took part in the debate. Aldo Giannuli argued that the ambiguous equalisation between partisans and Fascists was aimed at removing the intrinsic value of the Resistance in order to delegitimise the left in current political affairs (Giannuli 2001, p. 65). Gian Enrico Rusconi agreed with Pavone on subverting the question of equivalence between left and right violence to that of identity. For Rusconi, public discussions about Fascism and anti-Communism reflected the way in which these two positions formed during the Resistance and in the aftermath of the war. He feared that a rereading of the last 50 years of Italian history could dangerously erase those sets of values that had given meaning to twentieth century history. On the other hand, Rusconi was also convinced that all ideological taboos had to be shattered, purged from the national unconscious so that, once removed, the truth about the Resistance could finally be established (Rusconi 1998, p. 603).

IRRECONCILABLE MEMORIES: THE WAR FILMS

Pavone attempted to reaffirm the partisans' right to resist Fascism and

Nazism with the use of violence. He distinguished three different wars that were fought during the Resistance: the patriotic war, the civil war and the class war. The only war told on the screen was the civil war, reflecting the colonisation of Italian imaginary by this profound revisionism. Italian history films about the period 1943–45, or with references to the Resistance and anti-Fascism that were released in the 1990s and 2000s are *Io e il re* (Lucio Gaudino, 1995), *Nemici d'infanzia* (Luigi Magni, 1995), *I piccoli maestri* (Daniele Luchetti, 1997), *La stanza dello Scirocco* (Maurizio Sciarra, 1997), *Porzûs* (Renzo Martinelli, 1997), *Il partigiano Johnny* (Guido Chiesa, 2000) and *Placido Rizzotto* (Pasquale Scimeca, 2000). This last film needs a particular mention because, despite the fact that it is not specifically about the Resistance, in its second opening scene it connects the Resistance with class war. *Placido Rizzotto* is a film inspired by the real-life murder by the mafia of a union leader in Corleone in 1948. The film links three periods in Placido's life: the arrest of his father by the royal guards for conspiracy against the state when he was a child; his militancy in Northern Italy in the Resistance as a Communist; and finally his return to Corleone at the end of the war. The first two episodes serve as justification for Placido's political consciousness and determination to fight against the mafia's management of land ownership. *Concorrenza sleale* (Ettore Scola, 2000) metaphorically situates divisions among Italians in the competition between the owners of two textile shops in Rome in the late 1930s: Umberto (Diego Abatantuono) is Catholic and Leone (Sergio Castellitto) is Jewish. Even though the two families are drawn together by the enforcement of racial laws against Jews, the film ends with the Jewish family leaving their apartment for the Ghetto while Umberto and his family look on powerless. In *La finestra di fronte* (Ferzan Ozpetek, 2005), Davide (Massimo Girotti) suffers from amnesia. Little by little, his story is revealed: the war, homosexuality, the Jewish ghetto, the deportation to a concentration camp in Germany. However, there are essentially three films that portray the Resistance in its canonical setting, the battlefields in the mountains of Northern Italy: *I piccoli maestri*, *Porzûs* and *Il partigiano Johnny*.

Like *La notte di San Lorenzo* (Paolo and Vittorio Taviani, 1982), these films offer a view of the Resistance and anti-Fascism that highlights divisions that occurred in small communities between partisans themselves and between partisans and fascist militants. The 1990s characterisation of the partisan attempts to show people's humanity in the face of the war. Characters are self-doubting 'everyday people' who need a constant revision and affirmation of their own role in the Resistance. Often, they join the Resistance by chance or because it appears the only sensible thing to do in that chaotic period. Characters confess that they fear death and torture, and at the same time can hardly carry out executions of Fascists and Nazis. In *I piccoli maestri* the tidiness of the characters and the modernity of language are anachronisms that hint at 'young bourgeois, I can feel them closer to today's Italians, in some way I can identify with them', as director Daniele Luchetti said about his characters' representation.[7]

In *I piccoli maestri*, Marietto, while in hiding in Padua, compiles a list of known Fascists and collaborators with Fascism who should be executed at the end of the war, although Marietto says the problem is complicated by the presence of relatives. Gigi (interpreted by Stefano Accorsi) replies sharply: 'Do you have an attack of civil war? Why don't you kill them with the pen?' Gigi's answer comes as spoken from a 'future of the past' point of view, with an implied knowledge of the postwar political developments of the Italian republic. Importantly, the scene differs from Luigi Meneghello's autobiography, *I piccoli maestri*, to which the film was directly inspired. In the book, both Gigi and Marietto work on the list of traitors, setting up different punishments according to the role played by the collaborators during Fascism. In describing this episode, Meneghello recalls his attempt at finding ethical justification for the purge in Machiavelli, Tocqeville and Cuoco. Meneghello (the fictional Gigi) and Marietto concluded many times that their principles were correct, but still they felt unease at the thought of having to dispose of the traitors' bodies. At the end, Gigi suggests killing Fascists with ink, as this would resolve the problem of having to deal with too many corpses. Thus in the book, published in 1964, the idea that the actions of the partisans would be morally justified was still free from revisionist doubts, while in the film Gigi boldly refuses the idea of civil war, clearly representing the current view upheld by the left.[8]

Gigi's inference in using ink to get rid of Fascists and collaborators is that the persistence of Fascism in postwar society in the bureaucracy and right-wing parties should have been defeated with education and the spread of an anti-Fascist culture. The same moral stance recurs in one of the final scenes, after Padua has been liberated from German occupation and the partisans triumphantly march in the city streets. A butcher executes a Fascist, and a partisan attacks the butcher in a hopeless attempt to avoid useless personal revenge. The partisan accuses the butcher: 'Where have you been until now? Where did you hide?' thus opening the question of *attendismo* (waiting to see what happens) of Italians who randomly cooperated with Fascism through their apathy.

In *Il partigiano Johnny*, adapted from Beppe Fenoglio's autobiography which was published in 1968, after Fenoglio's death in 1963, Johnny is a young university student torn between the necessity for and the refusal of violence. In the opening segment, we see an original fragment from a *Cinegiornale* (the news bulletins produced by Istituto Luce) about the war. In the background, we hear news and propaganda from Radio Londra first and then the state radio channel. Images and sound work as counterpoints, contextualising the actions that we will see within the history of violence perpetrated by the state and the Fascists. In this, Chiesa attempts to provide a balanced, historically accurate image of the Resistance in Piedmont. The mobile camera work, the dull colours that are reduced to a dominance of light and dark provide an illusion of war reportage, supported by Chiesa's documentary research and the many documentaries that he has made about the Resistance.[9] The intense light contrast – the *chiaroscuro* technique – with shifts to uniform colours where the dominant colour is a grey, foggy background underline shifting moments in Johnny's psychology, from certainty about the justification of the Resistance and his decision to participate (stark contrast), to moments in which his choice does not seem so clear, and especially when it is difficult to make a decision about killing the enemy. In both *I piccoli maestri* and *Il partigiano Johnny*, the partisans' profound concern is that they fear the postwar period. They dread the possibility of forgetting the purpose of their sacrifices as partisans. After all, they are all young students who dream about freedom. Compared with the exhilarating life on the hills, the battles and the camaraderie, postwar Italy looms as normalcy and boredom: the Resistance is thus a rite of passage which will be lost forever if it is not accompanied by political consciousness and a sense of the reason as to why one should be a partisan, as Johnny's professor Cocito tells him. *Il partigiano Johnny* ends with a close-up of Johnny holding his gun towards the sky in a gesture of victory, similar to the photographic iconography of Communist fighters in the Spanish Civil War. The image leaves open the hopes of thousands of partisans at the end of the war for a free, anti-Fascist country.

Conversely, a new typology of the massacres sifted through oral histories, media debates, research and conferences. Along with the Nazis, who physically carried out massacres and torture, the partisans were made accountable for the death of innocent civilians and for the death of other partisans. Within this narrative, a unique account of the Resistance emerged. This was an episode of violence between two opposed partisan factions that occurred at the *malghe* (alpine huts) of Porzûs, at the border of Friuli–Venezia Giulia with former Yugoslavia. The groups involved were partisans from the Gruppi d'Azione Partigiana (GAP, Partisans Action Groups, mainly constituted by of communist militants) and the Osoppo Brigade, a Catholic group. This episode of violence, in which Pier Paolo Pasolini's brother Guido lost his life, was rendered in 1997 in a very controversial film, *Porzûs*, by director Renzo Martinelli. Much debate and many allegations followed. The director Renzo Martinelli, son of partisans himself, was accused of 'throwing mud' on the Resistance (Polo 1997, p. 5). Both *I piccoli maestri* and *Il partigiano Johnny* imply political divisions among the various groups in the Resistance, but these are reduced to some heated discussions among the partisans.[10] *Porzûs* stands out because it is the first film that openly challenges the canonical image of the heroic Resistance. Thus the film requires a more detailed analysis than *I piccoli maestri* and *Il partigiano Johnny*.

Porzûs was the taboo-film that reopened the painful memory of the civil war, not only between Fascists and anti-Fascists, but also between partisans of different political colours. It ignited a series of articles in the major Italian newspapers, and for this reason – beyond its debatable formal and aesthetic merits – *Porzûs* can be regarded as an imagined theatre of memory that provoked public discussion and confrontation (see Manin 1997; Kezich 1997; Kersevan 1997; Polo 1997). The protagonists of this massacre between partisans were the Communists of the GAP in one camp and the Osoppo Brigade (Catholic) in the opposite camp. Both the brigades had in common their anti-Fascism, but they were divided by their different views of the world and reciprocal distrust: the Communists, who during the last winter of the war, in 1944, were under the command of the Slovenian army, suspected the Catholic brigade of an alliance with the Fascists; the Catholics, on the other hand, feared the military expansion of Tito's army into Italy with the subsequent annexation of Italian territories by Yugoslavia and thus refused to join in the Slovenian army. This clash between different visions of politics concluded in the massacre at Porzûs.

Guido Pasolini, Pier Paolo's brother, was with the 22 partisans of the Osoppo Brigades who were killed. A novel written by Carlo Sgorlon, *La malga di Sir*, was also published in 1997, months before the release of the film in Venice. The focus of the novel is the interpretation of the massacre in a broad context of international Communist politics. According to Sgorlon, the order for the massacre came from the Communist leadership, 'as to say, Togliatti, who was in exile in Russia and somehow prisoner of the Bolshevik system' (Sgorlon 1997, p. 7). Sgorlon says that, for the Leninist and Stalinist Communists, the end justified the means; thus the order to kill at Porzûs was given in accordance with the predominant Stalinist and Leninist mentality in the PCI.

The film starts in 1945 with two children running in a forest. They run into half-buried corpses in a mass grave. From here, the film goes forward to 1980. In the Slovenian village of Krapina, an old man named Storno, the ex-commander of the Osoppo Brigades, looks for another man, the fictional Geko, the ex-commander of the Garibaldi Brigades. Storno confronts Geko, who is close to death from an incurable disease. In a mix of reciprocal accusations, reminiscences and debates over the morality of the Resistance, the two characters dialectically reconstruct the facts of the winter of 1944–45. Martinelli's choice to set the story in 1980 is significant in that the film tries to decontextualise the mnemonic recollection of this massacre from contemporary revisionist debates. The story is thus set in a time in which Yugoslavia was not yet shattered into ethnic wars and, importantly, before the fall of the Berlin Wall. The director's intent was to search for truth transcending the historical context, because it 'is a story that must be told' (Martinelli 1997, p. 3).

The film is structured in eight flashbacks. This particular form of film language engages with the juncture between past and present, in which the concepts of memory and history are implied. In this film, the flashbacks work as counterpoints to the violent altercations between Geko and Storno in their 1980 encounter. The flashbacks are the mimetic representation of the re-emergence of memory. The dialectic construction between what is remembered and who is remembering on the one hand, and the alleged factuality of the past (in the flashback) problematises the relationship between history and subjective memory. In the same way, Geko and Storno are opposed. The first is the bloody executioner of a Grand Guignol massacre, while the second incarnates the humanism of the Resistance. The extreme confrontation of the characters and the shifts back and forward in time constructs the film as a detective fiction, with the investigation conducted as in a courtroom trial. In fact, the film relied heavily on the documents of the trial that started in 1947 and ended in 1952 with Mario Toffanin (Geko), the material executioner of the massacre, sentenced to prison.

Porzûs clearly situates the two main characters within the dilemma of morally acceptable violence on the one hand, and the notion that all violence is unjustifiable on the other. Geko's portrait is that of a bloodthirsty, politically and ideologically fanatic communist militant, while Storno's character remains suspended in doubt about his collaboration with the Fascists. The film does not offer a resolution to this dilemma in the last flashback, in one of the last dialogues between Spaccaossa, a 'good' Communist, and Geko. Spaccaossa, disillusioned, voluntarily walks into the grave where the partisans of the Osoppo Brigade have been shot. Spaccaossa asks Geko what he will say when the truth surfaces. Geko answers that the truth is on the side of those killed by Fascists, implying that it is on the side of partisans' martyrdom. The final word is Spaccaossa's: he proclaims his Communist ideal, but fears those like Geko because if Geko can do what he is doing during the war, then he would also be able to do it after the war. Spaccaossa does not want Geko's Communism. The film resolves this confrontation between Communists themselves by resorting to the intervention of a foreigner: the 'humanist' Communist Spaccaossa is then killed by a Russian comrade of the Red Army.

It is clear that, from the 1990s, a narrative of division dominates the Resistance discourse. This came to be known as *memoria divisa* (divided memory), which can be summarised as the reopening of a complex sedimentation of subsequent contextual and political factors, in which the Cold War played a crucial role. Studies of Fascist and Nazi massacres of civilian populations in response to violent action by partisans have raised complex issues of guilt and responsibility, and ethical debates which question the pure and heroic image of the Resistance. In the 50 years since the end of the war, the construction of a narrative of the Resistance was tightly managed by the PCI's official accounts, and by other democratic parties which used the Resistance as a date for state celebrations and as a façade of democratic unity. But the Resistance constituted a problematic point of reference for Italians since the beginning, and failed in its significant ritual and symbolic function as a common tradition of democratic Italy.

The shift to an introspective cinema narrating the personal memories of individuals coincided with a general international shift and with the demise of the grand ideologies of socialist tradition. The historical films produced in the last two decades of the twentieth century clearly privileged individual memories, which were often controversial and divisive. Part of a larger revisionist project, the historical film has come to function in the public sphere as mediator between academic history and popular memory — that is, versions of the past told by family and friends. In privileging individual memory and the autobiographical mode, the historical film has closed the gap between those included and those excluded from history.

THE ITALIAN HOLOCAUST

Thousands of documentaries based on interviews with the survivors, books and many fictional films have transformed the Holocaust into a historical genre. The appropriate language for its representation was tragedy, while the victim–perpetrator relationship was the focus of the narrative. The enormous success of *La vita è bella* in the United States and worldwide can certainly be explained in relation to the growth of American sensibility toward the Holocaust after the opening of the United States Holocaust Memorial Museum and the release of *Schindler's List* (Steven Spielberg, 1993). Both events point to the Americanisation of the Holocaust, which was already preceded by the US television series *Holocaust*, which was an unprecedented success in Germany in 1979.

In Italy, the process of revision involved not only a critique of the myths of the Resistance but also the exploration of new themes which disturbed and muddied the traditional categories of victims and perpetrators. As in the case of the Resistance, discussions about the Holocaust have raised issues of historical interpretation as well as questions about the appropriate way to talk about it or represent it. After more than 50 years, historians are still divided about the definition of victims, perpetrators and bystanders, while in the arts debates centre on the appropriate forms of visualising or narrating the Shoah.

As with the Resistance, there has been a recent historical shift in the representation of the Holocaust. A number of memoirs published over the last twenty years have shifted their focus from the victim–perpetrator relationship to the survivor–rescuer relationship. There has been a similar shift in film. In the literary and cinematic representations of the Holocaust, the protagonists are no longer hopeless victims but survivors, the bystanders are reformed rescuers and the Nazis now occupy the background. This new paradigm has made possible the use of different languages, such as that of comedy.

We must return for a moment to the broad process of historical revisionism. In 1987, historian Renzo de Felice claimed that Italian anti-Semitism was an internal phenomenon not to be confused with German anti-Semitism, and that Italian Fascists did not perpetrate the Holocaust while Germans did (in Bosworth 1993, p. 137). Generally, responsibility for the Shoah is attributed to Germany, and Italy has been free of guilt. It is well known that, during World War II, Italian Jews were in a better situation than their counterparts in other European countries, where they were not only persecuted but also handed over to the Germans for deportation to the death camps. However, the situation in Italy changed dramatically after the armistice of 8 September 1943, when the German army occupied Italy. Acting on their own initiative, bands of Fascists in the Muti Legion and militarised squads like the 72 thousand men in the National Fascist Guard, the 22 thousand in the Black Brigades and the 20 thousand in the Italian SS arrested, murdered and tortured Jews and anti-Fascists. After the constitution of the Fascist Republic of Salò, Mussolini never took a stand against the actions of these bands. The Italian government did not withdraw the racial laws and the Vatican never openly condemned the arrests and deportations of Jews. In addition, informers and ordinary Italian citizens turned in Jews in hiding to the Italian police or the SS in order to gain cash rewards. So the period from 1943 until the end of 1944 can be called the Italian Holocaust in its own right. As Zucotti said in response to De Felice, the Holocaust was not a purely German affair (Zucotti 1987, p. 200). This previously hidden chapter of Italian national history emerged in the 1990s as a signifier of national guilt.

In Italy, the Holocaust did not claim the dramatic numbers of dead recorded in other European countries. In fact, before the racial laws of 1938, the small Jewish community was thoroughly assimilated into the Italian community. They were so assimilated that intermarriage became more common, even in the early Fascist period. Some Jews even joined the Fascist National Party and participated in the march on Rome, when the Fascists seized power. Some Jews were high-ranking officers in the Italian army, until the promulgation of the racial laws in 1938 forced them to relinquish their posts (Zucotti 1987).

Benigni's image of the Italian Jew, who is not different from other Italians, reflects the level of assimilation among Italian Jews. The character of Guido (played by Benigni) is presented as a jolly peasant who wants to seek his fortune in the city, and only well into the film do the spectators discover that he is a Jew. His uncle's horse is daubed with graffiti, proclaiming it a 'Jew horse'. It is only after this incident that Guido becomes conscious of his difference. This conforms to the experience of Primo Levi who, before the racial laws, never thought of himself as a Jew, but only as an Italian.[11] It was the racial laws of 1938 that determined Jews' otherness from the rest of the Italian community for the first time since the unification of the country in 1861, when the existing racial laws and ghettoes were abolished.

In the period between 1960 and 1975, a number of films dealing with the legacy of Fascism and the Holocaust were made in Italy. This wave of films was produced in a climate of left-wing activism and militant anti-Fascism. Among these films are Gillo Pontecorvo's *Kapò* (1960), Carlo Lizzani's *L'oro di Roma* (1961), Vittorio De Sica's *I sequestrati di Altona* (1962) and *Il giardino dei Finzi-Contini* (1970), Luchino Visconti's *Vaghe stelle dell'Orsa* (1965) and *La caduta degli dei* (1969), Bernardo Bertolucci's *Il conformista* (1970), Liliana Cavani's *Il portiere di notte* (1974) and Lina Wertmuller's *Pasqualino Settebellezze* (1975). The resurgence of Holocaust films in Italy in the 1990s occurred in a very different climate, one marked by decline in political activism, widespread disillusion with left-wing ideology and neo-conservative revival. The

Holocaust came to represent the last bastion of left-wing political commitment. Roberto Benigni, the director and star of *La vita è bella*, is such a man of the left. Before he became a film director, he was a stand-up comedian and comic actor who, in the 1980s, attracted large audiences to his theatrical one-man shows attacking right-wing politicians, parties and policies. Among his targets were the powerful nationalist politician Silvio Berlusconi, the corrupt socialist politician Bettino Craxi and the Christian Democrats.

La vita è bella is essentially based on the individual experience of Guido and his efforts to ensure the bodily and spiritual survival of his young son in the concentration camp. The game that will sustain Giosuè, his son, and enable his survival, with a toy tank as its final reward, is based on a historical fallacy. Auschwitz was actually liberated by Soviet Russian forces, but in the film it is an American GI who arrives at the deserted camp in his tank on a glorious sunny day. It is perhaps going too far to claim that this ending was specifically designed for the American market. However, the positive resolution of the narrative does conform to the Hollywood approach to World War II and the Holocaust. When the American GI enters Auschwitz, collects Giosuè and helps him reunite with his surviving mother under blue skies (symbolising happiness and hope for the future), we may well be reminded of the triumphal ending of Hollywood war films. Furthermore, the film employs a classical narrative structure in which the actions of the protagonist determine the final outcome. It is based on the premises of motivation and character choice that elevate the main character – Guido – to the status of hero. It is thus possible to say that *La vita è bella* is unorthodox in its use of comic language, but classical in its narrative. And yet the film is unorthodox in its depiction of the Jew who can mastermind his son's survival.

La vita è bella attracted international debate because it repositions and subverts the victim–perpetrator relationship. The clear division between good and evil, victim and perpetrator, was already problematised in the 1970s in films showing the victim being compelled to become a perpetrator him/herself. The existence of such cases is attested to by Primo Levi in *Se*

Questo è un uomo (*This is a Man*) and in *I sommersi e i salvati* (*The Drowned and the Saved*), where he reveals the existence of a 'grey zone' between collaboration and survival tactics. Nevertheless, Levi is critical of attempts to justify collaboration. He objected to Liliana Cavani's film *Il portiere di notte* (1974), which transgressively employed a decadent and erotic approach to the relationship between Holocaust victims and perpetrators. Levi maintained that confusing victims with their assassins is 'a moral disease or an aesthetic affectation or a sinister signal of complicity'.¹² Lina Wertmuller's film *Pasqualino Settebellezze* (1976) also aroused controversy for transgressing the boundaries of good taste and for questionable morality in its grotesque portrayal of the victim-turned-perpetrator in the battle for survival.

This raises the problem of the acceptable norms of Holocaust representations, a problem which resurfaced in the response to *La vita è bella*. In Italy, the Resistance is still a very sensitive subject that must be treated with a serious and respectful attitude, but Italian critics were quite prepared to accept a comic treatment of the Holocaust. In their view, the elements of slapstick comedy and romantic comedy that were skilfully employed by Benigni in the film were quite acceptable and attractive. They could relate his comedy to that of Jewish comedians like Woody Allen, whose films are popular with Italians – especially those on the left. But perhaps most importantly, we can trace the origins of the coupling of the comic with the tragic in *La vita è bella* to the classic Italian comedies of the 1960s, especially those starring the actors Alberto Sordi and Vittorio Gassman. These actors portrayed a type of opportunistic and selfish Italian who performs dirty tricks in schemes to get rich quickly in a period of fast economic growth. Despite their ignoble characters, these films enabled them to become heroes – to display their adaptability and capacity to change for the better, ultimately sacrificing their material wealth and even their lives in random acts of generosity — by shifting from comic to tragic mode.

Much of the controversy that *La vita è bella* attracted centres on its lack of *authenticity* in its departures from the accepted or canonical representation of the Holocaust, which is based on historical truth, realism and tragedy. Critics of the film found its use of comedy disrespectful to the victims of the Shoah, and saw it ultimately as an attempt to deny the genocide. Benigni counter-claimed that *La vita è bella* is not a comedy about the Holocaust but 'a movie by a comedian about the Holocaust' (Milvy 1998). On his own admission, it was inspired by his father, who was a prisoner of war in a German camp; he subsequently told his children about his experience in a jocular fashion so as not to scare them (Te Koha, 1998, p 15). In this way, Benigni could make a claim for the authenticity of his story.

Paradoxically, the realism in *La vita è bella* can be located in its overt artificiality – its status as fiction. Its reconstructed Auschwitz is clearly a film set, and the situations in the camp are patently absurd. In this sense, *La vita è bella* is not an illusionist film. In the film, the hero's wishes are magically fulfilled: princesses drop from the sky; the villain is bombarded with eggs; guard dogs abandon their search on Guido's command. In a word, *La vita è bella* constantly reminds the spectators that they are watching a film. In this sense, it cannot be confused with the illusory verisimilitude of *Schindler's List,* as mimetic realism was not Benigni's concern. This is especially evident in the only reference to the Shoah in the film, which is represented by a theatrical backdrop on which the corpses of the victims are painted in black and white. This sheet emerges from the darkness and the fog, in silence, when Guido walks back to his hut after serving as a waiter at a Nazi dinner party. This scene can be compared to the silence of the true victims described by Primo Levi in this passage in *The Drowned and the Saved*:

> We, the survivors, are not the true witnesses. This is an uncomfortable notion of which I have become conscious little by little, reading the memoirs of others and reading mine at a distance of years ... Those who saw the Gorgon have not returned to tell about it or have returned mute; they are ... the drowned, the complete witnesses, the ones whose depositions would have a general significance. They are the rule, we are the exception.[13]

The revelation through the painting prompts Guido's knowledge of the dimension of the catastrophe and, because he will die at the end of the film in his ultimate sacrifice to save his son's life, his silent testimony can be equated with the silenced and silent voices of the drowned, the real witnesses in Levi's terms.

The power of this scene derives from the evocative nature of the painting, rather than from a realistic representation of corpses or mass murders. In a similar fashion to Lanzmann's documentary film *Shoah* (1985), *La vita è bella* relies on 'what one should "know" in order to understand what one "sees"' (Loshitzky 1995, p. 112). In this sense, the scene of the painted corpses is the place of the absent, those who cannot be represented. In this way, *La vita è bella* remains true to Primo Levi's statement that there are no words and no images to represent Auschwitz.

Also, by avoiding images of real dead bodies, the film stresses the gap between seeing and comprehending. In both *Se questo è un uomo* and *La tregua* Levi describes how, in the concentration camp universe, the inmates maintained this gap, and saw the surrounding horror only partially or obliquely. The oblique gaze is a means of survival, a way of becoming impermeable to the horror. Similarly, in *La tregua* (Francesco Rosi, 1996), Rosi holds back from foregrounding dead bodies in the opening segment. The viewer only sees the bodies in the background while Levi, impersonated by a sorrowful John Turturro, in the foreground registers the presence of the Russian soldiers by looking up. This choice again stresses the split between seeing and meaning in a way that can be likened to the scene of the painted sheet in *La vita è bella*.

Benigni has also been criticised for depicting a Jew in control of his own life in a concentration camp. In the death camps, it was a daily struggle to survive physically, to stay alive, let alone maintaining a sense of humour. However, there are memoirs of survivors of the Nazi camps in which the function of humour as a means of coping with the horror and the condition of sub-humanity to which they were reduced is highlighted. Levi writes that:

> To sink is the easiest of matters; it is enough to carry out all the

orders one receives, to eat only the rations, to observe the discipline of the work and the camp. Experience showed that only exceptionally could one survive more than three months in this way. (Levi 1987, p. 91)

In Levi's opinion, in order to survive or cope with life in the camp, one had to invent some kind of special ability. The prisoner had to rise above the multitude and create a status for him/herself. Guido's special ability is his humour, which enables him to adapt to the camp's life and discipline.

Before he made *La vita è bella*, Benigni collaborated with another filmmaker, Roberto Faenza, on the film *Jona che visse nella balena*, released in 1993. This film was adapted from the autobiography of Jonah Oberski, who is a nuclear physicist in Amsterdam. When he was four years old, he was deported together with his parents to Bergen Belsen, a concentration camp. The story focuses on Oberski's memories of his parents' love and their efforts to make his life in the camp as happy as possible. However, after the liberation Jonah's mother cannot cope with the memory of the concentration camp and she suicides. It is perhaps this film that constituted the pre-text of, and inspiration for, *La vita è bella*, the second part of which is similarly focused on the attempt of a father to shelter his son from the horror of Auschwitz.

Even before *La vita è bella*, Benigni had challenged the acceptable uses of comedy in his film *Il mostro* (1994), a comedy about female dismemberment which was based on a true story of serial murders in Tuscany over the previous three decades. But even more pointedly, *La vita è bella* has two illustrious predecessors: Chaplin's *The Great Dictator* (1940) and Lubitsch's *To Be or Not to Be* (1942), which was remade in 1983 by Mel Brooks. Benigni pays express homage to Chaplin by wearing the same number (0737) on his prisoner's uniform as Chaplin did in *The Great Dictator*. Like *La vita è bella*, both of these films encountered some criticism in their time. Both films are based on the juxtaposition of farce and melodrama, and the comedy that arises from role-playing and role-switching. Chaplin plays two characters, the Dictator (a parody of Hitler) and the victimised Jewish barber. In *To Be or Not to Be*, Jack Benny plays a Polish actor (hamming up Hamlet) who impersonates a Nazi spy, and constantly switches identities. Importantly, both of these films were released at a time when the extent of the devastation caused by Nazism was not widely known. Images of the concentration camps, either in documentary footage or photographs, had yet to be circulated. These films ridiculed Nazism and its anti-Semitism in the absence of knowledge of the Holocaust.

In *La vita è bella*, the slapstick comedy of the first part turns into farce in the second part of the film, which unfolds in the concentration camp. The comedy here derives from the ironic use of language. Irony is used to highlight the absurdity of the situation in which Guido finds himself. Guido deliberately mistranslates Nazi orders to the prisoners so that he can conduct the game that will maintain his son's hopes. The irony, of course, resides in the audience's knowledge of the horror of the Holocaust. The positioning of the characters is also ironical, as here it is the Nazi officer who is the victim of the Jew's jokes. In both Lubitsch's *To Be or Not to Be* and Benigni's *La vita è bella*, the comedy is expressed through language, and in both films the Nazis are positioned as victims of the jokes. Nevertheless, comedy in films about the Holocaust appears to be possible only when the evocation of the Shoah is implicit rather than explicit.

In conclusion, *La vita è bella* is a mixture of conventional and unconventional elements. On one hand, the film can be situated within the tradition of Italian comedy, which is based on the complementarity of the comic and the tragic. This element helps to account for the film's acceptance by Italian audiences. On the other hand, the film's use of comedy and irony does not conform to the obligatory tragic perspective and verisimilitude in depictions of the Holocaust. Yet again, many elements in *La vita è bella* conform to the testimony of Primo Levi, whose credentials as a survivor and moralist are widely acknowledged as impeccable.

NOTES

1. Franco Piperno, one of the leaders of Autonomia Operaia, wrote from prison to

L'espresso, describing Bettino Craxi's public speeches as 'American style' (1979).

2. Interview with Kiko Stella, Milan, May 2000.

3. Interview with Kiko Stella.

4. Interview with Enzo Monteleone, May 2000.

5. For a thoroughly informed discussion of Italy's own fascination with food in the 1980s, the birth of the Slow Food movement, and the discovery of the politics of pleasure by militants of the Communist Party, see Leitch (2003).

6. See the cases of Civitella della Chiana and surrounding villages in Tuscany on 29 June 1944, when 203 people were killed in a few hours. The episode is comparable to the massacre of the notorious Fosse Ardeatine (335 hostages killed) in Rome and Marzabotto, near Bologna, where the Nazi troops killed 1,830 civilians. The story of the Civitella della Chiana's massacre was published in a book by historian Paolo Pezzino (1997). Other books related to ethical problems in the Resistance were by Paggi (1996) and Contini (1997).

6. See interview with Luchetti in Fusco (1998, p. 35).

8. In my article '*Open city: Rossellini and neo-realism, sixty years later*' (2006) I argue that the narrative of the Resistance constitutes a discourse in which categories and canons have been rewritten four times from the end of the war to the present time.

9. *Materiale resistente* (1995, co-directed with Davide Ferrario); *La memoria inquieta* (1995); *Partigiani* (co-directed with Davide Ferrario, 1997); *Una questione privata: Vita di Beppe Fenoglio* (1998); *Provini per un massacro* (2000).

10. Scoppola (1995) identifies in the almost immediate politicisation of partisan groups an important element of the division and fights among partisans. For Scoppola, this prevented the Resistance itself from becoming a catalyst for democratic instances of citizenry and national identity.

11. See the chapter 'Zinc' in Levi's autobiographical novel, *The Periodic Table* (1984, p. 35).

12. *The Drowned and the Saved* (English translation) is currently unavailable. The quotation is translated from the edition in original language. It can be found in the second chapter, 'The grey zone', p. 685.

13. This passage is to be found in the chapter 'Shame' in *The Drowned and the Saved*, p. 716.

6. THE MEMORY OF 1968 IN FRAGMENTS

The reflection on history that emerged in the 1990s produced a view that also questioned certain radical political practices, namely terrorism. Along with films about the Resistance and the Holocaust, the legacy of 1968 became a much-explored theme. The New Italian Cinema could be understood in terms of this convergence between the cultural relevance of the ideology of 1968 and the generation of the Baby Boomers. In fact, the New Italian Cinema, far from being the means of expression and self-representation of only a few young directors, on the contrary acquired a particular shape and logic of production thanks to films about the generation of the *sessantottini* (sixty-eighters). The history films that represent the events of 1968[1] and subsequent years of social and political unrest provide a public site for representation and identification for a specific audience, creating a generational trend. This chapter discusses the representational issues of the *sessantottini*, examining signs in the films that are terms of reference for this generation. My analysis traces the memory of 1968 and the 1970s in terms of the representation of what remained of that culture in the cinema of the 1990s and the new millennium. One of the most important problems that anguished the generation of 1968 was the phenomenon of repentance, established by decree 625/1979, subsequently converted into law, which aimed at dismantling political violence in Italy after the death of Aldo Moro. The law required the *pentito* (repentant) full confession and rupture of all contacts with individual terrorists and organisations. Ultimately, this law not only affected the *pentito*'s identity, but it also dramatically affected the collective identity of the generation of 1968 and their social and political relations. References to repentance emerge powerfully in many films produced in the 1990s and 2000s, signifying the profound consequences of repentance in the Italian community.

REPENTANCE

The phenomenon of repentance emerged with the arrest of the members of the group Autonomia Operaia (Workers' Autonomy) on 7 April 1979,[2] and gained momentum in 1984 with their trial. With the kidnapping and murder of the Christian Democratic Party Secretary Aldo Moro at the hands of the Red Brigades in 1978, the Italian government approved emergency legislation to defeat terrorism. It is generally recognised that the death of Aldo Moro marked the crisis of Italian red terrorism. Increasing defections left terrorist groups more and more isolated from intermediary groups and individuals who had provided logistic support while conducting a normal life. Ultimately, the Red Brigades became isolated from the entire left-wing spectrum. The arrests of 7 April 1979 were crucial to the end of the radical left and the opening of a period of political conformism which accelerated the wider process of historical revisionism.

On that day, former and current militants of the group Autonomia Operaia (Workers' Autonomy),[3] along with Antonio Negri, a professor of political theory at the university in Padua, were arrested. Later, other members of the terrorist group Prima Linea (Front Line) were also gaoled. It took four years, after much shifting of evidence and polemic, before 71 people were tried for 'promoting an insurrection, forming a subversive organisation and an armed band, performing several actions related to political violence' (Portelli 1985, p. 6). The case, which had great media coverage, came to be known as the '7 April' trial.

The arrest and trial of the 71 leaders, militants and university professors belonging to some of the most radical groups of the 1970s was in fact constructed against all Italian post-1968 radical movements (Portelli 1985). What the radical groups called 'proletarian war' or 'class war' was defined as terrorism and a conspiracy against the state; the judges and the media saw different groups as single organisations which coordinated terrorism with a subversive strategy. A fundamental role in the reconstruction or reinterpretation of the past (the 1970s) was played by the oral testimony of the so-called *pentiti* (repentants), former terrorists who denounced their past comrades, broke all relationships with them, repented their actions and thereby proved their will to collaborate with the judicial system. Those who were the heroes of the alleged revolutionary uprising were now disillusioned representatives of generational self-criticism.

The phenomenon of secularised repentance shares its basic principles in Catholicism and its biblical rituals. Features of repentance are self-confrontation, acknowledgment of sin and remorse, which leads to the awareness of having broken moral laws. From the viewpoint of the Italian judicial system, repentance was primarily a way to secure confessions from terrorists (Red Brigades and other groups) to enable the dismantling of the terrorist groups between the late 1970s and 1980s. As this proved a successful strategy, the law on *pentiti* became a backbone of Italian legislation and it was then extended to the Mafiosi, who were willing to collaborate with the judiciary. The law operated through confession, state forgiveness of the sin, and return of the repentant to the community after a reduced sentence to prison. Foucault directed his attention to confessional technologies and recognised the part it played in many areas, from justice to medicine, education, love and family relationships. Thus, following a Foucauldian interpretation of the confessional, secular repentance is an appropriate goal for punishment. It contains the idea of public admissions of guilt and acknowledges the legitimacy of the authority. David Moss (2001) has also interpreted the phenomenon of repentance in Italy from a socio-anthropological point of view, taking Marcel Mauss's theory of the gift as an interpretive tool that explains the exchange between the Italian institutions and the *pentiti*. The insider knowledge about underground structures and parallel structures that supported armed struggle became an item of exchange; valuable information also needed to be delivered in the hands of the judiciary with permanent and sincere detachment from violence. Importantly, as the 7 April trial became a highly mediated event with partial publication of the proceedings and confessions of the *pentiti*, repentance became a theatre that offered the spectacle of punishment and discipline, the ultimate and ironic defeat for the ex-terrorists. In fact, it must be noted that the Red Brigades initiated the ritual of confession with their proletarian trials of kidnapped people and daily release of communiqués to the media with the confessions of the prisoner. This practice was perfected during the kidnapping of Aldo Moro, as he was required by his abductors to confess his political sins. Red Brigades' communiqués and Moro's letters were released daily to the press, followed by government counter-press releases and declarations, transforming the kidnapping in spectacle.

The phenomenon of repentance produced a further fracture among the terrorists themselves, and between militants of the left and public opinion. On the one hand there were the so-called *irriducibili* (indomitables), the core group of the Red Brigades which had kidnapped and killed Aldo Moro (Mario Moretti was the leader), who continued to attack the state from prison; on the other was the group of some of the historical leaders of the Red Brigades, such as Alberto Franceschini and Roberto Ognibene, who wanted to put their past behind. This division further alienated the *irriducibili* from the rest of the left and public opinion, while the *pentiti* were able to talk to the media from prison and write articles for newspapers and current affairs weeklies. The narrative in Marco Bellocchio's *Il diavolo in corpo* (1986) is centred around the erotic tension created by the *irriducibili*, on the one hand, who hide with their bodies two other comrades who defiantly make love during a tribunal hearing, and on the other, the pathetic desire of return to normality declared in inane poems by the repentant terrorist.

A *j'accuse* against left-wing terrorism and repentance is to be found in the first segment of Nanni Moretti's film *Caro diario* (1993). While touring the streets of Rome on his Vespa, Moretti comments bitterly about the poor state of Italian cinema, remarking that during Summer it is only possible to find porn films, American B-grade and splatter films, or a certain kind of Italian films. At this point, Moretti inserts a fragment from an Italian film, which is a fake film that mocks the genre of films set in interiors, in which four characters sit in a lounge-room. They are all in their mid-forties, they are professionals, their are ageing and they self-commiserate about the mistakes they made when, in 1968 and the 1970s, they were political activists in radical left-wing movements. They regret their actions, reflect about the state of love relationships and comment: 'We're old, bitter, dishonest. We used to shout awful, violent slogans! Look how ugly we've gotten!' The film cuts back to Nanni Moretti who, back on his Vespa, proclaims: 'You shouted awful, violent slogans, you have gotten ugly. I shouted the right slogans and I am a splendid 40-year old.' *Caro diario* is essentially a film about minorities who are able to be propositional and can initiate certain processes of change. Nanni Moretti sides with the minority of people who in the 1970s were aware of the broader repercussions of extremism that would lead to the conservative backlash in the 1980s, and thus refused certain rhetorical slogans and the rigid orthodoxy of the false prophets of proletarian militancy. Through his comments against repentance, Moretti also makes a strong statement against the falsehood of repentance and redemption, so typical of Italian Catholic mentality and upbringing, and above all against the acceptance of the disciplinary power of repentance.

The 7 April trial terrorism, repentance and oblivion are also issues represented in Mimmo Calopresti's film *La seconda volta* (1995). In this film, Nanni Moretti – who also co-wrote the screenplay and produced the film – is Alberto, a professor of economics at the University of Turin. He was wounded in his apartment by a group of terrorists for, it is presumed, not being a political extremist. We don't know why he was chosen as a victim, but in fact many militants of the institutional left – namely the PCI and the unions – were, in the early stages of red terrorism, targets of terrorist attacks.

Alberto survived the attack, but is left with a bullet in his head. This bullet is the cause of his occasional blackouts, an allegory for the loss of memory. In *Deutscland, bleich Mutteri (Germany, Pale Mother,* Helma Sanders-Brahams, 1980), Lene's facial paralysis is an allegory for the division between the two Germanies and the Cold War. Lene's paralysis is the signifier of the blackout of a part of Germany and at the same time the reminder of the existence of the problem of the division. There is a similarity between Lene's paralysis and Alberto's bullet, in that the bullet is also a historical marker, and precisely, between remembering and forgetting. These are allegories of moral right and wrong. Despite the complex nature of existence, one in which Alberto had to make compromises, he is reassessing those compromises in the light of his own moral agenda based on a simplistic opposition of right and wrong that is a constant preoccupation in Moretti's films. However, in *La seconda volta*, things are not so simple.

This time, memory is triggered when he sees by chance his former attacker, Lisa, walking around the city streets. She is on day-release, has a job, her life seems normal, but at nine o'clock at night she must return to *Le Nuove*, Turin's gaol. Alberto then starts his obsessive reconstruction of the facts and the historical context of his attack by following Lisa, searching for his file and newspaper clippings about the 7 April trial and reading the books that Renato Curcio and Rosanna Faranda, two of the historical leaders of the Red Brigades, published while in prison. One of the most explanatory scenes of Alberto's indignation about ex-terrorists being on the centre-stage of cultural and media life occurs when Alberto reads an excerpt from one of these books. It is important to recall this excerpt entirely, as it well summarises the feeling of failure and defeat of the revolutionary left:

> One thing were the Red Brigades with their actions, and their revolutionary manifesto. Quite another thing is our duty to retain dignity in defeat. The merit of failed revolutions is that they avoid the faults of successful revolutions. All successful revolutions somehow betray their promises but the failed ones can only betray their motivations. All in all, this seems to me a lesser betrayal. On the other hand, the generosity shown by some of my generation in joining the risky political ideological fight represents a positive value for which we'll eventually be given credit. I say this without shame. Today I feel great

compassion for myself and for my defeated generation. This arises from the observation that we've been denied the freedom to live out the expectations we had when we joined society. We couldn't live in the way we had chosen because the previous generation brutally blocked our path by asking us to conform or die. So some died fighting, many died with heroin in their veins, and many more survived by killing off their dreams of change. In jail I received many letters from my peers who talk about their lives with great bitterness, having become aware of the defeat of their generation which no individual success can ever redeem.

The following day Alberto talks angrily to his sister: 'They are all out and about ... Red Brigades, Front Line ... They are all busy writing books. And they get published.'

Alberto meets with Lisa, but there is no successful closure to their encounter. The attempt at dialogue or understanding and forgiving is frustrated. Their story is that of two people with a common history who meet in a society that is profoundly changed and in which their story no longer matters or offers any interest. Despite the system of repentance put in place by the state, there is no forgiveness from the part of direct victims of terrorism. The film offers closure only at an individual level: Alberto leaves for Germany, supposedly to finally go under surgery to remove the bullet, and Lisa gives up her day-release, as she understands that there is no redemption for her past actions.

THE MEMORY OF 1968 IN FRAGMENTS

In 1979, following the Italian success of Cimino's film *Deer Hunter*, the national newspaper *Corriere della Sera* published an autobiographical article by Giuliano Zincone with the title 'Orfani' (Orphans) (Zincone 1979). The weekly magazine *L'espresso* picked up the story with an article in which five prominent intellectuals – Zincone himself, Umberto Eco and

Alberto Moravia among others – were invited to open a debate (P. Ch., 1979, p. 98). In the *Corriere della Sera* article, Zincone reflects on the fact that the generation of 1968 was left too early without parents. These parents – or better, father-like figures – were those figures who had inspired radical movements in the 1960s and countercultural movements in the United States and the rest of the world against the Vietnam War: Fidel Castro, Che Guevara, Marcuse, Jean-Paul Sartre, Daniel Cohn-Bendit. This metaphorical, and in some cases real, loss indicated the bewilderment of the sixty-eighters in front of Vietnam's invasion of Cambodia and the surfacing of Vietcong massacres against Americans and the Vietnam civilians during the Vietnam War. *Deer Hunter* was received in Italy with standing ovations at the end of the film. People also clapped during the scene of the Russian roulette torture (with Ho Chi Minh's portrait in the background), when De Niro turns the gun on the Vietcong soldiers and, with the help of the other American prisoner, kills their tormentors.

The film was screened in a period in which Italian historians started debating about partisan violence during the Resistance, and political and cultural myths were shattered after the kidnapping of Aldo Moro, his murder and the arrest of the leaders of Workers Autonomy. The 7 April arrests focused media attention and public opinion on only one of the aspects of the left-wing movements of the 1970s: terrorism. One of the results of this process was that 1968 and the 1970s became colonised by terrorism in subsequent historical accounts, while other significant experiences, such as feminism, were cancelled from common memory. This political amnesia erased the most promising cultural mutations brought about by 1968. The creative, carnivalesque, defiant aspects of 1968 and the cultural transformation that involved all the domains of human agency and of interpersonal relationships, from those between the sexes to customs and habits, were buried under the weight of the 'leaden years'. It must also be noted that neo-Fascist terrorism in the 1970s has hardly been explored in film. The so-called *trame nere*, the collusion between right-wing military and paramilitary forces, also linked to the secret services and the Masonic lodge P2, have not attracted much interest from Italian filmmakers and writers, with the exception of Marco Bechis' *Garage Olimpo* (2002), which displaces the threat of a neo-Fascist coup in the 1970s to the tragedy of the Argentinian *desaparecidos*. On the contrary, in the years leading up to and around the thirtieth anniversary of 1968, a large number of books were published about the bombing of Piazza Fontana in Milan on the 12 December 1969 and the strategy of tension.[4]

From a political viewpoint, the movements of 1968 cultivated the idea of overthrowing the moral, pedagogical and aesthetic restrictions of traditional life. In the absence of a dominant ideology – in spite of the militaristically organised groups of the extreme left, such as Trotskyists and those of Marxist-Leninist inspiration – the Italian 1968 movement did not offer itself to a process of institutionalisation or homologation, where the change corresponds with a change in political figures. However, later, on a personal level, many militants and protagonists of 1968 conformed with the neoliberal institutionalisation that started to manifest itself in the late 1970s. These are the protagonists of the quoted segment in *Caro diario* who are professionals, often employed in sectors they once despised: advertising, journalism, business, academia, architecture, and so on.

Many questions arise from the sense of loss and disorientation that pervaded the generation of 1968 in the 1980s: did this feeling of loss and angst prepare the ground for representation in film? To what extent does 1968 emerge in the themes of the films produced in the 1980s and 1990s? Are there recognisable codes, conventions or signs that could provide intelligibility, identification, pleasure? Is there a preferred reading of these films?

There are two phases in the films about 1968. One occurs in the 1980s and is characterised essentially by low production values and poverty of means; in the second phase, in the late 1990s and in the new millennium, some directors were able to raise their budgets with television and European funding, which in turn enabled securing state funding, and thus higher production values (*I cento passi, Il partigiano Johnny, Concorrenza sleale, Placido Rizzotto*). The pre-*Tangentopoli* cinematic interpretation of 1968 is delivered by fragmented film images that are like 'Polaroids', as Monteleone says,[5] 'hanging on the fridge of the kitchen', adds Serenellini

(1985, p. 116). These images are like a series of 'notes, a bit casual and dispersed, with a lot of longing for action and a lot of disillusionment: the beer bar, the disco and the countryside excursion are refuge-islands, the waiting for something that will come' (1985, p. 116). Failure is the central theme of the films produced in the big industrial cities of North Italy: *Venerdì sera, lunedì mattina* (Pianciola-Chiantaretto, 1983), set in Turin, tells the story of the failure of a commune in a city pervaded by angst caused by the economic crisis of Fiat and by tired political demonstrations, while in *Giulia in ottobre* (Silvio Soldini, 1985) it is the failure of a love story that indicates the failure of a generation. The films of the first half of the 1980s are set in what Serenellini calls 'Kitchen, one bedroom and a camera' (1985, p. 116), which indicates the claustrophobic aesthetic of the period, the retreat into interior spaces, into a minimalist, intimate and introspective cinema, and metaphorically, the retreat into the confessional where it is possible to repent. Above all, the aesthetic of the 1980s cinema indicates poverty of the means of production, small budgets that only allowed sketches and episodic films, which could be reworked later on by adding other segments whenever filmmakers could find funding. This was an autarchic cinema, which did not offer pleasure through spectacular special effects; it was a cinema which Italian film critics attacked and which existed at the margins of the 'empire' Hollywood.

If, in the 1980s and 1990s, the recounting of the 1968 movement as a failure was the political allusion, and 'the family video, the school photos in which a generation poses' were, for Zagarrio (1998, p. 13), aesthetic references, then music and comic books were cultural references. In fact, music played an important role of aggregation for the youth of the 1960s. Gundle observes that the replacement of the old 78-rpm record with the single 45-rpm, which was used in marketing rock'n'roll and pop genres, coincided with a boom in record buying (Gundle 2000, p. 109). In Italy in 1953, five million records were sold, eighteen million in 1958 and over 30 million in 1964. Italian philosopher Pietro Adamo points out that the most striking phenomenon of the years before 1968 is the coincidence and overlapping between the hit parade – commercial music – and experimentations in counter-culture, as the explosion of mass culture cannot be separated from that of counter-culture (Adamo 1998, p. 48). In fact, songs from commercial pop music (the Beach Boys, the Mamas and Papas, the Turtles) and those from the American counter-culture (The Doors, Bob Dylan, Pete Seeger and Jefferson Airplane) were present at the same time in the Italian hit parade. As Liliana Cavani said commenting on her film *I cannibali* (1969) (in Cremonini 1987, p. 75), 'the protest discourse was already a consumerist product in 1969–1970'. The music of the 1960s and 1970s returns in the films of the 1990s as the soundtrack for 1968, providing not only historical reference, but above all pleasure and identification.

Thus mnemonic recollections of 1968 operated through the recognition of common cultural codes. Disillusionment about the present, longing for the events of 1968, the subject's split between a pervasive consumerist present and the loss of political engagement were the disruptions in the equilibrium of the sixty-eighters' narrative discourse. Here, the dramatic conflict is internal to the characters rather than external. The discourses mobilised in this conflict are those of revolution, terrorism, fragmentation or dissolution of collective action, but also the transformation of the relationship between men and women with the destruction of sentimental relationships (this is a specific obsession in Nanni Moretti's film *Bianca*, 1984). The ritual of confession can take the form of autobiographical narratives, thus films about 1968 share elements that include a strong narcissistic impulse to tell one's story, informed by repentance and regret. These themes emerge over and over, making most of the cinematic output of the 1980s and 1990s into a collective giant act of repentance.

The view of 1968 as a crucial event in the country's history is epitomised especially in the collaboration between Gabriele Salvatores and Enzo Monteleone. Indeed, from their collaboration, which started in 1987 with the film *Kamikazen*, came a cinema that could better represent the generation of acculturated moviegoers and could rescue the Italian cinema from the production of soft-core porn comedies of the early 1980s.[6] With a group of actors who had been working with Salvatores since the theatrical experience of left-wing *Teatro dell'Elfo* in the 1970s in Milan, Salvatores chose the voyage as a metaphor for escape. From *Marrakech Express*, Salvatores' cinema becomes a cinema of experience and generational self-representation, in which the retrieval of historical memory involves an entire generation through the group of actors-friends. The trip, friendship, dreams, projects and utopian desires are all represented in this film, which tells the story of a group of friends who travel from Milan to Marrakech (one of the trendy holiday destinations for the sixty-eighters who became fascinated with exotic locations and cultures, including the Orient) to help a friend who is in prison for possessing hashish. The focus of the film is their friendship and their common experiences during the trip. These are viewed as the irreplaceable existential experiences that are opposed to the rampant individualism of Italian society of the 1980s.

In opposition to the minimalist films set in interiors, Salvatores follows a different narrative strategy and throws his characters on the road, thus moving from the minimalist and enclosed visual perspective of Italian cinema of the late 1980s. The conventions of *Marrakech Express*, typical of the road movie genre, are inspired by a film of the golden era of the Italian comedy, namely Dino Risi's *Il sorpasso* (1962). *Mediterraneo* also finds its blueprint in two of the most successful Italian comedies, *La grande guerra* (Mario Monicelli, 1959) and *Tutti a casa* (Luigi Comencini, 1960). *Mediterraneo*, written by Enzo Monteleone, reflects Monteleone's love for the history of Italian cinema, and specifically for the *commedia all'italiana*, a genre that had been chastised by Italian critics for long time as a lower quality cinema compared with *auteur* cinema. The *commedia all'italiana*, on the contrary, grew and multiplied at the margins of the more serious political cinema, nevertheless delivering vitriolic comments on the *italietta*, the little Italy of the petty bourgeoisie and narrow-minded conservatism. The bewilderment of the soldiers in *Mediterraneo* in the face of the news that Italy has surrendered to the Allies and that those 'who once were the enemy are now allies' mirrors Alberto Innocenzi in *Tutti a casa* when, ignoring the fact that General Badoglio has surrendered, he realises that the Germans are shooting at his platoon, thus he deduces that the Nazis must now be allied with the Americans. The depiction of accidental heroism in *La grande guerra* and *Tutti a casa* is represented by Sergeant Lo Russo in *Mediterraneo* (interpreted by Diego Abatantuono, a key actor in most of Salvatores' movies). Lo Russo, stranded on a tiny Greek island during World War II with seven other soldiers, initially finds it difficult to adapt to this situation of isolation from historical action. However, at the end of the film, in a flash-forward, we come to know that he had returned to the island once he realised that there was no possibility for change in postwar Italy: 'Life wasn't so good in Italy. They didn't let us change anything. Then, I told them: you win, but I won't be your accomplice. That's what I said, and I came here,' says Lo Russo to Lieutenant Montini 40 years after the end of the war.

The island is the signifier of Utopia, a place where instances of community, friendship and equality are achieved. The film's historical reference is 1941–44, but its subtext addresses the disillusionment of the generation that participated in the movement of 1968,[7] and the concept of failure refers to both postwar reconstruction and the demise of the 1968 movement. However, in *Mediterraneo* there is a shift from failure and self-criticism to a sense of frustration and betrayal, which will then transform in a new view about 1968 in some films of the new millennium. *Mediterraneo* displays contemporary dialogue, slogans, clothes and cultural habits common to the generation of the sixty-eighters. The soldiers are initiated to smoking hashish by a Turkish fisherman who arrives one night from the nearby Turkish coast. As the story unfolds, the Italian soldiers free themselves of the army uniforms and dress in local attire, which recalls the idea of the Orient as an alternative utopia, a neo-Orientalism, that characterised the 1970s.[8]

The link between the Resistance and 1968 – equally considered two failed revolutions – also becomes apparent in Daniele Luchetti's latest film, *Mio fratello è figlio unico* (2007). In April 2007, *Mio fratello è figlio unico* was at the top of the Italian box office. Nominated for eleven David of Donatello awards,[9] the film tells the story of two brothers divided by their political coterie. The story is set in Latina[10] and spans the period from the early 1960s to the 1970s. Manrico is an extreme left-wing militant who, in the early 1970s, succumbs to the charisma of a terrorist group, presumably the Red Brigades. His youngest brother, Antonello (nicknamed Accio), after a clumsy beginnings as a seminarian, traverses the political spectrum, from extreme right to left, but without the excesses of Manrico, finding at the end of the film balance and wisdom, while Manrico is killed by the police during his arrest.

Mio fratello è figlio unico can be regarded as a sequel to *I piccoli maestri*. Divisions among young partisans and partisans and Fascists in *I piccoli maestri* are placed in the 1960s within the family environment, in the political differences between the two brothers Manrico and Accio. In both of Luchetti's films, Italy and Italians appear to have been deeply divided for 40 years. Likewise, Marco Tullio Giordana's epic film, transformed in a television mini-series *La meglio gioventù* (2004), narrates the vicissitudes of a middle-class family from 1966 to Spring 2002.

Giordana is not new to films about 1968 and terrorism. He directed the first two films about the subject, *Maledetti vi amerò* (1980) and *La caduta degli angeli ribelli* (1981), both from an already revisionist and negative perspective of 1968 and the following decade. *La caduta degli angeli ribelli* tells the story of Vittorio, the main character, who repents his actions and therefore is condemned to death by his own ex-comrades. Vittorio hopes to free himself from his past through entertaining an erotic relationship with Cecilia, a young bourgeois woman, but eventually is killed by Cecilia, who can then return to her bourgeois environment. This film combines the motif of repentance with the aesthetics of enclosure to communicate a suffocating environment and a dangerous outside world.

In *La meglio gioventù*, Nicola and Matteo are two brothers with a profound affinity, but at the same time they are different. Nicola is an incurable optimist while Matteo is an introvert and has an instinctive dislike of authority. It is Summer 1966, the end of university exams. Matteo, Nicola and two other friends are about to travel to the North Cape – a trendy destination for the 1960s Italian middle-class male, as young women from North Europe were perceived as more liberated than Italian women. Matteo works part-time in a psychiatric hospital and meets Giorgia, a girl with obsessive compulsive disorder. When he realises that doctors use electroshock on Giorgia, he takes her out of the hospital and, with his brother Nicola, starts a trip north to deliver Giorgia to her father. The failure of this initiative profoundly marks the two brothers. The four friends will never make it together to the North Cape. Nicola takes a year off from his studies and travels to the North Cape, from where he writes regularly to Nicola, communicating him his decision to become a psychiatrist. Matteo leaves university and enters in the police. Nicola returns to Italy to help clean up after the Florence flood of 1968. Here he meets Giulia, a piano player and a student of mathematics from Turin. Nicola moves to Turin where he participates in the occupation of the university. The differences between Giulia and Nicola are clear from the beginning: Giulia would not hesitate to defend herself with violence from the police, while Nicola does not want to respond to violence with violence. Eventually Giulia becomes a terrorist, goes underground and leaves Nicola and their young daughter Sara.

The film traverses 30 years of Italian history, with the two brothers often on opposite sides: Nicola runs from the police during a violent demonstration in Turin while Matteo, as a policeman, represses the students' revolts. Giordana does not offer any explanation or justification for Matteo's angst and violence. The film suffers from many flaws and Matteo's behaviour can only be explained by Giordana's rational decision to offer, through Matteo, Pasolini's interpretation of the policeman as the true proletarian because policemen were the sons of peasants and workers from the south, who were the true proletariat, while radical students were the offspring of transformist bourgeoisie (Bozza 1995, p. 56; Fantoni Minnella 2004, p. 26). The left criticised Pier Paolo Pasolini for his idealistic siding with the police after the clash between police and students in Valle Giulia in March 1968. In *La meglio gioventù*, Nicola and his other friends embody the stereotypical youth of 1968, full of dreams and hopes, who eventually become *integrati*, integrated into society, by being absorbed into the professional class.

In the 1990s, the political divisions are rationalised in the historians' disagreements about historical revisionism. History films are an obvious representation of the 1990s struggle about memory: Who were the victims in World War II? Was the Resistance a liberation war or a civil war? Were the partisans legitimate fighters or could they be likened to the 1970s terrorists? Should we accept the link between Resistance and terrorism? In an interview released in 2000, Senator Giovanni Pellegrino, president from 1994 of the Commission into the inquiry on terrorism, made a link between the two events by explaining the Italian political and social cleavage in the 1970s as:

> A real civil war, although of low intensity. The civil war that in the 1950s and 1960s (I would say from the attempted murder of Togliatti onward) had remained in a state of potentiality, in the 1970s, after Piazza Fontana, re-ignited in a real and bloody socio-political clash. (Fasanella and Pellegrino 2000, p. 140)

Enrico Berlinguer, secretary of the PCI between 1972 and 1984, also addressed the question of equivalence between partisans and terrorist in his speech during the unions' demonstration of solidarity after the kidnapping of Aldo Moro. In this speech, shown in a segment in Bellocchio's *Buongiorno notte* (2003), Berlinguer refuses this equivalence by stamping the mark of '*professionisti del terrore*' (professional terrorists) on the Red Brigades, pointing out that:

> We are facing civil war, we've been through it before. This time, we are not in front of a small group of people fighting against another small group ... we are in front of a small group of assassins attacking the institutions and freedom.

A different view from terrorism as the reason for the end of radical politics emerges in *Radiofreccia* (1998), directed by popular songwriter Luciano Ligabue. The film is an adaptation from Ligabue's book *Fuori e dentro il borgo*. Here the Italian province, Emilia-Romagna in particular, is presented in contrast to the big cities of the north of Italy: a site of boredom and the quintessence of a lack of goals and ideals. This image of the Italian province is contrasted with the enthusiasm of a group of friends, including Freccia the protagonist who, with other friends, opens a *radio libera* (free radio). The protagonists see the free radio as an alternative to Rai, the state radio broadcaster. The free radio is a fundamental witness to the 1970s, a signifier of self-management, collectivisation and, importantly, militant information away from the dominant public broadcaster Rai. In *Radiofreccia* music works as a trigger of memory and as a sign of political coterie: the opening bars of *Black Market* by Weather Report, the theme of Radio Popolare's news since the 1970s,[11] and the songs of David Bowie, Elvis Presley, Credence Clearwater Revival, Iggy Pop and Brian Ferry reconnect the audience to their past.

The story is told in flashback. It is 1993. RadioFreccia is eighteen years old and is closing down. Its founder, Bruno, speaks to his audience for the last time from the darkness of the broadcasting studio, a confessional once again. He remembers the facts and circumstances that led him to open a free radio, hence the many flashbacks. The reason for the radio's closing down is not a lack of funding, but because 'it's time to close'. Bruno starts his story from the funeral of Freccia (Stefano Accorsi), the main protagonist, who died of a heroin overdose in 1975. The film then cuts to Freccia's funeral. The suggestion that 'it's time to close' points to the fact that, for the generation of 1968, it is time to bury and mourn the past. Freccia's funeral is in fact the closure for the 1968 movement, which collapsed under the spread of hard drugs.

The film depicts a number of characters, each of whom represents a different typology of the province, which recalls Fellini's portrayal of the Romagna province. The gathering place for this group of friends is the bar. Here, emotions, idiosyncratic characters, madness, sexism and boredom are displayed. The barman, played by Francesco Guccini, a famous songwriter who in the 1970s was an icon for the counter-culture movement, is a member of the Communist Party who longs for Stalin (the Emilia-Romagna region was traditionally Communist). Pluto, the village idiot, wanders around town and the countryside trying to catch voices from the dead on his tape recorder. One night, he records the angry voice of Enrico Berlinguer, the secretary of the Communist Party. His friends object that it is impossible because Enrico Berlinguer is not dead (in the film, we are in 1975). Pluto maintains that Enrico Berlinguer is saying that he will die around the year 2000; he is angry because the cause of his death (metaphorically the death of the Communist Party) is that 'nobody believed any longer, whether in God or in Communism'. It is an obvious pronouncement against a secularised consumerist culture, and against the death of grand ideologies.

RadioFreccia grossed $4.5 million domestically. Much of the advertising campaign was conducted on radio, and the fact that the film was censored and rated for viewing for over-fourteens (the film was marketed as the Italian *Trainspotting*) caused an exaggerated outrage, but in the end functioned as a good marketing strategy. The film opened in an uncut version at the Salone della Musica (Music Fair) in Turin in October 1998, where crowds clamoured to see it. On 15 October, the censorship commission lifted the ban on the film. It must be said that, despite its historical references, the film marketing strategy was aimed at the 15–34-year-old demographic, using the director's Luciano Ligabue's songs as a carrier for its advertising campaign.[12]

The emphasis of the film is on free radio stations as a form of participation in civic and social life and political engagement, while the use of heroin is seen – quite rightly – as one of the main causes for the disintegration of a generation and its hopes for a better society. Aside from terrorism, in fact, heroin and the use of hard drugs are commonly seen as another fundamental element of the defeat of the radical groups of the left. These themes can be found also in *I cento passi* (Marco Tullio Giordana, 2000). This film was directly inspired by the life of Peppino Impastato, a young militant in Democrazia Proletaria who was killed in 1978 by the mafia. His distant relative, Gaetano Badalamenti, a famous mafia boss, was finally incriminated for his murder in 1994. During the 1970s, Peppino Impastato was able to gather a group of radical left-wing militants around a free radio from which he denounced the mafia's collusion with government, its involvement in the building industry and its shift in those years into the hard drug trade. When Peppino decides to run for the council as a representative of Democrazia Proletaria, Badalamenti sends his men to kill him. The film makes it clear that it is only when Peppino decides to use the institutions from inside that the potential threat to the mafia becomes real. The film also hints at the PCI's lack of support and differences between radical groups from the big cities of the north – which, by the end of the 1970s, were oriented on freedom of the body and 'personal' issues – and Sicily, where a real battle was fought against the collusion between mafia and political parties which crippled normal civic life. As in *Radiofreccia*, Peppino's funeral – which Giordana shot in black and white to show its factual and historical truth – represents an occasion for the community to show unity, but at the same time it becomes a moment of collective mourning, alluding to the end of political radicalism in Italy.

For the new filmmakers, the *Tangentopoli* inquiry into corruption meant the adoption of a critical stance against the political establishment, and above all the need to tell the truth in regard to certain facts that had been too readily swept under the carpet by the Christian Democrats. The elevation of truth underpins such films as *Placido Rizzotto* and *I cento passi*, both inspired by real life events. They need a few further words of acknowledgment for their engagement with reality and their positive viewpoint of left-wing ideology. These two films have strong stories with a beginning, a middle and an end, presenting the possibility of conceiving a personal destiny and purpose. The two main characters' political commitment is seen as the only way to fight against the Mafia. The extreme corruption that happens at all levels in Sicily is only an exacerbated version of the Italian reality and a metaphor for the Christian Democratic Party's corruption, which makes credible and viable political commitment and gives back its dignity to the radical left-wing ideologies of postwar Italy and of the 1970s. Giordana refuses to be labelled a 'political filmmaker',[13] but his *I cento passi*, as well as Scimeca's *Placido Rizzotto,* produces counter-cultural discourses in the best tradition of Italian political filmmaking from the 1960s to the 1970s, where personal stories are able to represent metaphors more akin to certain cinema by Fassbinder.

TELEVISION AND 1968: AN AMBIGUOUS RELATIONSHIP

The generation of the sixty-eighters was the first generation of Italians to grow up in a world dominated by television and advertising. Their language and identity formed along with television language and the historical context of post-1968. Thus this generation had an ambiguous relationship with television which was expressed on the one hand in its ideological refusal – resistance – and on the other in its embracement of its aesthetics, discourses and practice – pleasure. This double interpretation of resistance and pleasure in post-1968 audience activity is certainly a provocative hypothesis, but is based on the knowledge of the fact that audiences are active and that they engage with media texts. In particular, engagement and pleasure can come also from resistance – that is, asserting autonomy in relation to a preferred reading of a text (Croteau and Hoynes 2003, p. 298). Moreover, the 1970s are the context in which postmodernism problematised grand narratives, objectivity, universality and totality. The 1980s witnessed the emergence of multiple and fragmented identities that found active agency in new environments: gay groups, green parties, food appreciation and connoisseurship. Commercial television, the importation of American soap operas (especially *Dallas*), 24-hour television flow and the increase in advertising all occurred in the decade between 1980 and 1990 – in a moment, it must be remembered, in which political commitment went out of fashion. The 1975 media deregulation slowly changed the Italian television system from scarcity to plenty, culminating in the 1980s abundance of local television stations. As already discussed in Chapter 5, since the 1980s Italian filmmakers have used television funding and opportunities for training as a way to survive in the industry. The rationalisation of Rai as film producer transformed the public broadcaster into a vertically integrated structure for the production, distribution and exhibition of films, with its new production structure Raicinema, while Berlusconi's investments in film production occurred through its production arm Medusa. This has had obvious consequences on film aesthetics and content. Because of the availability of material accumulated over 50 years of broadcasting, television's archives have become an enormous well of history fragments. This has heavily affected the retelling of the country's history as bits from news, current affairs, music programs, entertaining shows and documentaries are spliced into film to deliver an objective and factual understanding of the story that is told on the (small) screen, but also to induce recognition and pleasure.

This book discusses contemporary Italian cinema through its industrial and textual components as they emerge in the reconfiguration of space off and on screen, but it also argues that in the 1980s and 1990s cinema became a vehicle to express meaning and memory, functioning as a mnemonic recollection of ambience, clothes, atmosphere: in one word, it awakened viewers' pleasure of gazing at *come eravamo* (how we were). In this regard, it is important to stretch the argument to explore whether memory and history can assume new meanings when mediated by television. There are no systematic studies on the relationship between memory and television in Italy, but research conducted for Rai and Mediaset on their 1995 schedules found that memory was represented using repeated and classifiable formulas (Cardini 1997). Television uses re-runs, program clones, anthologies and stock programs to elicit recognition. In the 1980s, the popular programs *Schegge*, *Fuori orario* and *Blob* showed film fragments, authorial shorts and old news edited together with a satirical political commentary in voiceover. History films have since used the same montage-like technique to add meaning to subjective interpretation, and to make visible 1968 youth culture and politics, which had been wiped out by the disciplining element of repentance.

Enzo Monteleone's first film as director was *La vera vita di Antonio H.* (1994). The film is set in an empty theatre in which the actor Alessandro Haber pretends to be a failed actor and tells the story of his life – and in parallel, the history of Italy and its cinema – through videoed interviews with various other actors. These fragments go backwards and forwards between present time (Alessandro Haber in the theatre) and the past (the fake interviews with real actors and directors), and mix with real television footage. Through pastiche, *La vera vita di Antonio H.* constructs a fully illusionary double narrative played on *double entendre* of what is real and what is fictional.

Ormai è fatta (1999), is Montleone's second film as director. It is set in a prison, and is adapted from the autobiography of Horst Fantazzini, the son of Libero Fantazzini (played by Francesco Guccini), an Anarchist partisan who fought in the Resistance in Emilia Romagna. This film is set in 1973. It unfolds during one day, from the morning of the attempted escape of Horst Fantazzini from the Fossano prison, near Cuneo, to the dramatic epilogue in which Fantazzini is nearly killed by the police marksman. The story is told in flashback by his wife to a journalist, while Horst Fantazzini lies on an operating table, perforated by many bullets. Horst Fantazzini, a self-proclaimed individualist anarchist, became famous in the 1960s as *ladro gentiluomo*, the gentleman robber, because he robbed banks with a toy gun. Unlike his father Libero, Horst has a distorted sense of the so-called *esproprio proletario* (proletarian expropriation). This is the topic of a strong discussion between father and son, in which Libero clarifies the difference between his robberies to finance the Resistance movement and Horst's actions, aimed at satisfying his own needs. Despite the fact that Horst never killed or wounded anybody, he was sentenced to 30 years in prison.

The film bears striking similarities to the narrative structure of Sidney Lumet's *Dog Day Afternoon* (1975). This film had a cultural significance on Monteleone's generation for its criticism of American society.[14] Like *Dog Day Afternoon*, in *Ormai è fatta* there is the constant presence of media, especially with television news footage of the period. Monteleone, through cinema verité style, constructs a dialectical reportage of the events inside the prison (Fantazzini, after an attempted escape, is barricaded in a room with two guards as hostages from where he negotiates his release) and those outside the prison. Monteleone uses footage from television news to project the outside world, add factuality and objectivity to its fictional reconstruction of a true story and, importantly, project images of the past which reconnect his personal interpretation of history with the rest of society. In these images taken from current affairs of nightly news, masses reappear in the form of unconscious actors. These crowds of Italian tourists and holiday-makers bathing on the popular and crowded beaches of the Adriatic Sea appear in a montage-like editing to highlight the thoughtless prosperity of middle class in 1973 while a drama is unfolding in the prison. The historical, social and cultural contexts of the 1970s are introduced in the opening shots with television news footage: the secretary of the Christian Democrats, Aldo Moro, the Beatles, street demonstrations, the popular Italian singer Caterina Caselli, workers leaving the factory, clashes between students and police, the Vietnam War, soccer. These images are spliced with real newspaper titles related to the gentleman robber, Horst Fantazzini. The mix of images is commented by songs of the period: Caterina Caselli, Patty Pravo and the Beatles, as the soundtrack of the 1960s.

Television news from one of Berlusconi's networks features in Nanni Moretti's *Aprile* (1998) to document the historical watershed of the Communist Party with the victory of Silvio Berlusconi at the 1994 elections. There are four elements connected in a cause-and-effect relationship in this film: the role of television in the life of Italians; the rise of Berlusconi to power, which causes Moretti's own inability to make a film; and the defeat of the left in the 1994 elections. In the opening scene, Nanni Moretti watches the special program about the 1994 elections on one of Berlusconi's networks and bitterly remarks on the delay of the PDS in calling a press conference to comment on its defeat. Segments of nightly news are also cross-edited with fictional scenes in Marco Tullio Giordana's *Pasolini, un delitto italiano* (1995) and Giuseppe Ferrara's *Il caso Moro* (1985). Giordana's film was in fact criticised for this mixing of different media. The critic Gianluigi Bozza defined it as 'a marginally convincing film-inquiry of historical popularisation' (Bozza 1995, p. 58). The use of the particular typology of the *film-inchiesta* through the use of material from television news with fictional scenes prevented an 'emotional reconstruction of the figure of Pier Paolo Pasolini' and especially, in Bozza's opinion, did not transmit the significance of the effect of Pasolini's death on contemporary culture. However, the film's *giallo* format, which uses *noir* conventions, suggest disfunctionality in Italian society at both the time of Pasolini's death and of the production of the film twenty years later. The film avoids the trap of suggesting a conspiracy hypothesis, even though it does not exclude the possibility of a political murder. The death of Pasolini is taken as an event of the past which occurred at a particular point in time. This is a signifier of an era, and real footage is used as the pro-filmic event to trigger the visual memory of the audience through its realism. This narrative construction reveals a Freudian methodology (or an inductive-deductive paradigm): through gaps, inconsistencies and contradictions of witnesses, judges, police investigators and distortions by the media, the film sets out to achieve a *possible* knowledge of history.

Buongiorno, notte (Marco Bellocchio, 2003) is a psychodrama of Aldo Moro's kidnapping and his captivity in a 'people's prison'. In this film, Bellocchio neither offers a historical or political perspective, nor is he interested in reconstructing the phases of the kidnapping in an investigative manner, which is instead the motivation behind Ferrara's examination of the kidnapping in *Il caso Moro* (1986). *Buongiorno, notte* is centred on the character of Chiara, inspired to the Red Brigades' Anna Laura Braghetti, the only female terrorist involved in the imprisonment of Aldo Moro. Through Chiara, Bellocchio wants to challenge history by proposing a fluidity of history. Chiara is the only character in the film who can still dream, and through her dreams she is able to reinvent the tragic ending of the kidnapping. In fact, the film ends with Aldo Moro leaving his prison, walking in the streets of EUR. Apart from proposing once more the element of repentance, through Chiara's increasing doubts about the political validity of killing Aldo Moro, Bellocchio uses footage from television to fill in the factual gaps: the Pope's address to the Red Brigades, Berlinguer's speech in support of national solidarity against terrorism, Aldo Moro's funerals (with Pink Floyd's opening bars of *Shine on you crazy diamond*). Bellocchio's use of fragments from the Saturday night show with Raffaella Carrà, and segments of military parades from Stalinist Russia, indicates the ambiguity of the identity formation of the militants of the Red Brigades, caught between pleasure through entertainment and bold Communism.

Luisa Passerini defined 1968 as a conceptual triangle formed by 'subjectivity, desire, utopia' (Passerini 2002, p. 13). These terms have re-emerged powerfully in the 1980s and 1990s films in various ways, with the common elements of nostalgia for rebellion and the utopian tension of 1968. While in the last twenty years capitalism offered new ways to understand utopia, with flexible and nomadic networks and jobs, tolerance of differences, and removal of the boundaries between the personal and the political through the media exposure of events that have involved political figures (Diana's life and death, Bill Clinton's sexual life), Italian directors felt the urge to dig the past inquiring into a range of possibilities for utopia. Unfortunately, the focus on terrorism curtailed any other propositional feature of 1968, directing filmic inquiry into the moral and existential dilemma of propaganda by the deed.

NOTES

1. I use 1968 as a symbolic year, not as a specific date. Many waves of rebellion, more or less organised, such as the 1977 youth movement in Bologna, extended 1968 into the late 1970s, until the kidnapping of Aldo Moro. Also, the Italian feminist movement emerged in the middle of 1970s. Thus 1968 stands for a long wave of political protests inspired by radical groups of the left.

2. For a discussion of the significance of the 7 April trial in Italian political imaginary of the time, see Portelli (1985).

3. Among the most important leaders arrested were Oreste Scalzone, Franco Piperno, Emilio Vesce, Manzio Sturaro, Ivo Galimberti, Luciano Ferrari-Bravo and Carmela di Rocco.

4. See selectively on the strategy of tension, Cucchiarelli and Giannuli (1997) *Lo stato parallelo*, which finds the origins of the strategy of tension from the expulsion of the PCI from government in 1947, with a consequent purge of communist bureaucrats, teachers, union leaders and activist workers from industries and state institutions (1997). Fasanella et al. (2000) look at the strategy of tension in the geopolitical context of the opposition of the two blocs East–West, and in tensions in the Mediterranean area. On the bomb in

Piazza Fontana on 12 December 1969, see Boatti (1993), where the events of 12 December 1969 are seen as a war fought between the hidden power of the secret services and part of the Italian population that wanted social change. Dianese and Bettin's (1999) book, *La strage: Piazza Fontana. Verità e memoria* is a historical reconstruction for younger generations and a handbook of memory for the older generation. *Il malore attivo dell'anarchico Pinelli* (1996) is the record of the sentence that closed the trial on the death of the anarchist Giuseppe Pinelli on 15 December 1969 at the Milan police headquarters. The book was distributed with a video by Pier Paolo Pasolini, made on the 12 of December 1969. Di Giovanni and Ligini's (2000) book, *La strage di stato*, is a militant counter-inquiry about the bomb in Piazza Fontana, media manipulation and links between secret services and neo-Fascist groups.

5. Interview with Enzo Monteleone, Rome, May 2000.
6. Italian films available at the beginning of the 1980s were comedies with a soft-core pornographic touch that catered to popular and adolescent audiences. Ex-cabaret entertainers, popular singers such as Adriano Celentano and Johnny Dorelli played the leading role in such comedies. Lino Banfi and Edwige Fenech were a typical couple in B-grade soft-core comedies.
7. Interview with Enzo Montaleone, Rome, May 2000.
8. I refer to a concept of neo-Orientalism, following Edward Said's critique of Orientalism as a discursive formation.
9. The David di Donatello is the Italian equivalent of the Oscar.
10. The closeness of the city to the south of Rome, where Cinecittà is located, makes it a viable alternative to the expensive studios, which are used for post-production.
11. Radio Popolare was one of the first free radio stations founded in Milan in the mid-1970s by radical left-wing groups. Despite the fact that the management has had economic problems, it is one of the very few radio stations from that period that has survived to the present day.
12. Interview with Maurizio Colombo, Marketing Director of Medusa Film, Milan, May 2000.
13. Interview with Marco Tullio Giordana, in Fantoni Minnella (2004, p. 280).
14. Interview with Enzo Montaleone.

PART III

SCREEN SPACES

7. INTIMACY, OTHERNESS AND SPACE

During the 1980s and 1990s, Italian cinema dealt with boundaries between inside and outside. On the one hand, films' aesthetics and themes concentrated on the intimate space (domestic interiors with self-reflexive micro-stories), and on the other they focused on the outside, the landscape, particularly with on-the-road films. The landscape films will be discussed in Chapter 8 with regard to representations of the Mediterranean Sea. This chapter discusses the relationship between cinema and television with reference to the rationalisation of production practices by both public and commercial networks from the 1980s. As it is essential to view the transformation of content and aesthetics of films made for television, this chapter also discusses the aesthetics of the close-up – the intimate space – in relation to the social function of television. Also, it acknowledges the contribution that women directors made to the film industry in the 1980s by working in the restricted environment of television, which has systematically been overlooked by scholarly works and film criticism. In summary, the relationship between television and film is complex, and it entails different points of analysis at the levels of aesthetics, industry, content, gender, technology, and so on.

The intimate-space films served two functions. First, the micro-stories were suitable for television, as in the 1980s both public and private networks became almost the only production option available to directors. The second function was economic, as the minimalist stories born out of the intimate style could be made with very low budgets that were covered by a third or even half of television pre-sales. There is evidence that television and cinema have often interacted in a symbiotic manner, but from the deregulation of the broadcasting system and the crisis in the film industry, their relationship has increasingly and inevitably drawn closer as the Italian mediascape has progressively become more integrated. The use of television archive and historical images, as discussed in the previous chapter, is an evidence of this integration.

Chapter 5 discussed the contextual and industrial elements that forced Italian filmmakers to make minimalist films 'in progress' as funding became available. In this chapter, I argue that stories filmed in interiors and the visualisation of the domestic space was a visualisation of everyday life of routine and repetition, which exists outside large-scale historical events. Films for television or funded by television thus suited a specific content and a specific aesthetic. A more naturalistic cinema emerged, breaking away from traditional art cinema, which even Pier Paolo Pasolini had criticised because it had become as conventional as Hollywood.

The naturalistic approach to film aesthetics emerged in films made by both male and female directors, and thus Italian movies were often described as '*carini*' (cute films) by dismissive critics. The domestic interiors – a feminine aesthetics – as well as the content of the stories (everyday life, micro-stories) and low-key technology nevertheless ensured the survival of Italian cinema through the bleak period of the 1980s.

SPACES OF CINEMA ON TELEVISION

There are two evaluations to be made in relation to spaces of film on the public broadcaster Rai and Berlusconi's television networks. The first is related to the accessibility of production and distribution opportunities, and the number of films broadcast. The second has to do with changes in film aesthetics in the 1980s and the development of intimate films. They are strongly interconnected, and thus the following discussion considers the relationship between film and television as it developed from the 1980s.

The great divide of broadcasting deregulation in 1974 caused significant changes in the public broadcasting system. Existing highbrow aesthetic and qualitative categories, usually connected with concepts of originality, innovation and criticism, were used to construct public and commercial television as oppositional. Seen retrospectively, pre-1974 television became 'good television' because, from the 1960s, following the traditional understanding and model of television that derived from the British BBC, Italian public television strived to become a cultural educative and moral force for the improvement of taste, knowledge and manners. The adoption of standard Italian language was an element aimed at promoting a unifying language and sense of nationhood. Literary classics were adapted for television, and cinema directors were called to direct them. It was the period of the growth of the *sceneggiato*, or *teleromanzo*, which fulfilled the 'educational mission' (Buonanno 2005, p. 49) of the public broadcaster. As examples of these many quality programs, it is enough to mention films and series such as *La prise du pouvoir par Louis XIV* (Roberto Rossellini, 1966), an Italo-French co-production between ORTF and Rai; *Il conte di Montecristo* (Edmo Fenoglio,1966); *L'Odissea* (Franco Rossi, 1968), produced by Dino De Laurentiis; *Vita di Leonardo* (Renato Castellani, 1971); and *Gesù di Nazareth* (Franco Zeffirelli, 1977).

With the proliferation of local commercial stations from the late 1970s – often created solely for the advertising and selling of local products from small and medium enterprises, filled with cheap American imports – public television came to occupy a space in which it was allowed to be 'good'. 'Bad' television is usually commercial television, which is seen as a time waster, a cultural invader, a taste debaser, as having bad influence on audiences and as reducing mental capabilities.[1] Therefore, 'good' television is constructed from the memory of television pre-1974. The most striking difference between television pre-1975 and after the deregulation lies in the percentage of Italian films broadcast. In the period 1950–79, 63 per cent of the movies broadcast on television were Italian, while from 1980 to the period 1990–99, this percentage fell progressively to a low 13 per cent in prime time (ANICA 2006). In 2006, there was an increase to 25 per cent between the three public channels, but Berlusconi's networks programmed 54 per cent of Italian films in prime time. This confirms the fact that Berlusconi's commercial networks function in synergy and in a vertically integrated relationship with Fininvest's production company Medusa. This means that Fininvest owns the entire film cycle, from production to theatre exhibition, television and DVD rights.

Tables 7.1, 7.2 and 7.3 illustrate film scheduling on commercial and public television. Table 7.2 shows that the United States not only dominates distribution in picture theatres, but also on the small screen. Table 10.3 shows the top ten films broadcast in the period 2000–04. Two interesting things should be noted: first, the top film in terms of share is *La vita è bella*, a comedy, and second, only two films broadcast on Canale 5 are of Italian nationality. The conclusion is that, despite the increase of Italian films, audiences still prefer US production and commercial television's quota of domestic films is only a response to broadcasting regulations.

Throughout the 1980s and 1990s Rai produced quality programs, but it was also influenced by the politics pursued by commercial networks which, unlike Rai, were free from political influences tied to factional tensions inside parties. To capture the widest audience possible, Rai became a *televisione generalista* (generalist television), thus maintaining an ambiguous profile between continuing to fulfil its public mandate and

TABLE 7.1 ITALIAN FILMS ON TELEVISION, 2000–04

Network/channel	Number of films broadcast	Number of Italian films
Rai 1	2,626	987
Rai 2	903	151
Rai 3	3,054	1,171
Canale 5	1,844	313
Italia 1	3,400	988
Rete 4	7,096	3,241
TMC-La Sette	3,688	1,108
Total	22,611	7,959

Source: Il mercato cinematografico italiano, 2000–04, pp. 132–35.

TABLE 7.2 FILMS BROADCAST ACCORDING TO NATIONALITY (2000-2004)

Nationality	Number of films broadcast
United States	10,958
Italy	7,959
Great Britain	1,102
France	1,117
Germany	180
Spain	147
Other	1,148
Total	22,611

Source: Il mercato cinematografico italiano, 2000–04, p. 145.

TABLE 7.3 TOP 10 FILM ON TELEVISION – PRIME TIME, 2000–2004

Original title	Channel	Nationality	Share %
La vita è bella	Rai 1	Italy	53.34
Titanic	Canale 5	United States	51.72
Gladiator	Canale 5	United States	43.89
Tre uomini e una gamba	Canale 5	Italy	39.92
Così è la vita	Canale 5	Italy	37.73
My Best Friend's Wedding	Canale 5	United States	36.46
La vita è bella (replay)	Rai 1	Italy	33,61
101 Dalmatians	Rai 1	United States	33.92
Erin Brokovich	Canale 5	United States	33.92
Pretty Woman	Rai 1	United States	33,23

Adapted from: Il mercato cinematografico in Italia, 2000–04, p. 146.

struggling to retain high audience numbers. On the other hand, commercial television also funded quality projects, such as *Ladri di saponette* (Maurizio Nichetti, 1989), a satire about how commercials disrupt and change films' narrative, and especially religious-historical mini-series such as *Padre Pio* (2000), with Sergio Castellitto in the lead role.

Just as validated art forms had legitimised cinema in its early history, the television movie was meant to legitimate good television. A derivative of the *sceneggiato* – which, as we have seen, was enormously popular in the 1950s and 1960s – the production of *film per la televisione* became a way in which the Italian film industry reorganised itself in the 1980s. With the *sceneggiato*, television had already borrowed conventions, producers, directors and aesthetics from cinema. Rossellini, Comencini, De Seta, Zeffirelli, Montaldo, Bolognini, Lizzani, Damiani, Lattuada, the Taviani Brothers and Amelio made *sceneggiati* and films for television from the 1960s throughout the 1970s and 1980s. This group of directors broke the period of opposition between the two media (Cereda 1996, p. 240), inaugurating the period of gradual interconnection. Elsaesser (1998, p. 203) argues that the narrative feature film is not only a familiar commodity, but also a remarkably stable product; thus, following the crisis in the sector, in the 1980s film production in Italy shifted from large production companies and Cinecittà to small production companies working for the public broadcaster or in co-production with Rai.

Later in the decade, Berlusconi's film production arm, Penta, was founded in partnership with the Cecchi Gori Group, formalising the final synergy and collaboration between cinema and television. Also, broadcasting networks – both public and commercial – became major exhibitors of films. From the middle of the 1980s, over 6,000 films a year were screened on television, making broadcasting the highest source of income for a film in Italy – a situation unlike that in other countries.

In 2000, Rai Cinema – which had effectively started operating from 1999 – was officially created. Like Fininvest's Medusa, Rai – now one of the largest film producers in Italy – has morphed into a vertically integrated structure for the production and distribution of films. Acknowledging market's imperatives, Rai Cinema operates as a buyer of film, fiction and animation, a producer, a distributor in theatres and a buyer of copyrights both in Italy and internationally. The distribution arm operates through 01 Distribution, a company founded in 2001 which was managed in partnership with Studio Canal until 2003, becoming completely controlled by Rai from that year. Between 1999 and 2007, Rai has helped in the production, funding and distribution of 148 films, shorts and documentaries. Marco Tullio Giordana, Marco Bellocchio, Gianni Amelio, Pasquale Scimeca, Wilma Labate, Marco Bechis and Nanni Moretti have all benefited from television financial and distribution support.

In the 1980s and 1990s, the formal involvement of the public broadcaster ensured that film production numbers remained relatively high.[2] In the 1980s, Rai promoted a politics of the *auteur* (with the Taviani brothers, Olmi, Nanni Moretti and Gianni Amelio, but also Iosselliani and Michalkov) (Crespi, 1990; Miscuglio 1988, p. 161), as well as addressing commercial imperatives forced by Fininvest's competition. As Rai and Fininvest privileged production with directors who had already established their careers in the 1970s, relegating young directors to low-budget programs for television, the duopoly Rai-Fininvest curbed experimentation. Nevertheless, state television had taken on the role of talent scout, guaranteeing at least a showing on television. Both networks produced with independent producers, who usually made their profit from their fee as executive producers, before the release of the film on to the market. The release of the film at this point was of secondary importance. It is not possible to understand the dynamics of Italian cinema of the 1980s without taking into consideration this perverse mechanism which led to the phenomenon of the 'produced and abandoned' films, and which exacerbated the crisis in the sector. Basically, small producers were after quick and easy earnings, rather than being concerned with seriously addressing the issue of the crisis.

However, the situation slowly improved from the late 1980s, as American television imports declined in popularity because 'the saturation point had finally been reached' (Buonanno 2005, p. 51). In addition, the 1996 reform on television introduced by the centre-left government that forced public television to invest 20 per cent of licence fees into the production of drama for television or theatre has guaranteed the return of Italian fiction and films for television in prime time. Private networks must also devote 10 per cent of their advertising revenues to the production or purchase of European drama (*Il settore cinematografico italiano*, 1998, p. 193). However, the most important feature of Rai's intervention in the film industry was the public broadcaster's discreet participation as a partner, which left full autonomy to producers. In this way, Rai fed the generational renewal of directors that Cinecittà lacked in the 1970s. The idea of good television was fully embraced by Rai when it helped quality films such as *Lamerica, Senza pelle* (Alessandro D'Alatri, 1994), *La vera vita di Antonio H., L'amore molesto* (Mario Martone, 1995), *Pasolini – Un delitto italiano* (Marco Tullio Giordana), *Sostiene Pereira* (Roberto Faenza, 1995), *Nitrato d'argento* (Marco Ferreri, 1996) and *Le affinità elettive* (Paolo and Vittorio Taviani, 1996) to get off the ground. Undoubtedly, this transitional phase of Rai was instrumental in re-shifting the camera focus from domestic interiors and navel-gazer films to a recovery of taste and content against the candyfloss world of commercial television.

The other important producer of films for theatrical release, and ultimately to fill television schedules, is Fininvest. In the 1980s, Fininvest's first objective was to buy film and television fiction rights in the Italian market and then in the US market, in order to feed its three television networks. In the middle of the 1980s, the company entered film production operating through Reteitalia. The first films produced and presented in Venice in 1987 were *Gli occhiali d'oro* (Giuliano Montaldo) and in 1988 *Paura e amore* (Margarethe von Trotta) (Cereda 1996, p. 245). In 1989, Fininvest founded Penta, which expanded in the United States with Pentamerica, buying distribution rights from Orion, Columbia and Tristar.

In 1994 Penta closed down, and in 1995 Fininvest bought a new company, Medusa Film, which inherited from Penta the production and distribution arm of Fininvest. Medusa Film was a sister company of Mediaset and operated as subsidiary of Fininvest until 2007. In 1999, for the first time, Medusa turned a profit of US$122.5 million (Rooney 2000), and in the period 2000–01, Medusa held 21 per cent of the Italian film market. Medusa's rationale is to invest in different genres of films, both for

Italian and international production and distribution, supporting directors as diverse as Aldo, Giovanni and Giacomo, Ferzan Ozpetek, Gabriele Muccino and Leonardo Pieraccioni. In this way, the company can cater for a diversified market and especially can secure rights for the three differentiated television networks that belong to Fininvest.[3] Up to 2007, Medusa Film has distributed and produced 249 national and international films.

The development of production practices, content and the social function of television provides evidence of the fact that television has not only become the privileged referent in the construction of popular/national identity, where the Italian community is for the first time effectively united by the production of a shared sense of reality, but also that the progressively integrated mediascape between cinema and television has transformed the aesthetics of recent filmmaking. *Recent Italian Cinema* evaluates the hybrid of the telemovie positively because the cultural gamble by television in movie production makes sense in economic terms, in that it may pay off at the box office, earn international awards (see *Cinema Paradiso*) and it may secure broadcasting rights over new feature films.

THE SPACE OF THE CLOSE-UP

The second contested element in the relationship between television and cinema is the adoption of television's aesthetics by film directors. Chapter 5 pointed out that the regular practice of splicing fragments from television archival footage in recent films substantiates objective and factual positions adopted by the filmmakers (Rossellini also used newsreel footage to this effect). The use of television footage in film functions as a mnemonic recollection of ambience, clothes and atmosphere (in a similar way to Polaroids on the refrigerator); however, this practice also reveals an economic factor: it is an inexpensive way to insert crowds, historical references and ambiance into individual contemporary stories. It is thus legitimate to ask how film conventions have been affected further by television in the 1980s. As we have seen, in Italy the synergy between cinema and television for the production of mini-series dates back to the 1960s; however, it is only since broadcasting deregulation in 1974 that the presence of films on television has expanded dramatically. The production of telemovies increased the involvement of Rai in film production and became, for the directors of the early 1980s, a conventional mode of production.

With this production option, filmmakers started to privilege the use of the close-up and interior settings, and avoided deep-staging. On television, the zooming-in shot, a technique that was deemed to enrich the visual language of art cinema, became fixed on close-ups. The close-up typically addresses issues of personal emotions, memory and empathy, melancholy, frustration and angst, inviting recognition from the audience and estrangement from the outside world. Typically, close-ups are associated with soap operas and telenovelas, which became very popular in Italy in the 1980s. *Dallas*, broadcast from 1981 to 1992, first on Rete 1 and then Canale 5 and Retequattro, is the epitome of the success US soap operas enjoyed in Italy. An ironic statement against the cultural desolation of American soap operas is to be found in the scene on Stromboli in Nanni Moretti's *Caro Diario*. In the second episode, set in the Eolian Islands, the barren, black and rocky landscape of the volcano functions symbolically as a sterile counterpoint to the conversation between Nanni Moretti, his friend and a group of Americans about *The Bold and the Beautiful*, which started in 1990 on the public channel Raidue, and moved to Canale 5 in 1993.

Pierre Sorlin sees the use of close-ups in Italian television as a convention that has lowered film quality, but especially a high notion of film aesthetics that derives from neorealism and the art film (Sorlin 1996, p. 127). He writes: 'While ostensibly mourning the glorious decades of the Italian studios, *Interview* and *Ginger and Fred* pointed to another era. A certain form and quality of films were over but moving images still amused and interested large audiences.' (Sorlin 1996, p. 127) In the 1980s, some 80 per cent of films were produced by the duopoly Rai-Fininvest, and this led to 'conformist themes and linguistic levelling' (Morandini 1996, p. 21). The concept of levelling is also brought up by Sorlin (1996, pp. 119–20), who suggests that the increased use of close-ups in films for television leads to the levelling of the image, and thus of meaning. A second argument that Sorlin makes against close-ups in film is through the connection between aesthetic transformation in films made for television and cultural transformations in society. If we look at the social use of television, Sorlin argues, close-ups and the use of television in a domestic context are linked because the function of the television set is that of a domestic appliance (Sorlin 1996, p. 152). Television is in fact conceived as a talking medium (as it replaced radio), where meaning is conveyed by dialogue. This does not mean that television is confined to speech. Feelings of self-identification, intimacy and authenticity are also important, and emotion is an important element of the close-up. Its use on television conveys above all simplicity, so for the viewer it is easy to catch glimpses of the screen and then readily to synthesise visual and verbal information with an impression of direct participation. This argument mirrors Silvia Harvey's (1996) analysis of the difference between television and cinema in the viewing experience. By reflecting upon Bazin's concept of the photographic image as special, or ontological, Harvey (1996) speaks especially of the concentrated attention span required in watching a film in the picture theatre and of the 'sacred' character of the filmic image that television lacks. Harvey thus links the quality of the image to that of experience, where low quality equates with the low experience of television. This circular argument thus goes back to the contention that from the 1980s the aura of cinema was lost forever.

Adriano Aprà, writing in *il Patalogo tre* in 1981, well sums up the interconnection between quality and quantity arguments about films on television:

> Because everything is available, nothing is available. From the angst of the lost film we shift too quickly to the aboulia of the indiscriminate availability. Mass consumption, which I cannot condemn, risks to make all films all the same. It is not only the well known low definition of cinema seen on television to intervene in this process; it is the sum of the collapse of values, and the consciousness that exists, somewhere, a warehouse

where everything is preserved and then, sooner or later, jumps out. (Aprà, in Grasso 2000, p. 370)

As television has specific ratio requirements, another way to transform the cinematic spectacle into a televisual spectacle is through narrative construction, with an alternation between exterior and interior shots. For example, *Il postino*, produced by Penta Films, is a sequence of perfectly alternated shots of interiors and exteriors. Interior shots are characterised by the dominance of close-ups, while landscape shots are framed with the actors (Massimo Troisi and Philip Noiret) at the centre of the scene – staying in what Steven Neale defines as the 'safe area' (Neale 1998, p. 133) so that this formal choice sidesteps panning and scanning techniques, as the image can easily be cut at the margins of the frame to fit in the television ratio. In *Lamerica*, Amelio's choice to place the main characters Gino and Spiro in the middle of the frame with Albanians in the background and around the margins symbolises the centrality of the Italian story. On the big screen, Gino and Spiro shift slowly from the foreground to mingle with the Albanian refugees, but on the small screen this subtle change of position, which indicates the shifting identities of the Italian characters, is lost.

The transformation of television aesthetics can only be understood in a context of economic pressures brought about by the consolidation of commercial television, and the subsequent competition between the public and commercial networks. It is important to remember that, throughout the 1960s, it was television that borrowed from cinema the tradition of the filmic spectacle with high-budget historical-epic productions. Thus what was resented in the polemic about film on television was that it was television's aesthetics and requirements that influenced filmmaking, and not the reverse. The aesthetic changes in filmmaking were thus an economic and historical contingency.

WOMEN'S SPACES IN CINEMA

Unfortunately, Italian women's cinema still remains under-researched and undefined, with the exception of small individual biographies and filmographies.[4] In her essay published in *Off Screen: Women and Film in Italy*, Annabella Miscuglio pointedly questions the ambiguous notion of women's cinema, as there are at least four different ways in which it is possible to speak about a 'women's cinema' in Italy. The first is an analytical history of women directors. The second is about the access to filmmaking, and thus the number of women directors and production opportunities. The third has to do with the representation of women and how central female characters are to the film narrative, with their desires and their dilemmas. The final way concerns women's relationship with their own image – that is, the way in which the work of a woman director is unconsciously 'influenced by the fact of her being female, given that her own body, the image of her identity, faces her on screen as image, as object of the look, as "impossible" body' (Melchiori 1988, p. 27). The areas of analysis converge, as they open up a space for the discussion of female representation and identity when the camera is in the hands of a female director, extending the study to female spectators and identification. In the past, male directors – for example, Antonioni – have put women at the centre of their narratives. However, as Paternò suggests, in the past as well as in the present, women's role were confined to those of wife, mother or lover, a tradition rooted in the Italian comedy, the comic cinema, the family melodrama[5] and the intellectual *auteur* cinema (Paternò 2006, p. 136), as the case of Antonioni demonstrates. However, things seem to be changing, as a number of male directors have recently focused their cameras on strong women characters and roles. Roberto Faenza has adapted Dacia Maraini's novel *Marianna Ucrìa*, which tells of Marianna's painful and hard path to freedom in eighteenth century Palermo. Also Gabriele Salvatores, in his recent noir *Quo Vadis, baby?*, cast a woman with a strong attitude and strong traits in the centre of the narrative. Emanuele Crialese focuses on an unstable and subversive woman in *Respiro* (2002), and the frustrated housewife in *Pane e Tulipani* (Silvio Soldini) takes over her life, abandoning husband and children.

In the context of this book, I wish to explore spaces on screen and off screen that are connected with women's contribution to the film industry in the 1980s and with a change in the aesthetic of film. The access to filmmaking and funding by women directors is fundamental in assessing the position and representation of women in Italian cinema. However, as far as the 1970s and 1980s are concerned, this was not only problematic for women directors. In fact, after the crisis of Cinecittà and the relocation or closure of Carlo Ponti, Dino De Laurentiis and Titanus, the Italian film industry lacked infrastructure that could ensure the generational renewal of directors. Stefano Masi wrote in 1987 that there was no interest in renewing the industry because, for the professionals in the field, 'Italian cinema is in crisis' (Masi 1987, p. 51). Moreover, there was no real connection between film schools and the industry, as in the industry it was commonplace to employ relatives, perpetuating that system of patronage that pervades many aspects of Italian society and that Ginsborg named *familismo* (Ginsborg 1990, p. 2). According to Masi, a mythology recurrent in the film industry saw this protectionist system as similar to the apprenticeship of young artists in the Renaissance, who went *'a bottega'* (in the workshop) to learn with one of the great masters (Masi 1987, p. 52). Thus the commonplace was that, to learn the art and craft of filmmaking, it was mandatory to work 'hands on' for some time as an assistant to a known director.

A central argument of this chapter is based on the premise that the transition between the 1970s and the end of the 1990s – that is, the period of crisis in the film industry – was increasingly dominated by television's involvement in film production. This in turn influenced film aesthetics. But, most importantly, television provided spaces of production for new directors, and among them there were many women. Women were thus able to carve a space inside television, and this in turn provided the means for more experimental and independent work.

Women directors existed from the late 1960s, and they worked especially in documentary, experimental cinema and television. Anna Baldazzi, Alessandra Bocchetti, Maricla Boggio, Maria Bosio, Gaia Ceriana, Paola Faloja, Anna Lajolo, Annabella Miscuglio, Adriana Monti,

Virginia Onorato, Ludovica Ripa di Meana, Sofia Scandurra, Maria Serena Tait and Annamaria Tatò have worked regularly with television since the middle of the 1970s. One of the most innovative filmmakers was Annabella Miscuglio, who died in 2004. In 1967, Annabella co-founded Filmstudio, which helped to launch, among many others, Nanni Moretti; however, she was also an experimental filmmaker and a promoter, from the early 1970s, of the first *Collettivo di cinema femminista*. Among her best-known shorts are *Fughe lineari in progressione psichica* (1975) and *Puzzle Therapy* (1976). Annabella became famous with the first documentary produced by the Collettivo, *Processo per stupro* (1978), which was broadcast on Rete 2 on 26 April 1978, broadcasting for the first time on television a trial against a case of sexual assault which had occurred in Latina in the same year. The documentary was censored and the makers prosecuted. Annabella's subsequent *AAA Offresi* (1979) is a documentary filmed with a candid camera that shows a prostitute's dealings with her clients. Rai's executives also tried to prevent the broadcasting of this documentary.

Fundamental to the emergence of a feminist militant cinema was the adoption of the Super-8 format, which enabled low-cost production and more freedom in approach to the themes relevant to women: the body, repression and exploitation. Narcissism, intimacy and voyeuristic pleasure, as Miscuglio (1988, p. 157) puts it, characterised some aspects of that cinema. In the middle of the 1970s, when the Italian women's movement was at its height, and thanks to some women in executive positions in Rai, the public broadcaster opened its doors to documentaries made by women. The programs were outsourced by Rai to women directors who preferred to work as freelancers. In the 1980s, women's cinema was subsumed into the category of young cinema. Annabella Miscuglio continued to work in RAI as a free-lancer for programs such as *Chi l'ha visto?*

Cristiana Paternò (2006, p. 135) estimates that, today, around 30 per cent of the total number of Italian directors are women. In the past, the only names that resonated nationally and internationally were those of Liliana Cavani and Lina Wertmuller, and of screenwriter Suso Cecchi D'Amico. The list of women directors from 2001 includes Cristina

Comencini, Cecilia Calvi, Asia Argento, Anne Rita Ciccone, Roberta Torre, Isabella Sandri, Francesca Archibugi, Wilma Labate, Laura Muscardin, Francesca Comencini, Francesca Pirani, Monica Stambrini, Sabina Guzzanti, Federica Martino, Carola Spadoni, Nina di Majo, Antonietta De Lillo, Federica Pontremoli, Emanuela Piovano, Giada Colagrande, Costanza Quatriglio, Eleonora Giorgi, Valeria Bruni Tedeschi, Susanna Tamaro, Valia Santella, Catherine McGilvrey, Maria Martinelli, Anna Negri and Donatella Maiorca.

Women are also emerging in roles previously held by men. Among the producers, the most active are Elda Ferri, Donatella Botti, Rosanna Seregni, Tilde Corsi, Giuliana Del Punta, Donatella Palermo, Laura Cafiero and Mariella Li Sacchi. Also, following the example in Hollywood, actresses engaged in different production stages and who play a more decisional role in filmmaking include Laura Morante, Francesca Neri, Maria Grazia Cucinotta, Valeria Bruni Tedeschi, Sabina Guzzanti, Nicoletta Braschi, Ida Di Benedetto, Marta Bifano and Chiara Caselli (Paternò 2006, p. 141).

It is worth mentioning Francesca Archibugi because she was one of the first women filmmakers to shift the *look*, not only in terms of aesthetics but also content, starting to tell stories of teenagers in which young girls were always present, if not the main characters. As Melchiori suggests, in classical cinema, 'the phantasmagoric image constructed by the cinematic apparatus converge with the narrative content (the love story) into a perfect combination, closing the circle' (Melchiori 1988, p. 32). Women's identification is thus subsumed in the man's look as she responds to her own idealised image. Interestingly, Archibugi shows principally fragmented families in which children can exist outside the family circle – as real people, not just as children. Archibugi affirms that she likes 'films in which there are women, possibly young; and in those stories that have been able to treat truthfully the existential relationship between men and women, inevitably there are children involved' (Archibugi n.d.). Thus spectators' desires are frustrated as they are led to identify with images and stories of childhood in which the love story is denied and the look is directed by a child.

Aesthetically, Archibugi attempts a more naturalistic framing in which the camera work must be as invisible as possible. While making *Mignon è partita* (1988), a film about the discovery of love and friendship by a group of teenagers in Rome, with their weary 40-year-old parents in the background, she recalls asking herself: 'Are we setting up a shot?' (Archibugi n.d., p. 13), wishing instead that the characters would come to life on their own, without the 'authorial self-intoxication' typical of art film. This was obviously a difficult task, which cost Archibugi much criticism.

She was one of the first filmmakers to subvert aesthetic and content choices. Chapter 4 discussed how the culture of interiors and domestic spaces was an inevitable choice in films in the 1980s because it was linked to scarcity of funding and production spaces. As we also saw in Chapter 4, in the 1980s Italian film critics remained firm on traditional authorial paradigms, unable to frame the cinema that was being produced at the time. Domestic interiors and everyday life, away from large-scale events, were the symptoms of a poor cinema that was defined as 'minimalist' (Quaresima 1991, p. 38). Interestingly, Ettore Scola's films from *Una giornata particolare* (1977) have mostly been set in circumscribed spaces (a terrace in *La terrazza*, 1980; an apartment in *La famiglia*, 1987; the ballroom in *Ballando ballando*, 1984; a cinema in *Splendor*, 1989; a 1930s Roman street reconstructed in Cinecittà by set designer Dante Ferretti in *Concorrenza Sleale* (2001), but his choice is referred to as a stylistic unity in which the confined space becomes an essential part of the story (see Brunetta 1998, p. 387, who also quotes Bondanella). It is evident that, as Scola's reputation was established after the 1960s, the *auteur* argument is brought into the discussion, pointing to a specific phase in Scola's career in which he discards a cinema of spectacle in favour of a 'minimalist' cinema (Brunetta 1998, p. 389).

A different judgment was passed when the enclosed space appeared in the low-budget films of the 1980s. The visualisation of the domestic space, which exists in the small scale of day-to-day survival, can be likened to the same ambivalence of criticism in painting. In the past, higher genres of painting dealt with history, landscape and large-scale events, while a lower genre – the still life for example – was concerned with what Pliny labelled 'rhyparography' (Bryson 1990, p. 137), or the painting of filth and waste, which was at Pliny's time the domestic sphere, and hence connected with woman. As the meaning of seventeenth century artistic paradigms, based on the fusion of Greek classical thought, humanism and Christian religion, was transferred to that of the mechanically reproduced visual image, prejudices about what constitutes high and popular art continued to be applied to creative production. Despite the dismantling of traditional canons of high and low culture in the 1960s, *auteur* cinema contributed to the recreation and persistence of aesthetic and formal canons. Thus prejudices in Italian film criticism that derived from past artistic paradigms smeared the autobiographical, domestic, minimalist, feminine cinema against a higher concept of cinema, which embedded anthropological and sociological explorations of Italian society.

THE SPACE OF THE 'OTHER'

We have seen how a new generation of filmmakers responded to the profound changes in economy and politics that were occurring in the 1980s, with self-reflexive narratives that coincided with the world of a cohort of spectators. In these films, the experience of the self is expressed in a work of mourning of collective experiences that finds its space in the intimate screen. Italian cinema established a relationship with its audience through television and produced a cinema of experience based on daily life and routine that catered to a politically motivated, albeit disillusioned, group of spectators. Women filmmakers found a niche in television, which they used as a launching pad for other independent film projects. In the 1990s and in the new millennium, Italian women filmmakers have emerged as a new creative force which is also involved in production of quality films. In contrast, this last section of the chapter discusses a new marginality that is being explored in Italian cinema: the immigrant as the 'other' and the space that they occupy.

While the left questioned itself about the past, in the society witnessed a profound change brought about ⌐⸗ immigration from North Africa and Eastern Europe. For the first time, Italian society confronted a different 'other': from being a country of migrants, Italy became a country of immigration, and films in which the voice of the 'other' emerges must be accounted for. Similarly, in spite of Italy's bigoted Catholicism and homophobia emanating from the Vatican, homosexual themes successfully crossed over into mainstream cinema with Ferzan Ozpetek's films. The director speaks from a double position at the margins, as an immigrant (from Turkey) and as a homosexual. In his best-known film, *Le fate ignoranti*, Ozpetek explores the community of Turkish political refugees along with the gay community in Rome. However, in two of his latest films (*La finestra di fronte* and *Cuore sacro*), Ozpetek is concerned with a more general concept of 'otherness'. In *La finestra di fronte*, Giovanna and Filippo are a couple in crisis. The arrival of Davide, an old man who has lost his short-term memory, forces Giovanna – who in the meantime has a brief relationship with the neighbour across the courtyard – to reconsider her life and disappointments. *La finestra di fronte* explores women's alienation and the sentimental difficulties that modern families encounter in Italy today. This film was released at the same time as *L'ultimo bacio*, and it can be considered the working-class answer to Muccino's film. In line with Ozpetek's other films, it is the arrival of an outsider which provokes the characters to confront their own frustrated aspirations. Davide, a Jewish gay who avoided Nazi deportation during the occupation of Rome, is the means to Giovanna's realisation of her dreams. In *Cuore sacro*, homeless people – rarely seen in current Italian cinema – become the object of interest of Irene, a rich and unscrupulous manager who abandons her life and transforms her parents' building in the centre of Rome into a soup kitchen for poor and destitute people. In the final segment, which is a direct reference to Rossellini and Pasolini, Irene strips herself bare in the subway, in an extreme gesture of spirituality.

However, both films are still concerned with Italians who are alienated from their own environments. Ozpetek's interest in marginalised people is not new in Italian cinema. Rossellini explored spiritual destitution in his film *Francesco Giullare di Dio* (1950), and De Sica famously cast Milan's homeless community in his masterpiece *Miracolo a Milano* (1951). The utopian ending in this film anticipates Third World and post-colonial theories which emerged a decade later in Europe, and which found their way into much 1960s Italian cinema. This corpus of films has been overlooked in Italian film scholarship; thus it is important to recall here the antecedent of current films that depict the difficult encounter between the 'other', or *extracomunitario*, and Italian people.

In the decade 1963–73, decolonisation and post-colonial theories inspired in European civil and political movements the hope that the revolution could have more potential to be realised in South America and in Third World countries. It was during this period that Frantz Fanon's *The Wretched of the Earth* (1961) became a key reading – one which, along with China's Cultural Revolution, instigated a critical consciousness in many artists and filmmakers. Third World politics inspired many films of this decade – indeed, there was even a film with the same title as Fanon's manifesto, Valentino Orsini's *I dannati della terra* (1969). This film simultaneously questioned Eurocentrism, masculinity and universal values, in an attempt to generate a critique of Western patriarchal culture that included Third World politics and gender politics.

There is very little, if any, analysis of Italian films about the Third World, as they are generically grouped as political films. This is a very rich *filone*[6] which has been often dismissed as a sub-element of the spaghetti Western genre.[7] A detailed analysis of these films is beyond the scope of this book; in fact, a discussion of films produced between 1963 and 1973 demands a more complex approach, because there are reciprocal influences between the political film genre, which addressed internal problems and depicted the south as a colonised land inside the peninsula, and the militant and Third World films. Chapter 8 explores some of the themes that have to do with this equation in relation to the Mediterranean Sea and Mediterranean cinema in the light of Franco Cassano's book *Il pensiero meridiano*.

A contemporary example of equivalence between the most backward expressions of Italian society and Third World politics is to be found in Roberto Faenza's *Alla luce del sole* (2005), a film directly inspired to the story of Don Pino Puglisi, killed by the mafia in 1993. The film is set in the Brancaccio suburb which, with its stone buildings, scorched squares, decay and fatalism, can be likened to a village of the undeveloped world. In one initial scene, Palermo's mafia boss warns the local boss in Brancaccio about the danger that Don Puglisi represents for the petty criminal business in the area: 'First [we had] a priest who thought that Sicily was Latino America, now we have Don Puglisi.' This Third World vision of Italian society is still based on a Marxist approach to the Western world, which symmetrically situates the reality of the Third World alongside the situation of the impoverished South.

Films about immigrants from the Third World approach the encounter between the two cultures as a clash. These films do not deny that there is racism in Italy, but they still confine the clash to isolated episodes of racism, avoiding a deeper analysis of the cultures involved, and avoiding the difficult depiction of migrants' world and community. Often the Filippino maid (in *Le fate ignoranti*) or the Eritrean lover who takes the place of the nurturing Italian wife – a disappeared genre in Italian society – the immigrant is a token reminder of Italy as melting pot.

In other films, the immigrant is seen as immersed in the social landscape of the country, yet in conflict with it. In recent Italian films, the immigrant represents the failure of all economic and political discourses that have attempted to address the inequalities between the First and Third Worlds over the past 30 years. It is not a coincidence that the Third World multitude of workers – regular and irregular – has entered Europe at the point of its economic instability and in a moment of ideological and historical crisis.[8]

Bernardo Bertolucci's film *L'assedio* (1998) questions and problematises European identity and supremacy through the appearance of Jason Kinsky (David Thewlis), an eccentric English piano player who lives in a decaying building in the centre of Rome. The film is set in the present, but its subtext points to the weight of European traditional high culture expressed in the problematic relationship between the two main characters. Shandurai, a black woman who is interpreted by Thandie Newton, is the housekeeper and lives in the basement of the building. The only means of communication (other than direct confrontation) is the internal lift that was once used by servants to send food up to the rich aristocratic owner. In the film, Jason sends down his clothes to be washed and ironed. This arrangement quite obviously addresses the problem of hierarchy between North and South of the world. The point of European decadence is aptly represented by the male's blackened teeth, cracks in the building's walls, and a dusty tapestry that hide scraped paint. Only when Jason sells his paintings, tapestry, sculptures and piano to pay for the liberation of Shandurai's husband held in prison in Africa – and thus symbolically rids himself of his cultural and philosophical inheritance that is embedded in his aesthetic experience of the world – can communication, and indeed love, between the two protagonists be established.

The invisibility of immigrants in Italy is metaphorically addressed in Michele Placido's *Pummarò* (1990) and Luigi Faccini's *Giamaica* (1999), inspired by the real-life story of Auro B., a young man burnt alive in an occupied social centre in 1991. In both films, the coloured immigrants are absent because they are dead. In *Giamaica*, it is a group of friends of the killed foreigner who search the town during the night to find traces of the friend that was burnt alive by a group of Naziskin. In *Pummarò* it is Kwaku, the victim's brother, who has come from Ghana to Naples; he wanders around the city searching for Pummarò. Kwaku moves from Naples to Rome, Verona and Frankfurt, and in each city his experience of Italy and Germany is different. In both *Giamaica* and *Pummarò*, the city enables the characters to experience at first hand the anonymity of the urban multitude. Their peripatetic search becomes the link between the dream city – the city that represented their hopes for social freedom from their country of origin – and the real city, where they experience first-hand what Laura Balbo (1992, p. 10) called 'ordinary racism'. Ordinary racism in fact defines a society that has shifted from episodes of racism to a situation of diffused racism. This is what is missing from current Italian cinema.

The disjuncture between dream and reality was depicted in Amelio's *Lamerica*, one of the best films of European contemporary cinema. In this case, the disjuncture addresses the dream country and the real country, in a parallel between what America represented for Italian migrants in the postwar era and what Italy represented in the 1990s for Albanian people. Until 1985, watching Italian television was prohibited by the regime and punished by seven years in prison (Mai 2001). After the death of Enver Hoxha in that year, watching Italian television – and in particular commercial television – became a national pastime. Thus the Italian media, whose signal could reach most of the coastal regions in Albania, were primarily responsible in creating this gap between illusion and reality.

In 1991, an influx of immigrants arrived on the Italian shore, in Apulia. Between 7 March and August 1991, some 45,700 Albanians crossed the Adriatic Sea to Otranto; at the end of 1997, a total of 83,807 Albanian immigrants were legally present in Italy (Mai 2001). The case of Albanian migration is interesting because in the beginning Albanians were considered Italy's own *extracomunitari*. The fact that Albania had been colonised by Mussolini and their geographical proximity through the Adriatic Sea suggested that Albanian people had to be considered as the 'other' side of Italy. Albania was likened to what, symbolically, Kuwait and East Germany represented to Iraq and West Germany respectively. Left-wing and right-wing newspapers in early 1991 felt very empathetic towards the plight of Albanians. Things started to shift when the influx became unsustainable, and when the first episodes of petty criminality by unemployed and desperate Albanians started to surface. These were followed by intolerance and racism.

The film tells at the same time the story of Albanian refugees who want to flee their country, Gino's personal story of arrogance and ignorance of Italy's own history, the story of Gino and Spiro's relationship, and finally the story of Italian corruption and racism. Framing and camera movements foreground alternatively these stories which, at the end of the film, all mingle in the character of Gino, who has lost his passport and has become similar to the Albanian refugees. *Lamerica*'s rich and layered subtext and aesthetics point not only to the history of Italian migration, but especially to forms of cultural and economic imperialism sustained by global capitalism and the centrality of its financial form.

The gap between the dream country and the real country is also explored in Armando Manni's *Elvjs e Mariljn* (1998), which explores the illusion of a Romanian couple who leave their country to follow the dream of the promised land. This illusion is metaphorically represented by the spectacle that they improvise, in which they play Elvis Presley and Marilyn Monroe, whose (real) premature death in turn represents the failure of the dream-First World and its myths. Their trip takes them through shattered ex-Yugoslavia, in which they start to experience the crumbling of their illusion. Once in Italy, they come into contact with Italians' ordinary racism, which will prompt their consciousness as unwanted foreigners.

Stefano Rulli and Sandro Petraglia were the screenwriters for *Pummarò*. They also co-signed with Marco Tullio Giordana the screenplay for *Quando sei nato non puoi più nasconderti* (Marco Tullio Giordana, 2005). This film, which was the only Italian feature presented at the Cannes Film Festival in 2005, was inspired by a book of the same title by Maria Pace Ottieri. The film tells the story of Sandro, a twelve-year-old boy who lives in Brescia, among the privileges of the rich bourgeoisie. His father is a small entrepreneur who has, like many others in Italy, started from the bottom of the social ladder and climbed to the top with hard work. Sandro, during a holiday on his father's sailing boat, falls into the sea and is rescued by one of the people on a boat that is transporting migrants to Italy. Like Gino in *Lamerica*, Sandro experiences at first hand the world of illegal migrants both on the boat then when he arrives in a refugee centre on the Apulian shore. During the film, he tries desperately to save Alina, a young girl, from the world of prostitution to which she is destined.

This is Giordana's first film about contemporary social reality, after many movies dedicated to 1968 and terrorism. The use of a teenager's point of view was a device, in Giordana's (in Zanardi, 2005) words, aimed at avoiding preconceptions and ideological influences in the story. Also, the fact that the story evolves by exploring the friendship between Sandro and Alina, and the way in which Sandro sees the world of adults, situates this film within a new perspective on neorealist conventions, which have too often been conveniently employed in the films of the new millennium. Also, Giordana's film focuses once more on migrants from Eastern Europe, from ex-Communist countries, and mixes together illegal Romanians with Gypsies Roms in his depiction of a Third World ghetto in Milan where Sandro finds Alina, the prey of internet child abuse.

Unlike France and Germany, which had debated for years about models of integration or assimilation of Third World immigrants, for many years Italy ignored or avoided talking publicly about the phenomenon of immigration and the process of globalisation of the fabric of Italian society. This lack of debate and political and civic responsibility towards immigrants, and the settling of intolerance and racism, is reflected in the superficiality of much of contemporary cinematic output that addresses the problem. The presence of the 'other' in Italian society is treated in film only on the surface, where the director dusts up some neorealist conventions in order to make up for the incapacity to address the postcolonial discourse. A different approach to the presence of the other emerges in films made by southern directors about the south of Italy, where the idea of the outsider – whether Italian or foreigner – is explored in a much more complex way. This is perhaps because the *questione meridionale* (the southern question) has been debated for as long as the Italian state exists. In the middle of the 1990s, a new philosophical approach to Mediterranean appeared in the writings of Franco Cassano, which is discussed in the following chapter.

NOTES

1. Charlotte Brunsdon (1989) discussed the problem with quality in British television shortly before the opening of the British airwaves to satellite television.

2. However, the number of films had, in comparison, very little to do with the number of films produced twenty years earlier. Nowell-Smith (1996, pp. 159–60) reports 139 domestic productions plus 106 co-productions in 1962, while in 1982 these were reduced to 99 national films and 15 co-productions.

3. Canale 5 caters to mass audience, Italia 1 is directed mainly to a younger audience and Rete 4 is aimed at women.

4. Giuliana Bruno has filled a historical vacuum with her extraordinary biography of Elvira Notari, *Streetwalking on a Ruined Map* (1993) and her collection of writings published in *Off Screen: Women and Film In Italy* (1988).

5. For a discussion of the family melodrama as a genre of Italian cinema, see Günsberg (2005).

6. A list would include *Congo Vivo* (Giuseppe Bennati, 1962), *La battaglia di Algeri* (Gillo Pontecorvo, 1966), *Quien Sabe?* (Damiano Damiani, 1966), *El Che Guevara* (Paolo Huesch, 1969), *Queimada* (Gillo Pontecorvo, 1969), the already mentioned *I dannati della terra* (Valerio Orsini, 1969), *Sierra maestra* (Ansano Giannarelli, 1969), *Vamos a matar compañeros* (Sergio Corbucci, 1970). Finally, it is worth mentioning Ugo Gregoretti's documentary *Vietnam, scene dal dopoguerra* (1975), and a series of feature films and documentaries made between 1969 and 2007 about the life of Che Guevara.

7. This is how Nowell-Smith, Hay and Volpe (1996) classify the Third World films, while a better culturally grounded analysis is to be found in Fantoni Minnella (2004).

8. For a discussion of the new global political order and of new forms of solidarity, see Hardt and Negri's book *Empire* (2000).

8. MEDITTERANEAN LANDSCAPES

Films that provide pleasure through the aesthetic consumption of landscape are the counterpoint to the intimate film set in interiors. The importance of landscape to local cultures has obvious implications for the continuation of a sense of place in the communication revolution that annihilates place and distance. However, the aural images of Italian landscape serve also as a means for international audiences to *experience* and know Italy. The landscape film thus functions in a context of the cultural economy of space, especially linked to the tourism industry. Chapter 3 discussed the function of the urban landscape in films set in Turin, as well as the city's cultural economy, driven by cultural policy, that has clustered around the film and television industry since the late 1990s. As Levebvre (1991) points out, space is the result of a process of production, sedimentation and accumulation of history, people, numbers, technologies and so on. If society produces a space, and each society produces its *own* space, then representations of that space also have a role in this processes of production because they contribute to the construction of imaginary understandings and functions of the space, modifying what is informed by effective knowledge. Historically, the Mediterranean has been subject to this transformation as an ensemble of localities in which to consume leisure. It is a place of idleness and exotic eroticism, consumed in the shadow of thousands of years of history. Thus, in regard to Lefebvre's concept of production of space, the Mediterranean region is a commodified space tied to the relations of production imposed by external economic and social forces. In the current historical context, the south and the Mediterranean Sea also appear as sites of authenticity and innocence (*Mediterraneo, Il ladro di bambini, Il postino, Preferisco il rumore del mare*), and as places where one can escape from the corrupt and alienating north (*Verso Sud*, *Figli di Annibale*, and again *Il ladro di bambini* and *Preferisco il rumore del mare*). However, the Mediterranean region has recently been the object of a critical conceptual rethinking, through the work of Franco Cassano. In his book *Pensiero Meridiano*, Cassano (2007) elaborates a critique of capitalism informed by post-colonial thought. He calls for a different intellectual and moral attitude towards the south that would give autonomy, centrality and dignity back to the region. Thus this chapter considers films about the south in terms of the way they engage in a conversation with southern culture, rather than reproducing stereotypes. In the geographical redefinition of Italian cinema in the 1980s and 1990s, the south plays an important role, as it not only emerges as a location in many films, but it was also part of a new regional redistribution of production. In fact, many new directors emerged in Naples, Puglia and Sicily, contributing substantially to what was defined the new wave of Italian cinema. While Naples has traditionally been a cinematic city – it was after all one of the three poles of Italian film production in the silent era, along with Turin and Milan – for Sicily and Apulia, these clusters of production are a new asset which is supported by the interplay of local culture and policy at a European level. As Zagarrio states (1999), it is not possible to understand contemporary Italian cinema without taking into account the different realities and production networks that have developed throughout the peninsula, especially in the Napolitan area.

CONCEPTIONS AND REPRESENTATIONS OF THE SOUTH

Historically, the representation of Italian landscape in film has relied on a cognitive experience of Italy through images of its rich architecture that circulated internationally since early cinema through *vedutismo* (views): monuments, the countryside, backward villages, the Mediterranean Sea and its islands. Early history films such as the blockbuster *Cabiria* (Giovanni Pastrone, 1914) and other classics – *La caduta di Troia*

(Giovanni Pastrone, 1911), the various re-makes of *Gli ultimi giorni di Pompei* (1908, 1913, 1926) – were produced in a context of resurgence of national pride and glorification of the Italian monarchy and Rome, the capital of Italy. These films provided a narrative for the construction of a national discourse that found its referent in the ancient glories of the Roman Empire. In fact, the interest of the young Italian state in the Mediterranean basin culminated in the Libyan war in 1911. *Cabiria* locates evil in the city of Cartage, the historic (now imaginary) city located on the opposite Mediterranean shore. Its inhabitants attend pagan rituals and human sacrifices; thus the films constructs an idea of the Mediterranean Sea as the frontier between a primitive and backward place and civilisation. The southern landscape is also dangerous, as it is the eruption of the Etna that sets *Cabiria*'s narrative in motion.

Italian early history films were functional to exporting the idea of Rome which dominated the Mediterranean basin, in an effort to establish Italian claims to hegemony in the area. Giuseppe Mazzini himself had emphasised the germ contained in the idea of Rome opening the road to civilisation in the south of Europe against barbarianism, stressing that Italy, once having defined her borders in Europe, should stretch into the Mediterranean area (Chabod 1976, p. 224). With their lavish costumes, life-size sets built in natural locations, which increased the realist illusion and magnified the effect of depth, and interior decors filled with mirrors, beds, sofas, brocades and curtains, Italian silent history films focused on the glory of Rome were also able to inspire decadent images of artificial and exotic paradises for national and international bourgeois audiences. The construction of the south as something *not yet* civilised in relation to modernity, where the only possible model of development was technological and industrial, started with the formation of Italy as a unified country.

The films of the second postwar period continued the depiction of the south as backwards and primitive, although they followed different perspectives, genres and aesthetics. The tragic destiny of the south is depicted in neorealist films, which owe a lot to the South. *Sciuscià* (Vittorio De Sica, 1946) portrays the children of Naples as marginalised people trying to survive among the rubble left by World War II, and as ultimately doomed; *Paisà* must be remembered for its 'geography of history' (Bruno 2007, p. 365) as the travelling film through the peninsula, from the liberated south to the north still under Nazi occupation during the last stages of World War II. In *La terra trema* (1947), deemed a masterpiece of Italian neorealism, Luchino Visconti anticipates Frantz Fanon's manifesto of Third World politics, *The Wretched of the Earth*. Despite the film's aestheticisation of poverty, with extreme close-ups of the fishermen, *La terra trema* gives a voice to the men and women of Acitrezza, who are allowed to speak for themselves in their own dialect. For Fanon, the retention of language was a very important element of autonomy and cultural independence from colonial power. The mafia and the state's attempts at disciplining the south, which often found common goals and operated in a synergic manner – for example, with Cesare Mori's intervention during Fascism,[1] can be likened to colonial power. The Acitrezza fishermen are conscious about their exploitations: they depend on unscrupulous middle-men and are doomed by the inclemency of the weather. As the Valastro family loses everything, 'Ntoni's only possibility is to go back to the middle-men. For its political engagement with society, neorealism attempted to address the subaltern condition of southern Italy that was exacerbated by the war. But with the demise of the film movement from the early 1950s, issues of poverty and indigence were turned into spectacle in the genre of the *commedia all'italiana* (Italian comedy).

From *L'oro di Napoli* (Vittorio De Sica, 1954) and the trilogy *Pane, amore e …* (1953, 1954, 1955) to *Divorzio all'italiana* (Pietro Germi, 1961) and *Sedotta e abbandonata* (Pietro Germi, 1963), the south has become the metaphor symbolising the clash between an Italy that is changing and an Italy that does not want to change. The south is depicted as culturally static and stagnant – aptly represented by the sweltering heat, Marcello Mastroianni's sweaty face and the interminable, burnt Sicilian landscape in *Divorzio all'italiana*, and is locked in its traditions which prevent civic engagement and forward thinking. Southerners are viewed as the collateral damage of inaction, ineptitude and policies gone wrong within historic Italy. All the films produced in this period, from the comedy to Visconti's, Antonioni's and Fellini's films, express from different point of views, but in a complementary way, the passage from old to new, representing the trauma that this passage produces. The consolidation of neocapitalist integration and of the economic boom, which produced an affluent society (in the north), created at the same time the crisis of the relationship between the individual and reality, and exacerbated the economic and social gap between north and south.

In the 1960s and early 1970s, the condition of the south was depicted in many films that addressed different topics: migration, the mafia (this is the topic that inspired most of the so-called political films) and history. Both *Il gattopardo* (Luchino Visconti, 1963) and *Rocco e i suoi fratelli* (Luchino Visconti, 1960) are concerned with the south's resistance, the first against political change, and the second against modernisation. However, neither offers a simplistic reading of the south, as the films show the deep-seated responsibilities of the political class and of the north in maintaining the south in a subaltern condition. *Rocco e i suoi fratelli*, made during the massive migration from the south to the factories of the north, offers two alternatives for southern migrants: to succumb to the lure of civilisation and modernity of the north, which produces vice — aptly represented in the character of Simone – or to assimilate, with the loss of cultural memory and language – represented by the characters of Vincenzo and Ciro. The loss of language implicates the internalisation of the culture and the values of the north, creating a fundamental disjuncture between the migrants' consciousness and their subjectivity. Rocco's character does not offer a satisfactory alternative, as he is trapped between the tragedy of the separation from the land and its traditions, and the burden of having to continue these traditions in an alien environment. Rocco and his family move in the liminal space of Milan's periphery, although it is not the city itself that corrupts the values of the Parondi family, but the characters. Nadia is in fact a key element in the film, as the blame for corruption is shifted from the city to her (body). According to Fanon, violence purifies and destroys categories and dichotomies – specifically, black and white, or north and south – but in *Rocco and e i suoi Fratelli*, this violence can only be sublimated with boxing and can only be directed against the woman's body, as the montage-like segment of Nadia's murder and Rocco's boxing match skilfully demonstrates in the last part of the movie.

Countless films about the Mafia were made between the 1960s and the 1970s – including the films adapted from Leonardo Sciascia's books. Along with political thrillers, they offer themselves as a location for the construction of male power (Wood 2005, p. 1987), continuing in the tradition of the politically engaged film. Many films about Sicily and the mafia produced in this period adopt a reportage style, in an effort to avoid narration and dramatisation, hence foregrounding didactic aspects. The south is at the centre of Francesco Rosi's films. *Salvatore Giuliano* (1962), which follows a *cinegiornale*[2] form of narration, comments on the broad connections between Mafia and the government, and the responsibility of the mafia in many assassinations of communist militants and unionists. This theme is revisited in Pasquale Scimeca's *Placido Rizzotto*, in which there are several references to the massacre at Portello della Ginestra, famously portrayed in *Salvatore Giuliano*. In two occasions in *Placido Rizzotto*, Scimeca gives voice to the many unionists killed by the mafia by making his characters read aloud lists of names of dead comrades, thus circulating again in Italian collective memory the names of forgotten heroes.

Sciascia, who took Sicily as a metaphor for the whole of Italian society affected by corruption and *malgoverno* (bad government), defined *Salvatore Giuliano* as 'the truest work that cinema has ever dedicated to Sicily' (in Miccichè 2002, p. 157). In *Le mani sulla città* (1963), Rosi continues his refusal to narrate, once more adopting a reportage style to tell a story about corruption in Naples' building trade. Also, *Il giorno della civetta* (Damiano Damiani, 1968), adapted from Sciascia's book of the same title, shuns the easy folklore of the island and its inhabitants offered by comedy, as it follows the conventions of the *film inchiesta* (the investigative film), digging into the connection between mafia, power and corruption, and into the international ramifications of the mafia, as it emerges from Leonardo Sciascia's thrillers. Giuseppe Ferrara's *Il sasso in bocca* (1970), which traces the origins of the mafia in a chronicle mode of narration, exposes connections between North American multinationals and secret services that employ the mafia to maintain the public order.

These films were released in a period of economic euphoria and affluence for the north-west of Italy – the so-called economic miracle, which relied on migration of labourers from the south to the north. The industrial and technological development in the period between 1950 and 1970 forced Italy's modernisation of sexual mores, family and gender relationships, but this modernisation proved problematic for the Italian south, which continued to be represented as the pathological consequence of a defect of modernity.

A special mention must go to Paolo and Vittorio Taviani because of the evocative power of their landscape films. Tuscany features strongly in the Tavianis' films, but they travel further afield in the south in *Un uomo da bruciare* (1962), *Allosanfan* (1974), *Kaos* (1984) and *Il sole anche di notte* (1990), and in Sardinia in *Padre Padrone* (1977). In the Taviani brothers' films, the landscape not only forms the background, but is part of the symbols and metaphors that connote the films' meaning. The southern landscape functions in the narrative as a way to connote ways of life, customs, mentality, traditions and culture, without going beyond their geographical and ethnographic specificity. The sun-drenched Sicilian landscape is written on the clothes in *Kaos*, as they are worn and faded. Taviani's stories of the south are stories that bring a sense of defeat and mourning for Utopia. In this regard, they declare that:

> It is not an accident if the land as a central concern almost always shows up in our films. And it shows up in the most lacerating way for us Italians: the South. The South as an unresolved national problem, as an ethical, if not mythical heritage, as a tangle of expressive forces that condition out future – the South, we say, is rather our Moby Dick. (in Ferrucci 1995, p. 126)

The Tavianis' representation of the south as an unresolved problem for Italy originated from a conceptualisation of the south that emerged during the postwar reconstruction. The 1951 census showed that illiteracy rates in the south were 24.3 per cent, double the national average of 12.9 per cent. The image that emerged, then, was thus that of a very divided Italy. However, at the same time, southern Italy constituted a big unifying myth in the national imaginary, as the Tavianis mention above, as Italians not only thought that the *Mezzogiorno* had the potential to shake off its archaic heritage and get rid of illiteracy, but that it could also be Italy's own California (Clerici and Di Pietro 1991), as a modernised sunny land of groomed orange orchards, olive groves and vineyards, with an ever-expanding economy. The discursive narrative of the south was thus based on a pedagogical understanding of democracy and development, and on a firm belief in the modernising capacity of capitalism and economic and technological development.

RETHINKING THE MEDITERRANEAN

In the mainstream *Sabato, Domenica, Lunedì* (Lina Wertmuller, 1990), the cinematic south is again mythologised. The myth of the Great Mother is the focus of the film, which is also set in Pozzuoli. Rosa (Sophia Loren, the epitome of the Mediterranean woman) is identified as the mythical Great Mother. With an injection of magic realism, Rosa's emotions and feelings – either positive or negative – awaken the deep substratum of Pozzuoli. They are *'scosse d'assestamento'* (aftershocks), which help the Great Mother to find her harmony, and hence Sophia Loren's equilibrium within her family. A less transcendental myth of the south motivates Diego Abatantuono in *Figli di Annibale* to escape to Egypt with Silvio Orlando after a bank robbery, only to discover that Egypt, where they imagined a life of pleasure, is as expensive and consumerist as Italy and the money soon runs out.

A counter-cultural analysis about the south emerged with Franco

Cassano's Meridian thinking. In the 1980s, Franco Cassano started a reflection about the Mediterranean region which appeared first in various published essays. As Cassano writes in his preface to the 2005 edition of *Il Pensiero Meridiano*, the 1980s were for him 'much more than the elaboration of mourning, they were a febrile season of readings and reflections' (Cassano 2007, p. vi). It is evident that Cassano distances himself from the period of closure, repentance and demise of political commitment that dominated the 1980s, which was discussed in Chapter 6. Thus Cassano follows a conceptual and intellectual journey into post-colonial and subaltern literature, from Edward Said and Dipesh Chakrabarty to Homi Bhabha and Edgar Morin, elaborating a theory of the Mediterranean region that connects the south of Italy to all the souths of the world. Following this analysis, the south has been colonised, and thus has been thought by the west according to stereotypes that have contributed to maintain it in a subaltern condition. For Cassano, the south and the Mediterranean region are thought and represented as an unfinished business in relation to the north–west of the world, which is taken as the only model of development. According to the Meridian thinking, through a *'decostruzione simbolica'* (symbolic deconstruction), the Mediterranean states should reconsider their relationship with space and turn the focus on to their non-western origins, reconsider the notion of the frontier, call for political, social, religious and cultural changes that must also be based on the reorientation of the notion of time (slowness) and the refusal of the imperatives posed by what he calls *turbocapitalismo* (turbo-capitalism). As Cassano (2007, p. xv) suggests, the concept of slowness can be found in the cinema of Wim Wenders who, as discussed in Chapter 5, had great intellectual influence on the 1980s generation of Italian filmmakers, Werner Herzog, Theodoros Anghelopulos and Abbas Kiarostami, or in the literary work of Milan Kundera (1995), and of course in Carlo Petrini's revolution of Slow Food.

In summary, the Mediterranean can very well be compared with Said's Orientalist paradigm, as its representations – even the most sophisticated and alternative – are constrained within dualistic thought and oscillate between the paradigms of 'tourist paradise and a mafia hell' (Cassano 2007, p. xiii). Thus the reconsideration of space implies a symbolic connection between the European south – the Mediterrranean – and all the other souths of the world. As with the Orient, the south has helped to define the north as its counterpoint of language, images, ideas and experiences.

A renewed cinematic interest in the Mediterranean region surfaced from 1991, when the first Mediterranean cinema festival opened in Brussels. The second festival, in 1992, was organised by the French-speaking community in the Belgian capital, with the support of the European Commission. About 60 films from fifteen countries opening on to the Mediterranean were shown on that occasion, bringing together the concept of a cinema of frontier and of the Third World. In 1997, the European Union inaugurated Euromed Audiovisuel, a program dedicated to enhancing Euro-Mediterranean audiovisual cooperation with the goal of establishing peace, dialogue and stability in the area. Euromed Audiovisuel II has established a fund of fifteen million Euros for the last three years to help production in twelve Mediterranean countries. This is a resource that could broaden collaboration between Italian Mediterranean regions and the other countries which participate in the project.

In 2000, the Mediterranean Film Festival concentrated on the countries on the southern and eastern sides of the sea. In that occasion, social realist films such as *Mayis Sikintis* (*Clouds of May*, from Turkish director Nuri Bilge) were shown alongside 'classics' such as Salvatores' *Mediterraneo* (*Yomiury Shimbun/Daily Youmiuri*, 2000). In 2003, the Festival of European Cinema took place in Lecce (Puglia), home to one of the most innovative directors of the current generation, Edoardo Winspeare. A conference was also organised on the theme 'Il cinema meridiano',[3] in homage to Franco Cassano, who was also a keynote speaker at the conference. The key debates at the conference focused on the representation of the Mediterranean Sea in the cinema of the last decade. More importantly, the conference insisted on the difficulties of circulation created by the fact that Hollywood's majors control international distribution. To overcome these problems created by Los Angeles' cine-colonialism, but also as a way to contrast the strong competition of other international film festivals based on specialised niche markets, from 2007 the Taormina Film Festival has shifted its focus on to the Mediterranean basin, in the hope of attracting tourism and professionals from the Mediterranean area. Another initiative that aims to promote southern cinema, and especially the internationalisation of the Italian southern regions, called Cinesud, started a worldwide tour presenting thirteen titles, including documentaries and feature films. The initiative is supported by the Italian Ministry of Foreign Affairs in collaboration with API-FilmItalia. Its first screening was the documentary *Détour De Seta* at the Tribeca Film Festival. The Ministry of Foreign Affairs has set two goals for the project: the first is to show the changes that have occurred in the south in terms of modernisation; the second is to promote southern cinema in its own right. These initiatives, which have the noble intent of expanding the international reach of Mediterranean culture, are often accompanied or followed by the promotion of various industries and local produce, thus turning cultural diplomacy and promotion into profitable business deals.

SOCIAL AND ECONOMIC CONTEXTS

In the 1980s and 1990s, Italian cinema had to adapt to the cultural needs of a society that was going through a depoliticisation process. Also, the scarcity of investments in the film industry forced filmmakers to narrow their sets inside walls, delivering an intimate cinema. But the renewed interest in the Mediterranean region and in the road movie genre, whose characters' destination is always the south, or exotic Third World places, helped Italian cinema to come out of the impasse created by the scarcity of the means of production and ideas. Once more, politics of the Third World and migration issues seemed to be converging, both in society and in cultural representation. To understand this connection, various elements need to be taken into account. First, it is important to remember that in the 1980s and 1990s Italy was also undergoing a social transformation due to massive migration from African countries, and in the new millennium from Eastern Europe. Second, we must go back to the politics of 1968 and the way in which certain values and fascinations were transferred in the films of the 1980s and 1990s. The fascination with the Orient became predominant with the hippie generation, when a trip to India was *de rigueur*. The south and the Mediterranean region in general were also seen as a place of innocence, exotic experiences and haunting landscapes, an authentic 'other' where young generations of left-wingers spent their summer holidays looking for their 'California'. After the demise of the Greek Fascist regime, Greece became a cheap and exotic destination for the left-wing intelligentsia of the Italian north. Megisti, the island depicted in *Mediterraneo*, was discovered in the late 1970s by *alternative* tourists as its geographical position in the Mediterranean places it as the last bastion of the Western frontier before the 'true Orient': Turkey and the Middle East. Third, we must return to the geopolitics of film, to Hollywood and to Hollywood's judgment of what Italy is. There are textual and economic considerations to be taken into account here. Some of the films whose fundamental premise is the pleasurable view of the Mediterranean Sea – *Nuovo Cinema Paradiso, Il postino, Mediterraneo, Respiro* – found their way into wider distribution thanks to Hollywood's control of the international market. Only a few films make it on to this distribution circuit, and this has to do with the fact that the United States tightly and selectively controls film and television imports by adopting protectionist measures. Foreign films – European in this case – that make it on to the distribution circuit in the United States are very few compared with US exports of films to the European market. In 2000, receipts for European exports in North America were estimated at US$827 million, against $8.2 billion of North American revenues in Europe (European Audiovisual Observatory 2002). American distributors such as Miramax specialise in the marketing of local and cheap films for the US market. Traditional understandings of European cinema as art cinema and the exploitation of films whose narrative and aesthetic canons are readily recognisable by American audiences are fundamental elements of this process. Within a tradition of Italian filmmaking, films set in the Mediterranean are those that offer one of the two dominant stereotypes of the south – in this case, the leisure-oriented space that recalls the Grand Tour for industrialised Europe. This cognitive experience is elicited by images that give life to the Italian dream, connected to the aesthetic and ecstatic contemplation of the world. On this point, Lefebvre remarked that the Mediterranean perimeter had been redefined in the 1960s and 1970s as a 'non-work' space, thus acquiring a specific role in the social division of labour (Lefebvre 1991, p. 58).

Such role of non-work space dedicated to leisure and to the discovery of holiday sensuality was already typified by Tuscany in *Room with a View* (James Ivory, 1985), in which the danger in the streets of Florence, the city's intoxicating disorder and the sensuality of the surrounding landscape facilitate the rite of passage of the wealthy British young protagonists. *Tea with Mussolini* (Franco Zeffirelli, 1999) is a classic international film. An Italian-British co-production which depicts a community of English people living in Florence during Fascism, the film relies on visual imagery of Art Déco interiors, fashion and design, as well as Florence's museums and architecture, to reach international audiences. Other films depicting the Italian exotic charm and set in different parts of the country were produced in the 1990s. For example, *Enchanted April* (Mike Newell, 1992) is a British production filmed in Portofino in Liguria, and *The Talented Mr Ripley* (Anthony Minghella, 1999), a US production that was filmed in the south.

In fact, it was after the American success of *Nuovo Cinema Paradiso*, *Mediterraneo* and especially *Il postino*, thanks to a marketing campaign artfully orchestrated by Miramax, that the Mediterranean Sea has again become the stage of US film productions set in Italy. The fictitious filmic island in *Il postino*, the result of two different locations — Procida in front of Naples and Salina in the Eolian Islands – has created interest in white villages, blue skies and blue seas. Many locations were used for *The Talented Mr Ripley*: Naples, Ischia Island, Positano and Procida Island all formed an imaginary background for Mr Ripley's crimes. *A Good Woman*

(Mike Barker, 2004), an international co-production distributed in the United Kingdom, Germany, England, Italy, the United States and some Eastern European countries, was also filmed on the Amalfi Coast. But it was the film renaissance in Naples, with the development of ancillary industries and professional skills that attracted US productions, which could take advantage of cheaper labour costs in the production stage. The proximity to Cinecittà for post-production was a bonus.

Other co-productions, from *Ripley's Game* (Liliana Cavani, 2002), which is set in Veneto, to *My House in Umbria* (Richard Loncrain, 2003), an Italo-English-US co-production actually filmed in Siena (Tuscany), Cinecittà and Shepperton studios, contributed to construct a space that covers different geographies and cultures within Italy, but that has no specific cultural context, in the foreigner's view, as the rolling hills of the north and the centre and the bright colours of the south are all connotations of refined civilisation, reinvigoration and sensual discoveries. Following Lefebvre, these representations of space are tied to the relations of (film) production, constructing an imaginary site that it is called Italy, and thus effectively suppressing local cultures and imposing cine-colonisation.

THE TRANSFORMATIVE POWER OF MERIDIAN THINKING

It is legitimate to ask what the schemes of representation of the south are in contemporary films made by Italian filmmakers, to what extent these are subverted according to Cassano's philosophical rethinking of the Mediterranean region, and whether there are different sensibilities towards the south that can be detected in the films of the 1990s and those of the new millennium.

As we have seen, in an international setting Italy and its south are synonyms. Indeed, the perception of the country in the collective imagination on a global scale is the bright, passionate, enchanted and at times hard landscape of the Mediterranean. The success of national cinema at its local box office increases when it crosses borders and is recognised in an international setting – namely by the award of an Oscar®. In the postwar period, many Academy Awards in fact went to films displaying elements of the south (*Sciuscià*, 1947; *Ladri di biciclette*, 1949; *Divorzio all'Italiana*, 1961; *Ieri, oggi e domani*, 1964) and actresses who embodied southern sensuality and passion: Anna Magnani in 1955 and Sophia Loren, in 1961. *Nuovo Cinema Paradiso* and *Mediterraneo* secured two consecutive Oscars, in 1991 and 1992, while *Il postino* was nominated for five awards, winning in the Best Music, Original Dramatic Score in 1996. The three films have become a sort of mantra among academics and film critics because, with the exposure at the Academy Awards, they refocused international interest on Italian cinema after a long period of crisis and absence from international screens. Federico Fellini's *Amarcord* (1973) was in fact the last film that was awarded an Oscar® as Best Foreign Film in 1975.

The three films were undeniably able to speak to Italians about their culture, identity and history, but there is no doubt that the films also responded to an imaginary construction of what Italy is abroad. *Nuovo Cinema Paradiso*, for example, is the most engaging construction of the seductive myth of what the south is, for Tornatore constructs a fairytale and idealised picture of the past. On the occasion of the presentation of the Palm d'Or Award to Giuseppe Tornatore at the 1989 Cannes Film Festival – the first such presentation to an Italian director for eight years – Italian producers debated the state of Italian cinema. The Film Producers Association's vice-president, Mario Orfini, commented on the industry crisis, explaining that:

> It is not the audience's fault if it is fallen out of love with Italian cinema: for ten years they have been presented with a mass of firemen, *carabinieri*, nuns and all the other under-products of an Italian comedy that once was even glorious. (Bruzzone 1989)

Mario Cecchi Gori added that it was necessary for Italian cinema to go back to produce international films, whatever this may mean, to remain afloat in an industrial and economic environment in continuous evolution and in a moment, at the dawn of the Maastricht Treaty, particularly crucial for the audiovisual product (Bruzzone 1989). *Marrakech Express* (Gabriele Salvatores, 1989), *Nuovo Cinema Paradiso* and *Meri per sempre* (Marco Risi, 1989) were quoted as examples of the emergent cinema; coincidentally, these are all films set in the south or beyond the Mediterranean border (*Marrakech Express*).

Nuovo Cinema Paradiso, *Mediterraneo* and *Il postino* have been discussed from the point of view of landscapes of loss, with direct references to a narrative structured around a projection of politics on to romance (Galt 2002). The films ooze with nostalgia for the past as the location of authentic life. Their common characteristic is that they are history films. Chapter 6 discussed the importance of history in contemporary Italian cinema, and especially the role that specific historical events played in the directors' and audiences' imaginary. According to Higson (1993), a feature common to films which reconstruct the past is that, in response to a present that does not offer any viable alternative, they shun industrialised and chaotic society, and look nostalgically back to a period of innocence and authenticity. However, there is a more complex process at play in films set in the south and that deal with history. This process is formed by the interplay of layers of related affective elements: the questioning of society through a constructive historical revisionism; the emergence of a diasporic community of Italians within their own homeland; and the difficult but transformative relationship with displaced landscapes.

If we understand historical revisionism as a fundamental element of a dynamic society that constantly questions itself, its view of the world and its institutions (Castoriadis 1997, p. 281), the conflation of history, and views about the land and film result in a powerful cultural product – a public site that articulates not only anxieties in contemporary Italy about its past, but also a site of resistance for groups which are excluded and marginalised from other institutional spaces. The generation of new directors can very well be considered a diasporic community displaced and alienated in its own home, which it no longer recognises. Displacement and deterritorialisation thus become a narrative of belonging to an imagined community that is fictionalised in film. This constitutes the underlying sub-text in *Mediterraneo*, which is the second of a trilogy of films by Salvatores about escaping from the homeland because this can become oppressive and imprisoning. *Marrakech Express*, *Mediterraneo* and *Puerto Escondido* employ the *Fernweh*, the desire to escape from one's homeland – although, as Di Stefano explains, the '*Wonderlust* for other places can be just as insatiable and unrealizable as the desire to return to the homeland for those in exile' (Di Stefano 2002, p. 40). Thus, for Sergeant Lo Russo, the desire to return to Italy, to 'make a better Italy', is later transformed in voluntary exile because 'they did not let us change Italy'. Exile and the desire to return are visible in *Nuovo Cinema Paradiso*, as Salvatore is suddenly inundated by nostalgia and the desire to return to his land when he knows that Alfredo is dead, and in *Il postino* Pablo Neruda longs for Chile, his homeland. It is only when he returns to Mario's island and re-thinks his relationship with Mario, who is now dead, that he is filled with nostalgia for the island and the memories this symbolises.

Thus the three films use history selectively, constructing a narrative of decline, longing, loss and crisis. Postcard shots portraying the enchanted tranquillity of the Mediterranean Sea, but also the harsh, laconic noble landscape, as in *Nuovo Cinema Paradiso*, are inserted between scenes or as background. These pleasurable views of the sea and of the southern rural landscape, through their sensuous aspects, elicit not only the aesthetic consumption of the landscape by audiences, but also the desire to inhabit that image, and thus the past. However, all films end with death and disillusionment. In *Nuovo Cinema Paradiso*, Salvatore Di Vita, a successful film-maker who returns to his birthplace, Giancaldo, after Alfredo's death, the local cinema's former projectionist, witnesses the demolition of Cinema Paradiso to make way for a supermarket carpark. The rubble of the cinema symbolises the rubble left by something that went wrong in the past. Salvatore had left 30 years earlier, following

Alfredo's instructions, because Sicily was '*terra maligna*' (an evil land). In *Mediterraneo*, Sergeant Lo Russo looks hopefully to the future when it is time to leave the island, but he returns to Megisti almost immediately after the war. Also *Il postino* closes with the death of an ideal, symbolised by the death of Mario during a Communist demonstration.

If the three films present common themes that have to do with disillusionment and the loss of political projects, then they present different approaches to the symbolic value of the Mediterranean landscape. On the surface, they all seem to use the landscape as dislocation of history; however, a more culturally specific reading points to different assessments of the landscape. Rosalind Galt uses Krakauer's discussion of the function of a landscape image in a historical film to underline the friction and conflict between the reality and temporality of the landscape shot, and the historicity of the narrative (Galt 2002, p. 166). This is central to her argument of the landscape displacing the historical object in the three films, but both *Il postino* and *Mediterraneo* differ from *Nuovo Cinema Paradiso* in that they hint at the possibility of transformation.

Transformation, the acceptance of the 'other' and the dialogue that is being established between different cultures are at the core of Meridian cinema. In *Mediterraneo* and *Il postino*, we can glimpse some of this philosophical project of cultural hybridisation and mutual exchange that becomes very important in films about and set in the south. In *Nuovo Cinema Paradiso*, Sicily is '*terra maligna*', a place from which Salvatore must escape and to which he must never return. Accordingly, the Sicilian hills are seen through distancing aerial shots, stock frames visible in films about the Mafia of the 1960s. The village is the site of collective life, with its square, church and cafes, so evocative of the villages in *Divorzio all'italiana* (1961) and *Sedotta e abbandonata* (1963). Landscape here is used to evoke audiences' cognitive experience of Sicily. Thus, in *Cinema Paradiso*, Sicily does not have a transformative function, as it is only by leaving that Salvatore realises his dream. There is no encounter of different cultures, if we exclude what Descartes defined as two foreign cultures, the relationship between a society's present and its history: the final clash between the past – how Salvatore remembers Giancaldo – and the present – the arrival of modernisation, which produces only disillusionment.

On the contrary, in *Mediterraneo* and *Il postino*, the 'other' enters into dialogue with the local environment, and the result is a mutual transformation of the native and the other. In *Il postino*, Mario is transformed by Pablo Neruda's friendship, acquiring consciousness of his subjectivity. In turn, Pablo Neruda is transformed by the landscape, as seen, described and recorded by Mario. In *Mediterraneo*, within the temporal suspension from reality, as the radio broke during the soldiers' occupation of the island, the soldiers slowly adapt to the rhythm and customs of the island and its inhabitants.

Mediterraneo and *Il postino* were made before Cassano's book was published. They do not reflect on or represent Meridian thinking, but they certainly represent shifts in the perecpetions of the south by the left-wing generation of 1968, to which Cassano himself belongs. The transformative quality of place and the opening up of a dialogue between the south and the north are elements that can be found in some of Cassano's propositions:

> For the Meridian thinking in fact the South must not be separated from the others as if it were shameful. Epistemologically the South, with its slowness, with times and spaces that resist to the law of universal acceleration can become a resource ... Meridian thinking is that thinking that one starts feeling where the sea begins ... where the many differences touch and the game of the relationship with the other becomes difficult and true. (Cassano 2007, p. 7)

Born in Naples, Salvatores has a privileged relationship with the south. In *Sud* (1993), the main character, Ciro, embodies the empowerment and the reawakening of consciousness in psychological, cultural and civil terms. Ciro is unemployed and takes anti-depressants. His depression is at the same time the symptom and the symbol of his oppression. When he finds the courage to occupy an electoral booth in the local primary school, with two friends and an *extra-comunitario*,[4] a man from Eritrea with

Rastafarian dreadlocks, and especially when he discovers that the girl hostage, accidentally trapped in the school while voting, is the daughter of his enemy, Honourable Canavacciuolo, Ciro stops taking anti-depressants. His six months of depression without speaking are suddenly cured, and he takes the fight against Canavacciuolo and the police into his own hands. The first sequence of the film is the key to its interpretation: from the deep sub-strata of the earth, an earthquake wave traverses rocks and dirt, emerging to the surface under Ciro's dining-room floor. The change that occurs in Ciro is like an earthquake which reawakens his consciousness.

The film is set in the province of Salerno, but it was really made in Marzameni, a small village on the extreme Sicilian cape of Capo Passero. The semi-destroyed village in the film, real and fictitious, is literally propped up by posts and beams, thus resembling a theatre or film stage, reminding us of the fictionality of the story. However, it is also a metaphor for decades of neglect and corruption, which diverted the funds for the reconstruction following the earthquake to the pockets of Canavacciuolo, the fictional member of parliament. The film is set between the enclosed space of the school and the central square of the village, and tells a story of a failed rebellion (once again), but whose value lays in giving the picture of a rarely seen south – that is, a South that is able to react and take its destiny into its own hands. There are landscape shots that punctuate the narrative, although these are confined to a narrow strip of blue sea seen from the school terrace. These shots constitute the most traditional and folkloric image of the south, while music plays an important role here, as it is used as a critical counterpoint to the images. The music chosen by Salvatores is the *posse* of 99 Posse, Papa Ricky, Assalti Frontali and Possessione. The rap and raggamuffin add connotative meaning as they express contemporary social unrest in the *centri sociali*,[5] threatened by eviction. Tony Mitchell notes that the renewed interest in politics by Italian youth in the 1990s surfaces through transgressive popular music and youth culture that find expression in rap and ragamuffin music, in this way closing the 'gap between fiction and reality, desire and action' (Mitchell 1995, p. 333). Thus, in *Sud*, the music closes the gap between Ciro's desire to shake the political system and social relations in the village, based on patronage and corruption, and direct action, with the protest occupation of the electoral booth. Ciro has his own posse when a group of young unemployed turns up in the village square to support him with slogans and protest signs. More occupations occur in other electoral booths, as Ciro and his friends learn from the radio that other protesters have occupied electoral booths in other villages of the south, emulating Ciro's direct action.

The wheat fields of Basilicata are a key element in another film by Gabriele Salvatores set in the south, *Io non ho paura*, adapted from Niccolò Ammaniti's best-seller. The film is set at the end of the 1970s, when many children from rich families were kidnapped by the mafia, the *'ndrangheta*[6] or other criminal organisations. The film tells the story of Michele's passage from childhood to adolescence through the dramatic kidnapping for ransom of another child, Filippo, by Michele's father. The wheat fields in the land between Basilicata and Apulia are the playground of a group of children whose stories are followed by a mobile camera at child height. In one of the many excursions, Michele finds a hole; in the underground cave, Filippo is kept prisoner. Michele soon discovers that the whole village is somehow implicated in the kidnapping, and he will have to overcome his fear of darkness to save Filippo from being killed, as the police close in on those responsible for the kidnapping. The encounter between Filippo and Michele – children from very different social backgrounds – works its transformative power as Michele, completing his own rite of passage, finds the courage to go against the father and his authority.

ARTICULATING DIVERSITY IN THE 'ETHNOGRAPHIC' FEATURE FILM

The articulation of cultural differences and the transformative philosophy of Meridian thinking are the deeper elements characterising the films made by directors from the south who work predominantly in the south. Whether this cultural engagement is antagonistic or affiliative, it still reflects ongoing negotiations and forms of cultural hybridity that happen at the margins of authorised power. The margins and a new awareness of subject positions away from the 'singularities of "class" or "gender"', as Bhabha discusses, create an 'in-between' space, an interstice, or 'overlap and displacement of domains of difference' (Bhabha 1994, p. 2). Thus it is in the interstitial space of cultural hybridisation, and not within multiculturalism, that the subject is politically empowered and engaged in making their destiny.

Some features of Mediterranean cinema would simplistically dismiss it as neorealist cinema. Children, social and political themes, non-professional actors, realism and use of regional dialect are the features common to many of the films discussed and cited in this chapter. However, these conventions are only on the surface, as the films' texture has to do with the cinematic rendition of rituals, traditions and daily life connected with the culture of place. Goethe's description of a typical Italian sunset – 'The bells ring, the rosary is said, the maid enters the room with a lighted lamp and says *"Felicissima notte!"'* (in Bakhtin 1986, p. 31) is the disclosure of everyday life in which, as Bhabha (1994, p. 142) says, the 'vision of the microscopic, elementary, perhaps random, tolling of everyday life in Italy' represents realism over the romantic.

In fact, the best expression of the transformative power of Meridian thinking is to be found in films that foreground cultural tradition through the interplay of popular beliefs, culture, tradition and landscape as the source of the story. Giuseppe Gaudino (*Giro di lune tra terra e mare*, 1997), Edoardo Winspeare, Andrea Piva (*Lacapagira, 2000*), Vincenzo Marra (*Tornando a casa*, 2001), Salvatore Mereu (*Ballo a tre passi*, 2003) and Piero Sanna (*La destinazione*, 2003) have all explored Mediterranean magic and rituals. Cinematographic elements, drama techniques, *mise-en-scene* and spectacular elements are used as counterpoints to non-professional actors, lean dialogues and close-ups that express human feelings. This approach to storytelling is a reminder of the first documentaries by Robert Flaherty, *Nanook of the North* (1922) and *Man of Aran* (1934). Flaherty's influences are also to be found in the documentary *La storia del cammello che piange* (*The Weeping Camel*, 2005) by Luigi Falorni, another filmmaker who, like Edoardo Winspeare, graduated from the Munich Film School. In Gaudino's *Giro di lune tra terra e mare*, the history of Pozzuoli's seismic activity and the town's gradual slipping under the sea is mixed with the history of a family of fishermen, whose lives are turned upside down as they are forced to move home every time there is a seismic movement. This will inevitably lead to the breakdown of the family. The film is also a journey in the obscure and dramatic past of the region of the Campi Flegrei, with ghost-like appearances of Agrippina, killed by her son Nero, the oracles of the Sibilla Cumano and the young Christian martyr Artema, killed by his fellow students.

Returning to *Sud*, it is possible to appreciate how contemporary foreign influences have been translated in local music tradition with rap and raggamuffin. In the Italian context, certain music traditions are the expression of marginal cultures – of those who live in the interstices of the affluent and dominant society, and grow at the geographical margins of the peninsula, where unemployment is high and the corruption of the political class is most felt. The resurgent phenomenon of the *pizzica*, which is the narrative strategy in Edoardo Winspeare's first feature film *Pizzicata* (1996), and in his subsequent film *Sangue vivo* (2000), demonstrates the increased significance of popular music in Italian politics and social life. However, in *Il miracolo* (2003), the *pizzica* is not at the centre of the narrative, although Winspeare continues to explore popular beliefs and traditions of the south. In this film, Winspeare concentrates on the ordinary world of working-class characters, who believe in miracles performed by ordinary people. Lecce's proletarian landscape is the background to this story set around the harbour's docks and industrial suburbs. The magnificent baroque of Lecce's city centre is skilfully avoided so that pleasure through aesthetic contemplation is frustrated.

Pizzicata is set in 1943, in a village in the Salento peninsula, not far from the coast. Cosima is the middle of three sisters living with their widowed father, Carmine, owner of a small olive grove. An American fighter pilot born in a village in the same region, who migrated to the United States with his mother after the father died, parachutes himself before his aeroplane crashes into the sea. He is found unconscious by the younger sister, Franceschina. As it is wartime, and the Italian nation is allied with Hitler, Tony is an enemy; however, Carmine hides him because Tony reminds him of his own son, Donato, who is also at war, although on the opposite side. As Tony speaks Italian, he is easily passed as a fictitious cousin from Lecce. Cosima and Tony fall in love, but the son of the richest landowner in the region, Pasquale, is also in love with Cosima. He understands the deception and kills Tony during a *pizzica* party that the family throws for the return of Donato from war. After Tony's death, Cosima falls prey to the tremors typical of the tarantula's bite; a group of male musicians is called to play the *pizzica* for Cosima, so that she can dance and enter a state of trance. The film ends with the festival of Saint Paul in Galatina, with *tarantolati* from nearby villages entering in the church to demand grace from the Saint. It is believed in Galatina that Saint Paul protects the village's inhabitants from tarantulas' bites, so the phenomenon is circumscribed to the surrounding villages in the Salento region.

The Salento region is the place of the *pizzica*, and also the privileged set in Winspeare's films. The *pizzica* is the dance therapy that cures victims of the tarantula's bite which, as the tradition goes, occurred mostly during harvesting in the summertime. This phenomenon is called *Tarantismo*, and is defined as an historical and religious phenomenon with origins in Medieval times, but which characterised Apulia especially from the seventeenth century on. Every year on 29 and 30 June, in the church of Saint Paul in Galatina, the so-called *tarantolati* (those affected by *tarantolismo*) meet to ask the Saint to be graced. According to the tradition, those bitten by the tarantula fall in a state of general malaise: they sweat, tremble, are sad, refuse to talk and often indicate their heart is a place of pain. A group of men armed with their tamborines visit the *tarantolato's* house and play an obsessive music. The *tarantolato* dances frenetically, with convulsions similar to those of epilepsy, mimicking the movements of the insect, and reaching a state of trance. The dance is thus functional to reaching trance, which is the transformative element of the ritual.

There have been different theories about *tarantismo*, but Ernesto De Martino's cultural, historical and anthropological interpretation of the phenomenon is the most compelling as it grounds *tarantismo* in cultural and popular beliefs (De Martino 1961). According to De Martino, the crisis caused by the bite of the tarantula is part of popular and pagan traditions which have survived within Catholicism and is the result of imagination or hallucination. However, Catholicism has profoundly affected the ritual by exercising an hegemonic force in, for example, prohibiting the execution of music in the church. *Tarantismo* affects mainly women, as they are more oppressed by a society that imposes hard conditions on them, and represses their erotic desires and yearn of autonomy. In *Pizzicata*, *tarantismo* encroaches on the drama of a denied love relationship, reminding us that the phenomenon is mostly feminine, and thus linked to the hardship of the female condition in a peasant world. The arrival of Tony disrupts the community's world, and his death does not re-establish the equilibrium because Cosima does not accept the imposition on her sexuality, thus she becomes a *tarantolata*. The film leaves the ending open, as we do not know whether Cosima will be cured. In fact, according to the tradition, *tarantolati* have recurrent crises, which coincide with the celebrations of Saint Paul. Therefore the *pizzica*, far from re-establishing the equilibrium, shows how a society loses its equilibrium.

Winspeare's role in the resurgence of the *pizzica* has been fundamental as he has been researching the phenomenon and establishing relationships with all the tamborine players in the region since 1989. According to Winspeare (in Santoro and Torsello 2002, p. 172), the *pizzica* 'shakes, moves', so that it also makes a political statement about the fact that the south's own perception is shaken, therefore it is changing. Between 1992 and 1994, Winspeare organised at least 200 large events with musicians from all over the Salento region. At the same time, he discovered that other people in the area were undertaking similar operations, such as the Canzoniere di Terra d'Otranto and the Canzoniere Grecanico Salentino in Lecce. *Pizzicata* was thus the sum of this involvement in the roots of traditional culture in Apulia (in Santoro and Torsello 2002). Today, large *pizzica* festivals in the Salento region attract tens of thousands of young people.

Sangue Vivo continues the tradition of the *pizzica* as the musical expression and choreography of a story based on the clash of worlds through the clash between generations. The peasant world, represented by the father who died in mysterious circumstances, is destined to disappear, while contemporary reality is represented by Pino and Donato, two brothers who survive in the interstitial space between criminality and normality. Pino, the elder brother, tries to continue the cultural traditions of peasant civilisation, while Donato, the younger brother, is the symbol of a new society which tries to abandon past identity. Pino sells fruit at the markets, but his real activity is smuggling cigarettes and Albanian refugees on the Apulian coast. Donato is unemployed, with occasional jobs between shooting up heroin. The film is spoken in the dialect of the Salento region, and shows the interactions between different communities of illegal immigrants, peasants, musicians and the underworld with a sociological and ethnographical approach reminiscent of *Lacapagira* (Andrea Piva, 2000), but without the mean irony and satire of the latter.

NAPLES TO SICILY

The bloody and violent stereotype of the south, so common in the political films of the 1970s, is recast in the films of the 1990s and 2000s, but updated to the transformation of mafia and camorra that moved from the country to towns, from rural under-development to the urban decay. In this genre, some films that adopt a realistic aesthetic must be mentioned: *Mery per sempre* (Marco Risi, 1988), *La scorta* (1994, Ricky Tognazzi) and the recent *Alla luce del sole* (Roberto Faenza, 2005), inspired by the real story of Don Pino Puglisi, killed by the mafia in 1993.

Many other films that focus on the south and that subvert cinematic conventions deserve a mention. Post-Pasolinian cynicism is found in the surrealist provocations of Daniele Ciprì and Franco Maresco, who explore Palermo's underworld against a proletarian landscape in decay. Their depiction of Sicily is once again apocalyptic, a chronicle of the continuous death of the island's society. Sicily is the background for stories of misery and superstition that refuse conventional aesthetic codes and elements of seduction. Their film *Totò che visse due volte* (1998) represented a case of censorship unprecedented since *L'ultimo tango a Parigi* (Bernardo Bertolucci, 1972), with Catholic organisations and extreme right-wing associations boycotting the film, followed by parliamentary interrogations and withdrawal of state funding that had not yet been paid (Franco Maresco, in Fantoni Minnella 2004, p. 300).

Rubble and decay are also the backdrop in Roberta Torre's *Angela* (2002), a love story that develops between Angela, wife of a cocaine smuggler, Saro, and Masino, a young man who will become one of don Saro's offsiders. Roberta Torre's first feature, *Tano da morire* (1997), was presented at the Venice Film Festival among many polemics because the film is a satirical depiction of the mafia involved in the murder of Giuseppe Falcone and Paolo Borsellino. The film won a Nastro d'Argento and a David di Donatello as Best First Feature Film, and other awards for Best Music and Best Supporting Actress.

Finally, there are the films set in Naples. Giuliana Bruno has discussed in her commanding works *Streetwalking on a Ruined Map* (Bruno 1993) and *Atlas of Emotions* (Bruno 2007) the construction and representation of Naples as a cinematic city, from early films shot on location to the neorealist reinvention and documentation of Naples after World War II, to the urban cinema of the 1980s and 1990s. I will only mention the work of some directors who contributed, although in a very different stylistic and thematic way, to the renaissance of film in Naples and to that of Italian cinema in the 1990s in general: Pappi Corsicato (*Libera*, 1993; *I buchi neri*, 1995), Mario Martone (*Morte di un matematico napoletano*, 1992; *L'amore molesto*, 1995; *Teatro di guerra*, 1998), Antonietta de Lillo (*Matilda*, 1991; *Racconti di Vittoria*, 1996) and Antonio Capuano (*Vito e gli altri*, 1991; *Pianese Nunzio 14 anni a maggio*, 1996; *Polvere di Napoli*, 1998). All these films present a portrait of Naples in which sounds, voices, stories and memory mix together to give, once again, an anthropological view of the city and its inhabitants.

Among the recent films set in Naples and Sicily, *Domenica* (Wilma Labate, 2000) and *Respiro* (Emanuele Crialese, 2002) are worth mentioning for the way in which they ground their characters in the landscape. Both films are concerned with gender politics, as the main characters are a young girl (in *Domenica*) and a woman (in *Respiro*). *Domenica* is a classic film noir, and tells the story of Domenica, an orphan and a free-spirited teenager, who is raped in the streets of Naples. After a few months, the police need her to identify her alleged rapist at the morgue. The police version is that he threw himself out of the window in the police headquarters during the interrogation. The symbolic reference on the surface is to the alleged suicide of the Anarchist Giuseppe Pinelli in 1969 in police headquarters in Milan, but the value of the film lies in the unfolding of the story and of the relationship between Domenica and Sciarra, the retiring detective who was on her case when she was raped. Sciarra has only a few months to live, because his kidney cancer has returned. He is going to stay with his sister in Sicily, as he will become increasingly sick and unable to look after himself. He is leaving on that night, thus he has only one day to try to convince Domenica to identify the dead man, 'to finish the business'. The relationship between Domenica and Sciarra opens up as they wander through the labyrinthine and 'porous' (Block in Bruno 2007, p. 361) streets of Naples. In this film, there is no easy identification with an idealised Naples, as pleasurable, postcard views of the city are carefully avoided. As in *Lamerica*,[7] a filter tones the strong colours of the city to a vague, pale blue sky above Naples' rooftops. The mobile camera, which gives an illusion of observational documentary, follows Domenica in her daily business around town, showing us her mastering of the intricate and narrow streets, escaping from time to time from Sciarra. But her advantage slowly disappears, as she gets closer to the hospital morgue and closer to Sciarra. The film ends with Domenica accompanying the detective to the boat leaving for Sicily.

A completely opposite approach to landscape depiction is to be found in *Respiro.* This film is set in the late 1970s, on Lampedusa Island, which is 205 kilometres from Sicily and in fact closer to Tunisia. With a cast of mainly non-professional actors and spoken in dialect, the film tells the story of Grazia (Valeria Golino), mother of three – two boys and a teenage girl who suffers from wild mood swings. Grazia is either too happy or too sad, rebellious and unconventional, and life on Lampedusa is oppressive. In this film, symbols of oppression and male violence are even too evident: Grazia is forbidden to go on the husband's boat, like other wives do, as she was caught swimming naked by her husband returning from fishing. In response, Grazia entangles herself in a fishing net, making herself look even more ridiculous. Her female dog, Pastora, which follows her everywhere and sleeps with her, is killed by her husband, so Grazia frees all the stray dogs kept in the island's kennel. The following scene shows the village women running away from the dogs, which are killed by the men standing on the rooftops of the houses. In fact we don't see who is being shot; as we can hear the dogs' wild barking, we are led to imagine it is the women running away who are the target.

Grazia's elder son, Pasquale, roams the island with other children. Together they hunt for birds, fish and fight. What on the surface seem to be innocent children's games and scuffles are in fact a reflection of the violence of the land, sun-drenched and scarred by man's intervention. When family and neighbours become fed up with Grazia's antics, they decide to send Grazia to Milan to seek help from a psychiatrist, but she hides in a cave, helped by her son Pasquale. In fact, throughout the film the two sons show fierce loyalty to their mother, protecting her from the nosy neighbours and the accusing family. The relationship between sons and mother is so strong that it borders on sexual attraction. While in the cave, the village believes that Grazia is dead, but she is spotted by her husband while she is swimming. On the night of the patron saint festivity, she is finally rejoined by her husband and accepted in the community.

Lampedusa's aggressive beauty is softened by the sea, the element in which Grazia finds relief from her wild moods. Grazia is an outsider, a rebellious woman who cannot find a way to express her otherness, as she constantly comes up against mental and physical borders. Patty Pravo's song *La bambola* (1968), which Grazia plays constantly, is also an element of identification with rebelliousness, as Patty Pravo herself was a symbol of defiance of codes and morality in the late 1960s. Like *Pizzicata*, *Respiro* is a film about the life of a small community in which everybody is somehow related and knows everything about other people. In the first part, the film shows daily life and labour division between men and women, as the men go out fishing and the women work in the cannery, salting and canning anchovies, Lampedusa's traditional economy. As a place of gathering, the cannery is also a place for gossip. In fact, it is during her work at the cannery that Grazia hears about the plan to send her to Milan. Crialese wanted to end the film with the powerful imagery of the community entering in the water to reach out to Grazia, as the element in which 'you have no security, but it's there that human beings find each other, when they're all the same, floating and trying to understand what's going on' (Crialese, in Anderson 2003).

Water is thus the element that cements Lampedusa's community, as the island's economy depends on it. The Mediterranean Sea is a central force in Cassano's Meridian thinking because it represents an interface of mediation between the people who live around its borders. Therefore the Mediterranean Sea must no longer be seen as the border that separates north and continental Europe from Africa and Asia from the west, and that appears in the atlas only as a blue frontier between countries. Despite the many shots of the Mediterranean Sea as a static horizon, in *Il postino*, *Pizzicata*, *Mediterraneo* and *Lamerica* the 'other' comes from the horizon, creating in the community a multiplicity of voices and point of views. It is this key element that sets apart ethnographic films which give voice to the south in a positive way from films which are superficially interested in spectacular renditions of the landscape *tout court*.

NOTES

1.   Cesari Mori, called *il prefetto di ferro* (the iron prefect), was sent to Palermo

between 1925 and 1927 with special powers conferred by Mussolini to fight against the mafia. During his mandate, Mori arrested hundreds of law-ranking *mafiosi*. The war on the mafia closely resembled the war against forms of *brigantaggio* in the south during the early years of Italian unification. Mori's harsh methods earned him the name *prefetto di ferro*.

2. Before the arrival of television, the *cinegiornale* was the newsreel and current affairs program that was shown before the feature film.

3. The word *meridiano* makes reference to meridian, but also *meridionale* (Southerner) and *mezzogiorno*, which is another way of referring to southern Italy. The *Cassa del Mezzogiorno* was a public entity instituted in 1950 to oversee the development of public works in the south to increase social and economic development. It was abolished in 1986, after major scandals related to bribery, corruption and connections between the government and the mafia were discovered.

4. The term initially referred to the emigrants, illegal and legal, mainly from North Africa, who have arrived in Italy over the past twenty years. Later, the terms was applied to all citizens, legal or illegal, who were resident in Italy but not originating from any of the countries of the European Community. The 1990 Martelli Bill on immigration institutionalised the term, which was already in use in everyday language. The racist linguistic implication is obvious: the Italian dictionary *Zanichelli* defines the term as referring to job-searching emigrants, originally from *underdeveloped* countries (the italics are mine).

5. *Centri sociali* (social centres) are the only instance of 1970s radicalism that has survived through to the 1990s. The most important centre is the Leoncavallo, in Milan. The film ends with a dedication to the community centres throughout Italy.

6. The 'ndrangheta is another criminal organisation that operates in Calabria, while Apulia is the territory for the operations of the Sacra corona unita, and Naples for the camorra.

7. Luca Bigazzi, *Lamerica*'s cinematographer, purposely used a filter to tone down the striking beauty of the Albanian landscape, to avoid a pleasurable consumption of the landscape. (Interview with the author, Milan, December 1998).

9. CONCLUSION

The coming of age of recent Italian cinema followed two stages. From the late 1970s, a cinema that represented a cohort of the Italian audience emerged and evolved in the 1990s into what Italian film critics labelled 'New Italian Cinema'. The death of the author and the birth of self-reflexive subjectivity (in fact, an inflated version of the director as *auteur*) in the cinema of the 1970s were perceived as a break between generations of filmmakers. The death of Pier Paolo Pasolini first, and Federico Fellini later, were seen as markers of shifts in Italian cinema. Lino Micciché and other critics identified these shifts as the confused experimentation and refusal of aesthetics that originated in 1968. The habit of reading films through grand film theory inhibited the appreciation of complex systems of analysis of the country's industry in relation to generations of directors, modes and places of production, along with content. The self-indulgent approach to the discussion of Italian cinema through close textual analysis of authorial paradigms has continued in foreign scholarship, highlighting the poor understanding of wider economic and industrial implications. Analysis remains in the realm of representation, with postmodernist approaches to influences and encounters between Hollywood cinema and Italian cinema.

As in women's cinema, from the late 1970s the use of the Super-8 format allowed many young directors to experiment with themes and forms. In general, the proliferation of practices and aesthetics achieved in extremely low-budget films failed to create those processes of reiteration and repetition that constitute a genre, and which are highly productive in sustaining the national industry and ultimately cultural identity. In fact, the crisis of representation conflated with the industry's economic crisis and inability to sustain market differentiation.

With television and state financing, the Italian cinema of the early and mid-1980s found itself trapped in cultural and political issues, valuing intellectual content rather than entertainment. Some elements of the film industry responded through redefining audiences, reappropriating cinema as public space and restoring the element of 'quality' that traditionally had been attributed to Italian cinema. The triangulation filmmakers- audience- history supported a recovery of the industry which found in television a permanent space for collaboration. Since the late 1980s, television has not only offered a structure for training and funding, but it has also become a leading player in film production.

Part II of *Recent Italian Cinema* introduced the return of the event in the Italian cinema of the 1990s. In this, the New Italian Cinema must be recognised for its attempt to produce films that were nationally specific in their cultural and historical address. The history film, a traditionally stable genre in Italian cinema, became a thematic choice that reconnected a cohort of the Italian public with its collective imaginary, and hence with its cultural heritage. The Resistance and 1968 returned as events in a cinema of memory in an effort to return to strong stories. This approach projected in film a cultural shift in writing about history that had occurred from the middle of the 1970s.with the works of the historians Alessandro Portelli and Luisa Passerini. This shift was also motivated by a broader repositioning of the categories 'history' and 'memory'.

The shift into a minimalist, introspective cinema whose mode of narration was the individual mnemonic recollection of history is an indicator of a wide cultural shift which has occurred in Western societies in the last twenty years, and which coincides with the post-1970s demise of the grand ideologies of socialist tradition. The history films produced in the two decades of the 1980s and 1990s clearly privileged remembering and individual memories, which were often controversial and divisive. If seen as a part of a larger contemporary revisionist project, the history film in the public sphere has become the mediator between academic history and popular memory – that is, versions of the past told by family and friends.

In privileging individual memory and the autobiographical mode, the history film has closed the gap between those included in and those excluded from history. In the specific context of the period 1988–99, this conjunction between cinema and history can be interpreted as a return to politics in an environment of political disillusionment and restoration. In brief, cinema was able to recreate a conversation with its public through the coincidence between memory and personal narratives, as actors, directors and audiences coalesced around a set of texts which represented their own past.

The corollary of the public debate about the Resistance was that monolithic accounts of history and the position of professional historians were being questioned. With the much-proclaimed end of history, the public and authoritative function of the academic historian as the only legitimate storyteller of the past was under scrutiny. This became especially evident in the context of the exponential growth of the mass media system, which appropriated this function of the historian as the oracle of the nation. The debate then extended to the correct use of history, in contrast to the political use of history in which, it was feared, media would take away objective historical evidence in lieu of a partial, instrumental and popularised version of history.

The process of revisionism consisted not only of the critique of paradigms that were commonly accepted as founding features of the democratic republic, but also the themes that were explored. Often for the first time, the treatment on television of topics like the Italian population's collaboration with Fascism, the detention of Italian prisoners of war in German concentration camps, or of the soldiers who fought on the Russian front and never returned, attempted to rewrite Italy's own understanding and positioning of the notion of victims. Generally, these topics were seen in a broader context of international politics. As in the case of the Resistance, discussions about the Holocaust not only raised questions of historical understanding and interpretation, but also broader issues regarding the appropriate way to talk about or represent the Holocaust. After more than 50 years, historians are still confronted with providing definitions of victims, perpetrators and bystanders, while in the arts the issue is the appropriate form or language with which to visualise or recount the Shoah.

Historical debates about the Holocaust have opened different narratives of representation. In the literature and cinematic representations of the Holocaust, the protagonists are no longer hopeless victims, but survivors; the by-standers are reformed rescuers; and the Nazis now occupy the background. This new paradigm in telling the story of the Holocaust has thus made possible the use of different languages, such as that of comedy. Importantly, the return of the Holocaust in film, starting with *Schindler's List* and following with *Life is Beautiful*, has lent itself to commercial speculation, from a position which – like the grand historical epics of the past – accepts commodity status with the aura of history and culture.

Recent Italian Cinema has also focused on the discussion of space. A form of fetishised history has appeared in depictions of still landscapes. Similarly, *Cinema Paradiso, Mediterraneo* and *Il postino* represent a cinema of spectacle in which history is not only delivered through stories, but becomes a pro-filmic event because of the meanings that tradition layered on to landscape. 'Thus the sea stands for something else,' Mario tells Neruda in *Il postino*. Landscape is a metaphor, and its depiction of indolent backward villages freezes the past into an age of innocence because it is dialectically presented as authentic. Despite the stereotypical imagery, the exotic represented by the Mediterranean Sea, southern Italy or the Greek island of Castellorizo enabled a break into the international market by a cinema that was again seeking opportunities for national films. Conversely, the emergence of a Mediterranean cinema from the margins of global cine-colonialism has showed a distinct way to negotiate difference within Italy itself. However, conflicts between migrants from Eastern Europe and Italians, social victimisation and deprivation are now redirecting the gaze of the nation towards new margins and peripheries within Italy.

History films, social realism, popular comedies, biography, noir and romantic comedies have expressed the many Italies that have coexisted from the end of the millennium, in the delicate moment of transition from a nation of migrants to a nation of immigration. The move away from the categories of class and gender that dominated identity positions in the 1970s and part of the 1980s has resulted in a proliferation of identities and subject positions which inhabit different spaces and now provide terrain for the elaboration of different narratives and stories. This articulation of differences has been generated also by the decentralisation of film production in various parts of the peninsula, which in turn plays an important part in the development of a variety of images and sounds of screen spaces. Thus the intersection between history and space produces complex cinematic maps in which people, things and place make up for the experience of everyday life.

There is a sense of frustration when speaking of Italian cinema today. Its poor performance at the domestic box office does not reflect the richness, yet again, of a new generation of directors, actors and actresses. The interesting emergence of the documentary genre is also a welcome change in the Italian cinema industry. This book has not included documentary in its survey of current Italian cinema. A history of Italian documentary, and especially of the recent development of this format, has yet to be written. In fact, the twentieth century closed with a positive trend for the Italian documentary, thanks especially to the renewed interest of the public and television, and to investments by producers such as Domenico Procacci, who redirects some profits from international successes such as *L'ultimo bacio* to the production of documentaries. Television networks have been active in both buying and commissioning documentaries from film directors who have already made a name for themselves in the market or in the independent festivals arena. Directors such as Guido Chiesa, Marco Bellocchio, Bruno Bigoni, Marco Bechis, Ciprì e Maresco, Mario Martone, Enzo Monteleone and others have enthusiastically answered the call, often producing their best work in the documentary format. Many of these documentaries are the result of research that was being undertaken to make feature films centred on historical events.[1]

However, despite the positive signs that emerge also from crossovers between cinema, art, new media, theatre and new initiatives aimed at increasing the visibility of Italian cinema, the Italian public is eager to watch Hollywood blockbusters. In part, magazines and newspapers are to be blamed for the scarce exposure of Italian cinema among pages filled with local television starlets and Hollywood stars. In this regard, Monteleone writes that 'it isn't the public that does not want to see Italian films, but it is the press, television and the mass media that have decided to not to talk about Italian cinema, unless it's the cinema of comic actors' (Montaleone 2000, p. 11). Directors lament the paucity of support from the media and maintain that Italian cinema is reviewed and received with prejudice by the media and the public. Following a logical argument, it is hard to see why in turn a special effects Hollywood film is treated with respect, or German telemovies are broadcast in prime time on Saturday night, whereas Italian films never seem to be able to engender the favour of critics and public, inhabiting the graveyard television timeslot.

Sophisticated comedies such as Muccino's films are the exception. In fact, the period 2000–07 has marked the rapid rise and success of Gabriele Muccino, first in Italy and then in the United States. Muccino's case indicates that within an American-dominated cultural flow and manufacturing of taste transfer, the appearance of diversity within Hollywood is nothing less than the control and appropriation of national production and circulation of texts and labour by US transnationalism (Miller et al. 2000, p. 196). Naturally, Muccino's Hollywood films then top the Italian box office, messing up the concept of national cinema. What used to be a nationally dominated market that accommodated popular comedies, *auteur* and quality films have given in to the international spread of capitalistic production and conglomerates that dominate distribution. Hollywood-produced and distributed films have occupied national markets, pushing away the middle-range and quality films. In 2006, the average production cost of an Italian film was two million Euros, which indicates a fundamental problem in capital investment and policy support. This amount had remained basically constant since 2000, and is roughly half of a French film production budget, and four times lower than that of a co-production.

Conversely, Hollywood's average production cost for a film has been increasing steadily, reaching the US$53 million mark in 1997, and nearly half of this amount was spent on marketing (Miller et al. 2001, p. 196).

Italian cinema's subservience to Hollywood and the NICL is also expressed by the roller-coaster history of Cinecittà. Over the last two decades, the entire picture of film geography and film economics has changed. With the so-called new media – or, more accurately, new delivery systems – such as cable television, satellite, pay per view and the expansion of the video market, Hollywood has not only invested in distribution with the opening of multiplexes in Europe, and of course Italy, but it has also restructured by optimising its production. This has entailed increased flexibility and specialisation in the labour system, and especially in hiring overseas studios owned by countries such as Australia, Canada, the United Kingdom, Romania, France, Italy and so on. Cinecittà's privatisation and reorganisation from the middle of the 1990s exemplifies this current trend by European studios and production companies to attract large American investments. Thus, if on the one hand Italy no longer leads the market with spectacular high-budget productions, then on the other Cinecittà is concentrating on offering labour with specialised skills and technology. In this, Cinecittà's self-promotion resurrects the aura of Italian craftsmanship by offering an infrastructure of technical and artistic skills in several fields. Initially, this industrial shift proved effective in taking in commercial and international finance, especially from Miramax, and expanding small local ancillary companies. In reality, Cinecittà's studios languish when US productions pack up. The real cracks in Cinecittà's walls and scraped paint aptly symbolise the current state of affairs in Cinecittà.

In regard to the concept of and debate about national cinema, the third millennium has also witnessed the recasting of Carlo Verdone as a tragicomic anti-hero in the same vein as Alberto Sordi as anti-hero in the Italian comedy films of the 1960s. The so-called Christmas comedies continue to attract large audiences. If we have to measure the concept of national cinema against audience reception of domestic films, we should admit that Lino Banfi, Christian De Sica, Aldo, Vittorio and Giacomo express the soul of the nation. However, because of highbrow positions in Italian film criticism and academia, there is a resistance to accepting popular comedies as the true representation of the national imaginary – and when this is admitted, it is done in a sarcastic and accusatory tone.

The question that needs to be asked at this point is 'what next?' This book has shown that Italian cinema cannot be reviewed separately from Hollywood and from developments in the European and international film industry, especially in regard to the dispersion of production, and ownership concentration in the film industry and the media. The slight recovery of the Italian box office in 2006, which saw the return of the market share to 25 per cent from a low of 17 per cent in 2000, which in turn had collapsed from a 24 per cent in 1999, hardly indicates that Italian audiences are going back to the picture theatres to watch Italian films. It indicates that Italian audiences' appreciation of Italian films fluctuates in very short cycles which are linked to the release of a handful of popular films such as those by Gabriele Muccino and Carlo Verdone. It also indicates that Italian cinema follows the ups and downs of European cinema, and that the Italian film industry shows the same structural problems as other national cinemas: little visibility, high number of films produced and not distributed, smaller economic returns in comparison with American films, lack of infrastructures for the distribution and promotion of domestic cinematic output, and poor distribution outside the Italian market. At a European level, the main weakness is to be found in the fact that production, distribution and exhibition remain virtually within the national boundaries. Because the strongest film industry remains the French film industry, Italy has beefed up its co-productions with its cousins behind the Alps. Italian actors such as Laura Morante and Stefano Accorsi reside regularly in Paris where they can also find work opportunities in French films.

One predicament of the Italian film industry remains the tension between the production of a relatively high number of films, which represent opportunities for creativity and innovative ideas, and a lower filmic output, with higher production value and potential returns to sustain economic viability. A second predicament of Italian cinema –

which is a derivative of the first – involves content and rests on the constant conflict between the production of *auteur* films and popular films. Popular comedies that should be designed to fill gaps in between high-quality commercial films and authorial experimentation and first features become, on the contrary, the only films to top the domestic box-office. These films, along with Hollywood blockbusters, push aside the 'middle' quality films, which then have little visibility and almost no distribution nationwide. These predicaments force the production of many films which pretend to be *auteur* films, but which in reality are excellent works of professionals who can work in different genres and formats, but are never able to draw large crowds to the theatres or raise 'above the tree tops', to quote Andrew Sarris (1962).

The cultural map of Italian cinema is thus very complex, as it is intersected by tendencies that go in every direction. From the influence of television, with its aesthetic and formats, to the increasing use of literary adaptations, to the desperate search for genres and sub-genres that can reach the Italian imaginary, to new geographical scenarios that emerge in film, the best answer is perhaps promotion of Italian cinema to Italian audiences. The re-education – almost a form of cultural rehabilitation – of Italian audiences to the history of domestic cinema that is not served in the cup-cake format of *Nuovo Cinema Paradiso* is a new approach. From a promotional point of view, various initiatives – one of these is the *Centocittà* (One hundred cities) program – aim to educate audiences about the rich Italian filmic tradition. Centocittà is an initiative promoted by Cinecittà and Anec to sustain the circulation of Italian and European cinema in the picture theatres of cities with fewer than 150,000 inhabitants, where the local cinema *d'essai* is often the only cultural initiative in the area. The Department of Culture and Heritage invested 2.5 million Euros to be distributed to the theatres that committed to showing quality films for at least 270 days a year, while Cinecittà Holding contributed with 25,000 Euros for each theatre. This program takes packages of Italian films to the one hundred cities scattered throughout the peninsula, while other initiatives also promoted by Cinecittà and Italian trade offices in various parts of the world present retrospectives of Italian directors and actors, along with a handful of recent films.

This is a drop in the ocean if we compare Italian cinema with the way in which global Hollywood operates. All subsidy systems devised in the last twenty years by the Italian government through law decrees that all go by the name of 'Urgent measures for the audiovisual industry' have failed to deliver economic sustainability and viability because the film funding system is tied to the national economic performance. From the point of view of production, Italian cinema has been in a transition phase since the collapse of Cinecittà in the late 1960s, and various delusions of a rebirth of the domestic cinema have in reality only accounted for short periods of box office success of a handful of films. There is a need to find different avenues and different ways to sustain Italian national cinema. In a country that is culturally based on localism and regionalism, regional film commissions have proved useful to partially counter the squeezing power of global conglomerates, convergence in film, media and multimedia industries, and textual and economic cine-colonialism. More marginalised than any other form of entertainment in its own market, Italian cinema still lives in the heart of world cinema history for the contribution that it made with, often, the most subversive ideas. Looking back to the last twenty years, one can not separate the cinema of the 1990s from the transformations that occurred in the previous decades, from a cultural, political and industrial point of view. In its minimalist approach to filmmaking, recent Italian cinema has been able to make use of hybrid forms of story-telling in the best way that it could, considering the negative circumstances in which it has operated both domestically and internationally.

NOTE

1. See Enzo Monteleone's documentary about the survivors of El Alamein, Guido Chiesa's many documentaries about the Resistance and Marco Bellocchio's documentaries about terrorism.

APPENDIX: ABOVE OR BELOW THE LINE?

INTERVIEW WITH GIADA TRICOMI, ASSISTANT COSTUME DESIGNER, ROME, 14 MAY 2007

How did you start as costume designer?
I went to university, I studied Art History, and I graduated in Minor Arts. While I was writing my thesis, I understood that I wanted to go on a different pathway. I enrolled in the European Institute of Design, where I finished a Stylist Master. But this was still a theoretical course, so I attended stages in theatre and in advertising. I started working for free, but I was insured and had superannuation.

Tell me about your experience in the HBO series *Rome*.
I worked in the second series of *Rome*, between March to November 2006. *Rome* was co-produced by HBO and Fortuna Felix. Each part is directed by a different director and with different technicians. In Italy we don't have such big productions. The heads of department and workers were almost all Italian, while the costume designer, April Ferri, came from Los Angeles. For me, it was a positive experience because there were different skills and experiences that we exchanged. Americans are very professional and us Italians are very practical and we have a technical know-how at artisan-like level. There were 40 people working full time, plus many more working on a daily basis to dress hundreds of extras. Many departments were set up inside the theatres, just the costume departments had six sub-departments, from metals to tinting, from leather to sartorial. Everything was built in Cinecittà.

So, why do you think it was a positive experience?
Well, because Americans are very professional ...

In what way?
They invest a lot in a film. Italian films are really poor in comparison. American cinema has many more means. Then you could really breathe an international air; it was also very useful for networking.

How much were you paid?
Not much, because I was a second-level designer, so about 500 Euros before tax a week. Anyway, it is a good salary for my level and taking into account that I only have a year and half's experience. The rest of the crew, those at a higher level, were paid much more, naturally. Anyway, everybody – daily workers included – was paid very well.

Do you think that this experience was positive for your curriculum vitae?
Absolutely, there is a lot of competition in this job.

Do you think that the return of Hollywood from the end of the 1990s has created many expectations in the Italian film industry and thus created a surplus of workforce?
Absolutely. The offer of work in Italy is very low. You get in different sectors (theatre, advertising, spectacle in general). Sometimes you don't work for months. Well, I am at the beginning of this career, other people with more experience work all year around, maybe overseas. I finished working for *Rome* in November and I started again in March (with Riccardo Cocciante's musical, *Juliet and Romeo*, which will start in June in the Arena in Verona, nda).

How do you live when you are unemployed?
Well, I get organised. We know that this work is like this, but I do it because I am passionate about it. Anyway, I am not ashamed to say that in periods of unemployment I have also worked as a waitress.

Do you think that Hollywood's coming and going, the fact that the Americans use various studios around the world according to various

local professional skills, or for economic reasons, creates a state of precariousness for all the film industry, the Italian in particular?

Yes, I think so. *Rome* was conceived with other series until 2009, but they have made only two. When the production of the second started in March (2006, nda), the first was being broadcast. In Italy, the public did not like it, it did not stick, maybe because Italians now like more Italian fiction, or maybe because there was a mistake in the scheduling (it was scheduled on Friday night, nda). It was successful in the United States and in England, but the budget went up a lot and in my opinion they will go to film the other series somewhere else.

Getting back to the fall-out on the Italian cinema ...

I don't know if these big productions provoke a rise in the studio rent in a disproportionate way, or if the Italian crisis is due to the scarcity of investment. I don't think there is a relationship between the success of one and the crisis of the other.

There was a moment in which Cinecittà had a return.

Look, I don't know how they effectively invest money. The studios are falling apart, at a structural level. Cinecittà is wasted.

Maybe because Cinecittà is a private company, shareholders keep the money ...

I cannot answer this; certainly I can say that the money is not reinvested in local cinema. There are Italian films today that are finished, but they are never released.

INTERVIEW WITH SILVIA GUIDONI, ASSISTANT COSTUME DESIGNER (AGING), ROME, 10 MAY 2007

When did you start work as assistant costume designer?
From 1993.

Which are the productions you worked for?
Cold Mountain, Tim Burton's *Chocolate Factory*, Terry Gillian's *Brothers Grimm*, Mel Gibson's *Passion of the Christ*, which was filmed partly in Rome and Matera. I worked on *Rome*, then *Val Helsing*, then *Beowulf*, with Angelina Jolie, but it has not been released yet [the film was released in November 2007].

You worked a lot with Miramax. Did you work in Rome?
Almost all these films were made in other countries, between Prague and Romania.

How did you start? What kind of study did you do?
I went to the Fashion and Costume Academy, which no longer exists. Giulia Mafai was the director. Initially it was a course sponsored by Lazio Region, then funding ceased, thus it became a private school, and finally it closed down. As a school, it was really good; preparation was excellent. While you were studying, you could start straight away as a volunteer on the set, so it was important because you could meet many costume designers and could participate in tailoring workshops.

And now, are there other schools? What is the path that an aspiring costume designer has to follow?
There is a course at DAMS in Art and Costume.[1] Some girls I am working with at the moment come from the DAMS. It's a university course of three years plus two of specialisation, but all the girls are very unhappy; they say it is useless. Then there is another Academy of Fashion and Costume, directed by Pistolese, which lasts five years, very expensive, but it is not worth it. Lastly, there is the Centro Sperimentale di Cinematografia in

Rome, which is the only valid school. Piero Tosi teaches there. He is the costume designer *par excellence*: he did *The Leopard*.

Is there a lot of competition in your field?

Yes, there is a lot of competition. But at some point there is a natural selection: if you are good, you continue; it is not difficult to make a career out of it. There are very few good costume designers. If you are not good, you are dead. It all works through word of mouth. For example, I have started – like everybody else – through big laboratories, where there are a lot of costumes to build. The most experienced are the supervisors and then they call girls, the labourers, who are paid very little. In these laboratories, if you are good, you are called again and the supervisors recommend you to other costume designers. I am working with ten girls at the moment. Five of them are really good, so I have already referred them to other jobs. This is also how I started.

Can you say something about your experience on *Cold Mountain*? As I understand it, the costume designer gets the job and then she or he calls other assistants. So you end up working with different designers.

In Italy it all works through word of mouth and through the tailors you work with. In my opinion, the tailor's workshop where you start is very important. So if you start working with Tirelli, that works with many internationally renowned designers, automatically you get in contact with a certain kind of costume designer. If you work at Anna Mode or GP11, which does a lot of television, you enter into an entourage that works with television, opera, film for television.

You specialise in history films, where there are period costumes ...

I am lucky because I started with Tirelli, so I got in touch with excellent designers, and I speak fluent English, which is an advantage for when you have to travel abroad, or work with Americans. If you speak English you are ahead of everybody. Then I got in this entourage. Maurizio Millenotti was the first to call me to make big productions. Then he lives with Gabriella Pascucci, so automatically I am introduced to her. Gabriella works as assistant to Carlo Poggioli, who also has a big network, and so on.

How do you make the jump from assistant to costume designer?
With experience. But then it depends on many things. I am an assistant, but I do aging and tinting, and laboratories, which in Italy means to make hats, jewels, crowns, elaborations on costumes. So then from my specialisation you cannot become a designer, it's like being a cutter, as a cutter you will never become a designer. To become a costume designer you must be the assistant of the designer who follows her closely at rehearsals with the actors, to choose fabric, gets measurement, chooses models and design. The assistant also finds fabric samples, orders all the textiles, keeps everything organised. In large productions, there are over twenty assistants. Other assistants follow actors on the set, when costumes are finished. I work in the first phase, preparing them. In big films, I don't see the set.

In your opinion, is designing costumes a creative work? As designers work with actors, they probably also work with the director, or the producer ...
In cinema there is a division between the costume designer, the supervisor and then the assistants. The designer does the artistic work, the supervisor is the manager, follows the budget, decides the salaries of all those involved, and organises costumes to be ready for the day of shooting. It's office work, so the designer can concentrate with the production. But then it is obviously teamwork, because the costume designer must be aware of the budget.

Do you see the screenplay?
Yes I do, but I could not know about it, because what I see are the drawings that I get from the designer, and then it's the designer who explains to me what she or he wants.

You mentioned Piero Tosi, before, who is over 70 years old. How does the generational renewal happen? Is it difficult to enter in this world when those who worked in the 1960s are basically still working?
Yes, you are right, but as I said before, you are good at your work, you get work. Everybody needs hands to produce, so I work very often with Gabriella Pascucci. She is really good with ideas, but then needs somebody to realise them.

Let's go back to the large production. Is there any union in Italy like in the United States?

No, absolutely not. It's not like America. It's impossible for me to work there. If Gabriella is called to work in the United States, they give her the possibility to go with one assistant, and then she is obliged to employ Americans. For *Gangs of New York*, for example, they brought to Cinecittà whoever they wanted. Labourers are employed locally, but supervisors and close assistants are Americans. The same happens with Gabriella Pascucci. When we went to Prague, she brought people she had been working with for ten years. If you work with people for the first time you don't know if they are good.

Let's get into your profession more closely. How do you 'age' a costume? Have you been experimenting or there is a technique?

Well, this is passed on by older people. You age clothing with iron brushes and sandpaper, scratching with bleach. So when you start, your supervisor tells you, 'Scratch these pants', then when you get experience, you tell the youngest, 'Scratch these pants'. When a jacket is old the pockets, the collar and around the sleeves the fabric is faded, so to provoke this *chiaroscuro* we use bleach sprayed with an *aerografo* around the sleeves. It's like painting with watercolours. We spray bleach in some parts and darker colours in other parts, veiling colour, and then brush, and then tear and mend, and so on.

Tell me about your experience at Tirelli.

I work for Gabriella Pascucci, who is paid by the production, and she works at Tirelli, so I work at Tirelli, but I am not employed by Tirelli.

When they make a costume, does the garment remain at Tirelli?

Well, it depends. Often costumes are up for sale after film production, so it depends on the contract between Tirelli and the producer. Large production companies like Disney, which have warehouses, they re-use costumes, but small production companies throw them away or they auction them. For example, for the already mentioned *Gangs of New York*, when the film finished they did an auction of the costumes and a lot of tailor workshops went to buy costumes they were interested in. Today a lot of costumes are rented. It is not like in the 1960s when everything was made on purpose. For example, *The Leopard*'s pre-production lasted for a year, a year and half, and the costumes were all new. Essentially, today you make what you cannot find. You go around many tailors, not only in Italy but in other places – for example, Spain – and take what you need. You make new costumes when it is difficult to find specific costumes – for example, the Russian Army – and then it depends on the budget. For example, in *Cold Mountain* we had 1,200 soldiers, between the North and South Armies.

It's more expensive, though ...
Yes, but the production is in Romania, which is cheaper.

If the entire production crew moves to Romania, then do you make the costumes here and take them there, or do you make them in Romania?
No, we make them there. In Rome, you may be making the costumes for the actors, but not the extras. For example, costumes in *Cold Mountain* were made by Tirelli. Nicole Kidman's were nineteenth century, and they had to be beautiful, so we made them here at Tirelli. Everything else was made in Romania. This is why there were 25 of us there: two cutters for the ladies, two for the men, us doing the aging, plus assistants, and so on. And then in Romania there were another 25 labourers hired on the spot. So big productions like *Cold Mountain* have a costume department of 50 people.

NOTE

1. DAMS stands for Discipline delle Arti, della musica e dello spettacolo. It was instituted in Bologna in 1970/1971 within the Faculty of Humanities at the Bologna University. Today almost all universities in Italy have DAMS courses or similar.

FILMOGRAPHY

Note: Canal Plus appears as Canal+, Canal Plus Productions, Le Studio Canal Plus and Canal Plus Image International. Ministero or Dipartimento have been left according to the naming of government institutions at the time. The date indicates the year of release and not of production.

AAA Offresi (1979), Annabella Miscuglio. No production data are available.

Acrobate, Le (1997), Silvio Soldini. Production: Aran, Mediaset, Monogatari, Televisione Svizzera Italiana (TSI), Télévision Suisse-Romande (TSR), Vega Film Productions.

Affinità elettive, Le (1996), Paolo and Vittorio Taviani. Production: Filmtre, Gierrefilm, in collaboration with Raiuno, Florida-Movies-France 3, Canal+.

Alexander (2004), Oliver Stone. Production: Warner Bros. Pictures, Intermedia Films, Pacifica Films, Egmond Film & Television, France 3 Cinéma, IMF Internationale Medien und Film GmbH & Co. 3. Produktions KG, Pathé Renn Productions.

Al di là delle nuvole (1995), Wim Wenders and Michelangelo Antonioni. Production: Canal+, Cecchi Gori Group Tiger Cinematografica, Centre National de la Cinématographie (CNC), Ciné B, Degeto Film, Eurimages, France 3 Cin´ma, Road Movies Zweite Produktionen, Sunshine.

Alexandra's Project (2003), Rolf De Heer. Production: Vertigo Production, Australian Film Commission, Fandango Australia, Hendon Studios, Palace.

Alla luce del sole (2005), Roberto Faenza. Production: Cinecittà, Jean Vigo Italia, Mikado Film, Ministero per i Beni e le Attività Culturali, Rai Cinema.

Allosanfan (1974), Paolo and Vittorio Taviani. Production: Una cooperativa cinematografica.

Amarcord (1973), Federico Fellini. Production: Fc-Produzioni, Pecf.

Americanische Freund, De (The American Friend) (1977), Wim Wenders. Production: Les Films Du Losange, Moli Films, Road Movies

Filmproduktion, Westdeutscher Rundfunk 9WDR), Wim Wenders Productions.

Amiche, Le (1955), Michelangelo Antonioni. Production: Trionfalcine.

Amnesia (2001), Gabriele Salvatores. Production: Alquimia Cinema, Colorado Film Production, Medusa Produzione.

Amore molesto, L' (1995), Mario Martone. Production: Lucky Red, Teatri Uniti.

Angel Baby (1995), Michael Rymer. Production: Austral Films, Australian Film Commission, Australian Film Finance Corporation, Beyond Films, Meridian Films, Stamen.

Angela (2002), Roberta Torre. Production: Ministero per i Beni e le Attività Culturali, Movieweb Spa, Rita Rusic Co.

Anonimo veneziano (1970), Enrico Maria Salerno. Production: Ultra Film.

Aprile (1998), Nanni Moretti. Production: Bac Films, Canal+, La Sept Cinéma, Les Films Alain Sarde, Radiotelevisione Italiana, Sacher Film.

Assedio (1998), Bernardo Bertolucci. Production: Fiction, Navert Film, Mediaset, British Broadcasting Corporation (BBC).

Attila, flagello di Dio (1982-1983), Castellano e Pipolo.

Avventura, L' (1960), Michelangelo Antonioni. Production: Cino Del Duca Produzioni Cinematografiche, Europée Société Cinématographique Lyre.

Bad Boy Bubby (1993), Rolf De Heer. Production: Australian Film Finance Corporation (AFFC), Bubby Productions, Fandango.

Ballando ballando (1984), Ettore Scola. Production: Massfilm.

Ballo a tre passi (2003), Salvatore Mereu. Production: Eyescreen Srl, Lucky Red, Ministero per i Beni e le Attività Culturali.

Bianca (1984), Nanni Moretti. Production: Faso Film, Reteitalia.

Blob (1989), Television program, Raitre.

Blowup (1966), Michelangelo Antonioni. Production: Metro-Goldwyn-Mayer.

Boys don't Cry (1999), Kimberley Pierce. Production: Hart-Sharp Entertainment, Independent Film Channel (IFC), Killer Films.

Buchi neri, I (1995), Pappi Corsicato. Production: Filmauro.

Buongiorno notte (2003), Marco Bellocchio. Production: Filmalbatros, Rai Cinemafiction, Sky.

Cabiria (1914), Giovanni Pastrone. Production: Itala Film.

Caduta degli angeli ribelli, La (1981), Marco Tullio Giordana. Production: Filmalpha, Raidue.

Caduta degli dei, La (1969), Luchino Visconti. Production: Praesidens-Pegaso.

Caduta di Troia, La (1911), Giovanni Pastrone. Production: Itala.

Carbonara, La (2000), Luigi Magni. Production: Blu Film, Rai Cinemafiction.

Caro diario (1993), Nanni Moretti. Production: Sacher Film, Baufilm, La Sépt Cinema, Rai, Canal Plus Productions.

Cannibali, I (1969), Liliana Cavani. Production: Doria, San Marco Film.

Casanova di Federico Fellini, Il (1976), Federico Fellini. Production: Pea.

Casa in bilico, Una (1984), Antonietta de Lillo. Production: Giorgio Magliuolo.

Caso Moro, Il (1986), Giuseppe Ferrara. Production: Yarno Cinematografica.

Catene (1949), Raffaello Matarazzo. Production: Labor.

Caterina va in città (2003), Paolo Virzì. Production: Cattleya, Rai Cinemafiction.

Cento passi, I (2000), Marco Tullio Giordana. Production: Ministero per i Beni e le Attività Culturali, Radiotelevisione Italiana, Rai Cinemafiction, Tele+, Titti Film.

C'era una volta in America (1983), Sergio Leone. Production: Ladd Company.

Chi l'ha visto? (1989), teevision programme, Raitre.

Chiavi di casa, Le (2004), Gianni Amelio. Production: ACHAB Film, Pola Pandora Film, Arena Films, arte France Cinéma, 01 Rai Cinema, Bavaria Film, Bayerischer Rundfunk (BR), Bulbul Films, Canal+, Eurimages, Filmboard Berlin-Brandenburg (FBB), Filmförderungsanstalt (FFA), Jean Vigo Italia, Lakeshore Entertainment, Pandora Filmproduktion, Sky, ZZDF/Arte.

Cider House Rule (1999), Lasse Hallström. Production: FilmColony, Miramax, Nina Saxon Films.

Ciociara, La (1960), Vittorio De Sica. Production: Carlo Ponti, Titanus.

Cleopatra (1963), Joseph Mankiewicz. Production: Twentieth Century-Fox Film Corporation, MCL Films SA, Walwa Films SA.

Compagni, I (1963), Mario Monicelli. Production: Lux Film, Vides, Mediterrannée.

Con gli occhi chiusi (1995), Francesca Archibugi. Production: Canal+ España, Creativos Asociados de Radio y Televisión (CARTEL), MG Italian International Film, MG sri, Paradis Films, Radiotelevisione Italiana.

Concorrenza sleale (2001), Ettore Scola. Production: Filmtre, France 3 Cinéma,

Les Films Alain Sarde, Medusa, Telepiù.

Condanna, La (1990), Marco Bellocchio. Production: Cineuropa 92, Istituto Luce.

Conformista, Il (1970), Bernardo Bertolucci. Production: Maris Film, Marianne Production, Marau Film.

Conte di Montecristo, Il (1966), Edmo Fenoglio. Television series, eight parts. Rai.

Cosa, La (1990), Nanni Moretti. Production: Sacher Film.

Così ridevano (1998), Gianni Amelio. Production: Cecchi Gori Group Tiger Cinematografica, Pacific Films.

Crash (2004), Paul Haggis. Production: Bob Yari Productions, DEJ Production, Blackfriars Bridge Films, Harris Company, ApolloProScreen Filmproduktion, Bull's Eye Entertainment.

Dance Me to My Song (1998), Rolf De Heer. Production: Vertigo Ltd Pty.

Dannati della terra (1969), Vittorio Orsini. Production: Ager.

Deer Hunter (1979), Michael Cimino. Production: EMI Films, Universal Pictures.

Denti (2000), Gabriele Salvatores. Production: Cecchi Gori Group Tiger Cinematografica, Colorado Film Production.

Departed, The (2006), Martin Scorsese. Production: Warner Bros. Pictures, Plan B Entertainment, Initial Entertainment Group (IEG), Vertigo Entertainment, Media Asia Film.

Détour De Seta (2005), Savo Cuccia. Production: Palomar-Endemol.

Deutschland, bleiche Mutter (*Germany Pale Mother*) (1980), Helma Sanders Brahms. Production: Helma Sanders-Brahms Filmproduktion, Literarisches Colloquium, Westdeutscher Rundfunk (WDR).

Deux jours à Paris (2 Days in Paris) (2007), Julie Delpy. Production: Tempête Sous un Crâne, 3L Filmproduktion, Back Up Media, Polaris Film.

Deserto rosso (1964), Michelangelo Antonioni. Production: Federiz.

Destinazione, La (2003), Piero Sanna. Production: Ipotesi Cinema, Ministero per i Beni e le Attività Culturali, Rai Cinemafiction.

Diavolo in corpo, Il (1986), Marco Bellocchio. Production: Film Sextile, France 3 Cinéma, Istituto Luce, Ital-Noleggio Cinematografico, L.P. Film srl.

Die Bleierne Zeit (*Anni di piombo*) (1981), Margarethe von Trotta. Production: Bioskop Film, Sender Freies Berlin (SFB).

Divorzio all'italiana (1961), Pietro Germi. Production: Lux, Vides, Galatea.

Dog Day Afternoon (1975), Sydney Lumet. Production: Artists Entertainment Complex.

Domani accadrà (1988), Daniele Luchetti. Production: Nanni Moretti and Angelo Barbagallo for Sacher Film, Raiuno, SO.FI.NA.

Domenica (2000), Wilma Labate. Rai Cinemafiction, Sidecar Films & TV.

Don Camillo (1952), Julien Duvivier. Production: Rizzoli, Amato.

Don Camillo e l'onorevole Peppone (1955), Carmine Gallone. Production: Rizzoli Film.

Don Camillo e i giovani d'oggi (1972), Mario Camerini. Production: Rizzoli Film.

Donna della domenica (1975), Luigi Comencini. Production: Primex, Fox Europa.

Dopo mezzanotte (2003), Davide Ferrario. Production: Rossofuoco.

Doctor Zhivago (1965), David Lean. Production: Metro-Goldwyn-Mayer, Sostar S.A.

Dracula (1992), Francis Ford Coppola. American Zoetrope, Columbia Pictures Corporation, Osiris Films.

Ecce Bombo (1978), Nanni Moretti. Production Filmalpha, Alphabeta Film.

Eccezzziunale veramente (1982), Carlo Vanzina. Production: Cinemedia.

Eclisse, L' (1962), Michelangelo Antonioni. Production: Interopa, Cineriz, Paris Film.

Ehe der Maria Braun, Die (*The Marriage of Maria Braun*), (1979), Rainer Werner Fassbinder. Albatros Filmproduktion, Fengler Films, Filmverlag der Autoren, Tango Film, Trio Film, Westerdeutscher Rundfunk (WDR).

Epsilon (1997), Rolf De Heer. Production: Digital Arts, Fandango, Psilon Pty.

El-Alamein (2002), Enzo Montaleone. Cattleya, Ministero per i Beni e le Attività Culturali.

Enchanted April (1992), Mike Newell. Production: British Broadcasting Corporation (BBC), Curzon, Greenpoint Films.

Europa '51 (1952), Roberto Rossellini. Production: Ponti-De Laurentiis.

Fichissimi, I (1981), Carlo Vanzina. Production: Dean Film.

Fratelli e sorelle (1992), Pupi Avati. Production: A.M.A. Films.

Fate ignoranti (2001), Ferzan Ozpetek. Production: Les Films Balenciaga, Ministero per i Beni e le Attività Culturali, R&C Produzioni, TF1 International.

Figli di Annibale (1998), Davide Ferrario. Production: Colorado Film Production, Mediaset, Medusa Produzione.

Figli di nessuno, I (1951), Raffaello Matarazzo. Production: Labor Films, Titanus.

Finestra di fronte, La (2003), Ferzan Ozpetek. Production: AFS Film, Clap Filmes, R&C Produzioni, Redwave Films.

Fiorile (1993), Paolo and Vittorio Taviani. Production: Filmtre-Gierre Film, Florida Movies, K.S. Film (De), La Sept Cinéma, le Studio Canal+, Penta Film S.L. (Es), Roxy Films.

Frida (2002), Julie Taymor. Handprint Entertainment, Lions Gate Films, Miramax, Ventanarosa Productions.

Fughe lineari in progressione psichica (1975), Annabella Miscuglio.

Fuori orario (1988), Television program, RaiTre.

Garage Olimpo (1999), Marco Bechis. Production: Classic, Rai Cinemafiction, Tele+, Ministero per i Beni e le Attività Culturali.

Gattopardo, Il (1962), Luchino Visconti. Production: Titanus-Pathé Film.

Giamaica, (1998), Luigi Faccini. Rai Cinemafiction, Reiac Film.

Giardino dei Finzi-Contini (1970), Vittorio De Sica. Production: Central Cinema Company Film (CCC), Documento Film.

Giornata particolare, Una (1977), Ettore Scola. Production: Champion, Canafox.

Giulia in ottobre (1984), Silvio Soldini. Production: Bilico.

Gladiator (2000), Ridley Scott. Production: FreamWorks SKG, Universal Pictures, Scott Free Productions.

Good Woman, A (2004), Mile Barker. Production: Meltemi Entertainment, Thema Production, Buskin Film S.r.l., Kanzaman S.A., Beyond Films, Magic Hour Media.

Grande cocomero, Il (1993), Francesca Archibugi. Production: Canal+, Chrysalide Film, Ellepi Films, Moonlight Films.

Grande guerra, La (1959), Mario Monicelli. Production: De Laurentiis, Gray Film.

Gattopardo, Il (1963), Luchino Visconti. Production: Titanus, Société Nouvelle Pathé Cinéma, S.G.C.

Gesù di Nazareth (1977), television program, five parts, Franco Zeffirelli. Radiotelevisione Italiana.

Ginger and Fred (1985), Federico Fellini. Production:Pea, Istituto Luce.

Giorno della civetta, Il (1968), Damiano Damiani. Production: Corona Cinematografica, Euro International Film (EIA), Les Films Corona, Panda Società per l'Industria Cinematografica.

Giro di lune tra terra e mare (1997), Giuseppe Gaudino. Production: Gaundri Film.

Goddess of 1967, The (2000), Clara Law. Production: New South Wales Film & Television Office.

Great Dictator, The (1940), Charlie Chaplin. Production: Charlie Chaplin Production.

Hamam – Il bagno turco (1997) Ferzan Ozpetek. Production: Asbrell Productions, Promete Film, Sorpasso Film.

Hannibal (2001), Ridley Scott. Production: Dino De Laurentiis Company, Metro-Goldwyn-Mayer, Scott Free Production, Universal Pictures.

He Died with a Felafel in His hands (2001), Richard Lowenstein. Production: Fandango, Notorious Films Pty Ltd.

Hotel Colonial (1987), Cinzia Th. Torrini. Production: Hemdale Film, Legeis Theatrical.

Jack Frusciante è uscito dal gruppo (1996), Enza Negroni. Production: Brosfilm, Medusa Produzione.

Jona che visse nella balena (1993), Roberto Faenza. Production: Focus Film (I), French Productions, Jean Vigo International, Raiuno, Dipartimento del Turismmo e dello Spettacolo, Eurimages.

Kamikazen – Ultima notte a Milano (1987), Gabriele Salvatores. Production: Colorado Film Production, Eurovision-Italia, Reteitalia.

Kaos (1984), Paolo and Vittorio Taviani. Production: Raiuno.

Kapò (1960), Gillo Pontecorvo. Production: Vides, Zebra Film, Cineriz.

King Kong (1976), John Guillermin. Production: Dino De Laurentiis Company, Paramount Pictures.

Kingdom of Heaven (2005), Ridley Scott. Production: Twentieth Century-Fox Film Corporation, Scott Free Productions, Cahoca Productions, Dritte Babelsberg Film, Inside Track 3, Kanzaman S.A., Reino del Cielo.

Ieri, oggi e domani (1964), Vittorio De Sica. Production: Compagnia

Cinematografica Champion, Les Films Concordia.

Immacolata e Concetta (1979), Salvatore Piscicelli. Production: Antea, Ministero del Turismo e dello Spettacolo.

In the bedroom (2001), Todd Field. Production: Good Machine, GreeneStreet Films, Standard Film Company.

Intervista, L' (1988), Federico Fellini. Production: Raiuno.

Io e il re (1995), Lucio Gaudino. Production: Duea Film.

Io non ho paura (2003), Gabriele Salvatores. Production: Colorado Film Production, Medusa Produzione, Alquimia Cinema, The Producers Films, Cattleya, Ministero per i Beni e le Attivit¡a Culturali.

Io sono un autarchico (1976), Nanni Moretti. Production: Moretti Production.

Italia-Germania 4 a 3 (1990), Andrea Barzini. Production: Radiotelevisione Italiana ().

Lacapagira (2000), Andrea Piva. Production: Kubla Khan, Mumbut.

Ladri di biciclette (1949), Vittorio De Sica. Production: Pds.

Ladri di saponette (1989), Maurizio Nichetti. Production: Bambù, Reteitalia.

Ladro di bambini (1992), Gianni Amelio. Production: Angelo Rizzoli per Erre produzioni, Alia Film, in collaboration with Raidue.

Lamerica (1994), Gianni Amelio. Production: Alia Film, Cecchi Gori Group Tiger Cinematografica, Arena Films, Vega Film, Eurimages.

Lantana (2001), Ray Lawrence. Australian Film Finance Corporation (AFFC), Jan Chapman Productions, MBP (Germany).

Last Kiss, The (2006), Tony Goldwyn. Production: Lakeshore Enterteinment.

Lawrence of Arabia (1962), David Lean. Production: Horizon Pictures, Columbia Pictures Corporation.

Legend of 1900, The (*La leggenda del pianista sull'oceano*) (1998), Giuseppe Tornatore. Production: Medusa Film.

Lezioni di volo (2007), Francesca Archibugi. Production: Cattleya, Babe Film, Rai Cinema, Acquarius Film, Khussro Films, Ministero per i Beni e le Attività Culturali.

Libera (1993), Pappi Corsicato. Production: Hathor Film.

Liberate i pesci (2000), Cristina Comencini. Production: Cattleya, Ministero per i Beni e le Attività Culturali.

Looking for Alibrandi (2000), Kate Woods. Production: Robyn Kershaw Productions.

Maledetti vi amerò (1980), Marco Tullio Giordana. Production: Cooperativa Jean Vigo, Filmalpha, Radiotelevisione Italiana (Raidue).

Malena (2000), Giuseppe Tornatore. Production: Medusa Produzione, Miramax Films, Pacific Pictures.

Manila paloma bianca (1992), Daniele Segre. Production: I Cammelli Film.

Mambo (1954), Robert Rossen. Production: Dino De Laurentiis Cinematografica, Paramount Pictures.

Man of Aran (1934), Robert Flaherty. Production: Gainsborough Pictures.

Mani sulla città, Le (1963), Francesco Rosi. Production: Galatea Film.

Manuale d'amore (2005), Giovanni Veronesi. Production: Filmauro srl.

Manuale d'amore 2 – Capitoli successivi (2007),Giovanni Veronesi. Production: Fimauro srl.

Marianna Ucrìa (1996), Roberto Faenza. Production: Cecchi Gori Group Tiger Cinematografica, Arcturus Productions, France 2 Cinéma, Canal+, Fabrica de Imagens.

Marrakech Express (1989), Gabriele Salvatores. Production: A.M.A. Film, Cecchi Gori Group Tiger Cinematografica.

Maschera, La (1987), Fiorella Inascelli. Production: Best, Ital-Noleggio Cinematografico, Istituto Luce, Radiotelevisione Italiana (Rai).

Match Point (2005), Woody Allen. BBC Films, Thema Production, Jada Productions, Kudu Films, Bank of Ireland, Invicta Caapital.

Matilda (1991), Antonietta de Lillo, Giorgio Maglioulo. Production: AnGio Film, SoCoF.

Matrimonio all'italiana (1964), Vittorio De Sica. Production: Compagnia Cinematografica Champion, Les Films Concordia.

Mayis Sikintis (Clouds of May), (1999), Nuri Bilge Ceylan. Production: NBC Ajans.

Mediterraneo (1991), Gabriele Salvatores. Production: A.M.A. Film, Penta Film.

Meglio gioventù, La (2003), Marco Tullio Giordana. Production: BiBiFilm, Rai Cinemafiction.

Mery per sempre (1989), Marco Risi. Production: Int Sel, Numero Uno

International.

Messa è finita, La (1985), Nanni Moretti. Production: Faso Film srl.

Mia generazione, La (1996), Wilma Labate. Production: Radiotelevisione Italiana (Rai), Dania Film, Compact Productions.

Mignon è partita (1988), Francesca Archibugi. Production: Chrysalide Film, Ellepi Films.

Mio fratello è figlio unico (2007), Daniele Luchetti. Production: Cattleya, Babe Film.

Mio miglior nemico, Il (2006), Carlo Verdone. Production: Filmauro srl.

Miracolo, Il (2004), Edoardo Winspeare. Production: Rai Cinema, Sidecar Films & TV, Ministero per i Beni e le Attività Culturali.

Morte di un matematico napoletano (1992), Mario Martone. Production: AnGio Film, Radiotelevision Italiana (Raitre), Teatri Uniti.

Mostro, Il (1994), Roberto Benigni. Production: IRIS Films, La Sept Cinema, Melampo Cinematografica, UGC Images.

My House in Umbria (2003), Richard Loncrain. Production: Canine Films, Home Box Office (HBO), Panorama Films.

Nanook of the North (1922), Robert J. Flaherty. Production: Les Frères Revillon, Pathé Exchange.

Natale a New York (2006), Neri Parenti. Production: Filmauro srl.

Nemici d'infanzia (1995), Luigi Magni. Production: Istituto Luce, Radiotelevisione Italiana, Telecinestar Srl.

Nirvana (1997), Gabriele Salvatores. Production: Cecchi Gori Group Tiger Cinematografica, Colorado Films, Davis-Films.

Nitrato d'argento (1996), Marco Ferreri. Production: Salomé SA, Audifilm, Eurimages, Canal+, Le Centre National de la Cinématographie, Radiotelevisione Italiana, Hungarian Television.

Nome della rosa, Il (1986), Jean Jacques Annaud. Production: Cristaldifilm, France 3 Cinéma, Les Films Ariane, Neue Constantin Film, Rai Uno Radiotelevisione Italiana, Zweites Deutsches Fernsehen (ZDF).

Notte, La (1961), Michelangelo Antonioni.

Notte italiana (1987), Carlo Mazzacurati. Production: Angelo Barbagallo and Nanni Moretti.

Notte di San Lorenzo, La (1982), Paolo and Vittorio Taviani. Production:Ager, Rai.

Notti di Cabira (1957), Federico Fellini. Production: Dino de Laurentiis Cinematografica, Les Films Marceau.

Nuovo cinema Paradiso (1988), Giuseppe Tornatore. Production: Cristaldifilm, Films Ariane, Raitre, TF1 Film Production, with the collaboration of Forum Pictures.

Occasioni di Rosa, Le (1981), Salvatore Piscicelli. Production: Piscicelli, Salvatore.

Occhiali d'oro, Gli (1987), Giuliano Montaldo. Production: Reteitalia, L.P. Films srl, Paradis Films, Avala Film, DMV Distribuzione.

Odissea, L' (1968), Franco Rossi, television series, seven parts. Radiotelevisione Italiana.

Ormai è fatta (1999), Enzo Monteleone. Production: Hera International Film, Rai, Dipartimento dello Spettacolo e del Turismo, Ministero per i Beni e le Attività Culturali.

Oro di Napoli, L' (1954), Vittorio De Sica. Production: Ponti-De Laurentiis Cinematografica.

Oro di Roma, L' (1961), Carlo Lizzani. Production: Lux Film.

Padre Padrone (1977), Paolo and Vittorio Taviani. Production: Raidue, Cinema.

Padre Pio (2000), television program, three parts, Carlo Carlei. Canale 5.

Paisà (1947), Roberto Rossellini. Production: Mario Conti and Roberto Rossellini for the Organizzazione Film Internazionali, with the collaboration of Rod E. Geiger for Foreign Film Production.

Palombella rossa (1989), Nanni Moretti. Production: Sacher Film, Palmyre Film, Raiuno, So.Fin.A.

Pane, amore e... (1955), Dino Risi. Production: Titanus.

Pane, amore e fantasia (1953), Luigi Comencini. Production: Titanus, Girosi.

Pane, amore e gelosia (1954), Luigi Comencini. Production: Titanus.

Pane e tulipani (2000), Silvio Soldini. Production: Istituto Luce, Rai Cinemafiction, Amka Films Productions, Monogatari, Televisione Svizzera Italiana (TSI), Ministero per i Beni e le Attività Culturali.

Partigiano Johnny (2000), Guido Chiesa. Production: Fandango, MediaTrade, Ministero per i Beni e le Attività Culturali, Tele+.

Pasolini, un delitto italiano (1995), Marco Tullio Giordana. Production: CGG Leopold Srl, Cecchi Gori Group Tiger Cinematografica, Flach Film, Numero Cinque Srl, Tiger.

Pasqualino Settebellezze (1975), Lina Wertmuller. Production: Medusa.

Paura e amore (1988), Margarethe von Trotta. Production: Bioskop Film, Cinémax, Erre Produzioni, Westdeutscher Rundfunk (WDR).

Pesce innamorato, Il (1999), Leonardo Pieraccioni. Production: Cecchi Gori Entertainment Europa, Vertigo Film.

Pianese Nunzio 14 anni a maggio (1996), Antonio Capuano. Production: A.M.A. Film, GMF, Istituto Luce, Mediaset.

Piccoli fuochi (1985), Peter Dal Monte. Production: Produzioni Intersound.

Piccoli maestri, I (1998), Daniele Luchetti. Production: Cecchi Gori Group Tiger Cinematografica.

Piccolo mondo antico (1940), Mario Soldati. Production: Artisti Tecnici Associati (ATA), Industrie Cinematografiche Italiane (ICI).

Pizzicata (1996), Edoardo Winspeare. Production: Classic, Horres Film + TV, Süddeutscher Rundfunk (SDR).

Placido Rizzotto (2000), Pasquale Scimeca. Production: Arbash, Ministero per i Beni e le Attività Culturali, Rai Cinemafaction.

Polvere di Napoli (1998), Antonio Capuano. Production: A.M.A. Film, GMF, Radiotelevisione italiana.

Portaborse, Il (1991), Daniele Luchetti. Production: Sacher Film, Eidoscope Productions, Baufilm, Pyramide Productions, Ciné Cinq, Canal Plus Productions.

Portiere di notte (1974), Liliana Cavani. Production: Lotar Film.

Porzûs (1997), Renzo Martinelli. Production: Videomaura in collaboration with Progetto Immagine, Martinelli Film, Rai, Presidenza del Consiglio Dipartimento dello Spettacolo, European Script Fund (MEDIA program).

Postino, Il (1995), Michael Radford. Production: Cecchi Gori Group Tiger Cinematografica, Penta Film, Esterno Mediterraneo Film, Blue Dahlia Productions, K2TWO.

Poveri ma belli (1957), Dino Risi. Production: S.G.C., Titanus.

Preferisco il rumore del mare (2000), Mimmo Calopresti. Arcapix, Bianca Film,

Canal+, Mikado Film, Radiotelevisione Italiana.

Prise du pouvoir par Louis XIV (*La presa del potere di Luigi XIV*) (1966), Roberto Rossellini. Production: Radiodiffusion Française (ORTF), Radiotelevisione Italiana.

Processo per stupro (1978), Loredana Torti, Annabella Miscuglio. Radiotelevisione Italiana.

Professione: reporter (1975), Michelangelo Antonioni. Production: Compagnia Cinematografica Champion, CIPI Cinematografica SA, Les Films Concordia.

Puerto Escondido (1992), Gabriele Salvatores. Production: Colorado Film Production, Pentafilm, Silvio Berlusconi Communications.

Pummarò, (1990), Michele Placido. Production: CinEuropa 92, Numero Uno Cinematografica Srl, Radiotelevisione Italiana (Rai).

Pursuit of Happiness (2004), Gabriele Muccino. Production: Columbia Pictures Corporation, Relativity Media, Overbrook Entertainment, Escape Artists.

Puzzle Therapy (1976), Annabella Miscuglio.

Quo Vadis, Baby? (2006), Gabriele Salvatores. Production: Colorado Films.

Racconti di Vittoria (1996), Antonietta de Lillo. Production: Angio Fim, Bianca Film.

Radiofreccia (1998), Luciano Ligabue. Production: Domenico Procacci for Fandango, Medusa Film, Tele+.

Rain Main (1988), Barry Levinson. Production: United Artists, Guber-Peters Company, The, Mirage Entertainment, Star Partners II Ltd.

Ratataplan (1979), Maurizio Nichetti. Production: Vides.

Regalo di Natale (1986), Pupi Avati. Production: DMV Distribuzione, Duea Film.

Respiro (2002), Emanuele Crialese. Production: Eurimages, Fandango, Les Films des Tournelles, Medusa Produzione, Roissy Films, Rouse Films, TPS Cinéma, Telepiù.

Ricordati di me (2003), Gabriele Muccino. Production: Fandango, Medusa Produzione, Telepiù, Vice Versa Film.

Ripley's Game (2002), Liliana Cavani. Production: Baby Films, Cattleya, Mr. Mudd.

Riso amaro (1949), Giuseppe De Santis. Production: Lux Film.

Rocco e i suoi fratelli (1960), Luchino Visconti. Production: Titanus, Les Films Marceau.

Rome (2004-2006), television series, Home Box Office HBO.

Room with a View (1985), James Ivory. Production: Goldcrest Films International, National Film Finance Corporation (NFFC), Curzon Film Distributors, Film Four International, Merchant Ivory Productions.

Sabato, domenica e lunedì (1990), Lina Wertmuller. Production: Reteitalia.

Salò o le 120 giornate di Sodoma (1975), Pier Paolo Pasolini. Production: Pea, Artistes Associés.

Salvatore Giuliano (1962), Francesco Rosi. Production: Lux Vides, Galatea.

Sangue Vivo (2000), Edoardo Winspeare. Production: Ministero per i Beni e le Attività Culturali, Sidecar Film & TV.

Sasso in bocca, Il (1970), Giuliano Ferrara. Production: Cine 2000.

Saturno contro (2007), Ferzan Ozpetek. Production: AFS Film, Fars-Films, R&C Produzioni, UGCYM.

Schegge (1988), Television program, Raitre.

Schindler's List (1993), Steven Spielberg. Production: Universal Pictures, Amblin Entertainment.

Sciuscià (1946), Vittorio De Sica. Production: Alfa Cinematografica.

Scorta, La (1994), Rocky Tognazzi. Production: Claudio Bonivento Productions.

Seconda volta, La (1995), Mimmo Calopresti. Production: Banfilm, La Sept Cinéma, Sacher Film, Raiuno, Canal+.

Sedotta e abbandonata (1963), Pietro Germi.

Senso (1954), Luchino Visconti. Production: Lux Film.

Senza pelle (1994), Alessandro D'Alatri. Production: Istituto Luce, Radiotelevisione Italiana (Rai), Rodeo Drive.

Sequestrati di Altona, I (1962), Vittorio De Sica. Production: Titanus, Société Génnérale de Cinématographie.

Serpico (1973), Sydney Lumet. Production: Artists Entertainment Complex, Produzioni De Laurentiis International Manufacturing Company.

Seven Pounds (2009, pre-production), Gabriele Muccino. Production: Columbia Pictures, Escape Artists, Overbrook Entertainment.

Shoah (1985), Claude Lanzmann. Production: Historia, Les Films Aleph,

Ministère de la Culture de la Republique Française.

Silence of the Lambs, The (1991), Jonathan Demme. Production: Orion Pictures Corporation, Strong Heart/Demme Production.

Sodoma and Gomorrah (1962), Robert Aldrich. Production: Pathé Cinéma, S.G.C., Titanus.

Sole anche di notte, Il (1990), Paolo and Vittorio Taviani. Production: Capoul, Direkt-Film, Eurimages, Filmtre, Interpool, Rai Uno Radiotelevisione Italiana, Sara Film.

Sorpasso, Il (1962), Dino Risi. Production: Fair Film, Incei Film, Savero Film.

Sostiene Pereira (1995), Roberto Faenza. Production: Fàbrica de Imagens, Instituto Português da Arte Cinematográfica e Ausdiovisual (IPACA), Jean Vigo International, K.G. Productions.

Sovversivi (1967), Paolo and Vittorio Taviani. Production: Ager Cinematografica.

Splendor (1989), Ettore Scola. Production: Studi El, Gaumont.

Stanza del figlio, La (2000), Nanni Moretti. Production: Bac Films, Canal+, Rai Cinemafiction, Sacher Film, Telepiù.

Stanza dello scirocco (1997), Maurizio Sciarra. Production: Fandango.

Stazione, La (1990), Sergio Rubini. Production: Fandango, Ministero del Turismo e dello Spettacolo.

Stella che non c'è (2006), Gianni Amelio. Production: Cattleya, Babe Film, Rai Cinema, Radiotelevisione Svizzera Italiana (RTSI), Carac Films, ACHABB Film, Oak 3 Films, Ministero per i Beni e le Attività Culturali.

Storia del cammello che piange, La (2005), Byambasuren Davaa, Luigi Falorni. Production: Hochschule für Fernsehen und Film München (HFF), Bayerischer Rundfunk (BR), FilmFernsehFonds Bayern.

Strada, La (1954), Federico Fellini. Production: Ponti, De Laurentiis.

Sud (1993), Gabriele Salvatores. Production: Cecchi Gori Group Tiger Cinematografica, Colorado Film Production.

Sud Side Stori (2000), Roberta Torre. Production: Gam Films, Istituto Luce, Ministero per i Beni e le Attività Culturali.

Talented Mr Ripley, The (1999), Anthony Minghella. Production: Mirage Enterprises, Miramax Films, Paramount Pictures, Timnick Films.

Tano da morire (1997), Roberta Torre. Production: A.S.P. Srl, Dania Film, Lucky

Red, Radiotelevisione Italiana (Raitre), Tele+, VIP National Audiovisual.

Tea with Mussolini (*Te con Mussolini*) (1999), Franco Zeffirelli. Cattleya, Cineritmo, Film & General Productions Ltd., Medusa Produzione.

Teatro di guerra (1998), Mario Martone. Production: Lucky Red, Rai Cinemafiction, Teatri Uniti.

Terra trema, La (1948), Luchino Visconti. Production: Universalia Film.

Terrazza, La (1980), Ettore Scola. Production: Dean Film, International Dean, Les Films Marceau-Cocinor.

Three Days of the Condor (1975), Sydney Pollack. Production: Dino De Laurentiis Company, Paramount Pictures, Wildwood Enterprises.

Titus (1999), Julie Taymor. Production: Clear Blue Sky Productions, Overseas FilmGroup, Urania Pictures Srl, NDF International, Titus Productions Ltd.

To Be or not to Be (1942), Ernest Lubitsch. Production: Romain Film Corporation.

Tormento (1950), Raffaello Matarazzo. Production: Labor Film, Titanus.

Tornando a casa (2001), Vincenzo Marra. Production: Classic.

Totò che visse due volte (1998), Daniele Ciprì and Franco Maresco. Production: Istituto Luce, Lucky Red, Tea Nova.

Tracker, The (2002), Rolf De Heer. Production: Vertigo Productions Pty. Ltd.

Trasgredire (2000), Tinto Brass. Production: Lions Pictures.

Tre metri sopra il cielo (2004), Luca Lucini. Production: Cattleya.

Tregua, La (1996), Francesco Rosi. Production: Leo Pescarolo and Guido De Laurentiis for 3Emme Cinematografica, Stephan Films, UCG Images, T&Cfilm AG, DaZuFilm.

Troy (2004), Wolfgang Petersen. Production: Warner Bros. Pictures, Radiant Productions, Plan B Entertainment.

Turné (1990), Gabriele Salvatores. Production: A.M.A. Film, Reteitalia, Tiger Cinematografica.

Tutti a casa (1960), Luigi Comencini. Production: Dino De Laurentiis.

Tutti giù per terra (1997), Davide Ferrario. Production: Hera International Film.

U-571 (2000), John Mostow. Production: Canal Plus Image International, Universal Pictures.

Uccello dalle piume di cristallo (date), Dario Argento. Production: Central Cinema

Company Film (CCC), Glazier, Seda Spettacoli.

Ultimi giorni di Pompei, Gli (1908), Luigi Maggi. Production: Ambrosio.

Ultimi giorni di Pompei, Gli (1913), Eleuterio Rodolfi. Production: Società Anonima Ambrosio.

Ultimi giorni di Pompei, Gli (1926), Carmine Gallone, Amleto Palermi. Production: Società Italiana Grandi Film.

Ultimo bacio, L' (2001), Gabriele Muccino. Production: Fandango, Medusa Produzione.

Ultimo imperatore, L' (1987), Bernardo Bertolucci. Production: Yanco Films Limited, Recorded Picture Company (RPC), Screenframe Ltd, AAA Productions, Soprofilms, TAO Film.

Ultimo tango a Parigi (1972), Bernardo Bertolucci. Production: Produzioni Europee Associati (PEA), Les Productions Artistes Associés.

Umberto D (1952), Vittorio De Sica. Production: Amato Film, De Sica, Rizzoli Film.

Uomo da bruciare, Un (1962), Paolo and Vittorio Taviani. Ager Cinematografica, Alfa Cinematografica, Sancro Film.

Up at the villa (2000), Philip Haas. Production: Intermedia Films, Mirage Entertainment, October Films, Universal Pictures.

Va dove ti porta il cuore (1996), Cristina Comencini. Production: GMT Productions, Por-ject Filmproduktion, Videa.

Vaghe stelle dell'Orsa (1965), Luchino Visconti. Production: Vides.

Venerdì sera, lunedì mattina (1983), Pianciola-Chiantaretto.

Vera vita di Antonio H., La (1994), Enzo Monteleone. Production: Gianfranco Piccioli, Istituto Luce, Bellatrik Pictures.

Verso Sud (1992), Pasquale Pozzessere. Production: Demian Films.

Viaggio in Italia (1954), Roberto Rossellini. Production: Sveva Film, Junior Film, Italia Film, Francinex, Les Films Ariane, S.E.C.

Vita di Leonardo da Vinci, La (1971), television program, five parts, Renato Castellani. Rai.

Vita è bella, La (1997), Roberto Benigni. Production: Cecchi Gori Group Tiger Cinematografica, Melampo Cinematografica.

Vita coi figli (1990), Dino Risi. Production: International Video 80, Reteitalia.

Vito e gli altri (1991), Antonio Capuano. No production data are available.

Viulentemente (1982), Carlo Vanzina. Production: Horizon Productions srl, Paneuropean production Pictures.

War and Peace (1955), King Vidor. Production: Paramount Pictures, Ponti-De Laurentiis Cinematografica.

William Seakespeare's A Midsummer Night's Dream (1999), Michael Hoffman. Production: Fox Searchlight Pictures, Regency Enterprises, Taurus Film, Panoramica.

Zabriskie Point (1970), Michelangelo Antonioni. Production: Metro-Goldwyn-Mayer, Trianon Productions.

BIBLIOGRAPHY

Adamo, Pietro, 1998, 'La colonna musicale del 1968', *Bollettino Archivio G. Pinelli*, no. 11, pp. 48–50.

Allen, Robert C. and Gomery, Douglas, 1985, *Film History: Theory and Practice*, McGraw-Hill, New York.

Anderson, Jason, 2003, 'Island of lust dreams: Emanuele Crialese's *Respiro* offers Italian emotion and magnificent scenery', *Eye Weekly*, 7 December.

Associated Press, 'North Carolina wins studio war', *The Globe and Mail*, 16 .

Associazione Nazionale Industrie Cinematografiche Audiovisive e Multimediali (ANICA), 2004, *Il cinema italiano in numeri*.

Associazione Nazionale Industrie Cinematografiche Audiovisive e Multimediali (ANICA), 2006, *Il cinema italiano in numeri, 2000–2006*.

Associazione per l'economia della cultura, 2005, *Rapporto sull'economia della cultura in Italia, 1990–2000*, Roma. Available: www.primaonline.it Accessed 19/7/2007.

Bagella, Michele, 2000, 'L'economia latitante', in V. Zagarrio (ed.), *Il cinema della transizione: Scenari italiani degli anni Novanta*, Marsilio, Venezia, pp. 249–63.

Bakhtin, Mikhail, 1986, *Speech Genres and Other Late Essays*, University of Texas Press, Austin.

Baudrillard, Jean, 1988, *America*, Verso, London.

Benjamin, Walter, 1969, *Illuminations*, Schocken Books, New York.

Bernardini, Aldo, 1978, 'Nascita ed evoluzione delle strutture del primo cinema italiano', *Bianco e Nero*, no. 2, March/April, pp. 3–65.

Bertellini, Giorgio (ed.), 2004, *The Cinema of Italy*, Wallflower, London.

Betz, Mark, 2001, 'The name above the (Sub)title: Internationalism, coproduction, and polyglot European art cinema', *Camera Obscura*, vol. 16, no. 1, pp. 1–45. Special issue of *Marginality and Alterity in New European Cinemas*, Part 2.

Bibliography

Bhabha, Homi K., 1994, *The Location of Culture*, Routledge, London.

Bice, Kathrine, 1987, 'Worldwide link strengthen', *Financial Review*, 22 June, p. 40.

Bichon, Alain, 2000, 'Lo specchio rinnovato: per una valutazione del cinema italiano', in V. Zagarrio (ed.), *Il cinema della transizione: Scenari italiani degli anni Novanta*, Marsilio, Venezia, pp. 111–23.

Binetti, Vincenzo, 1997, 'Marginalità e appartenenza: la funzione dell'intellettuale tra sfera pubblica e privato nell'Italia del dopoguerra', *Italica*, vol. 74, no. 3, pp. 361–74.

Bo, Fabio, 1996, 'Dieci anni di solitudine. Dall'autobiografismo alla "desistenza" narrativa', in M. Sesti (ed.), *La 'scuola' italiana: Storia, strutture e immaginario di un altro cinema (1988–1996)*, Marsilio, Venezia, pp. 25–38.

Boatti, G., 1999 [1993], *Piazza Fontana: 12 dicembre 1969: il giorno dell'innocenza perduta*, Einaudi, Torino.

Bondanella, Peter, 2001 [1983], *From Neorealism to Present*, Continuum, London.

Bono, Francesco, 1995, 'Cinecittà – Italian motion picture studios', *UNESCO Courier*, July–August.

Bosworth, Richard, 1993, *Explaining Auschwitz and Hiroshima: History Writing and the Second World War 1945–1990*, Routledge, London.

Bozza, Gian Luigi, 1995, 'Pasolini: il peso di un'assenza', *Cineforum*, October, pp. 56–58.

Brunetta, Gian Piero, 1982, *Storia del cinema italiano: dal 1945 agli anni Ottanta*, Editori Riuniti, Roma.

Brunetta, Gian Piero, 1991, *Cent'anni di cinema italiano*, Laterza, Roma-Bari.

Brunetta, Gian Piero, 1993 (1982), *Storia del cinema italiano: il cinema muto 1895–1929*, vol. 1, Editori Riuniti, Roma.

Brunetta, Gian Piero, 1994, 'The long march of American cinema in Italy: From Fascism to the Cold War', in D.W. Ellwood and R. Kroes (eds), *Hollywood in Europe: Experiences of a Cultural Hegemony*, VU University Press, Amsterdam, pp. 139–54.

Brunetta, Gian Piero, 1998 [1982], *Storia del cinema italiano: dal neorealismo al miracolo economico 1945–1959*, vol. 3, Editori Riuniti, Roma.

Brunetta, Gian Piero, 1998 [1982], *Storia del cinema italiano: dal miracolo economico agli anni Novanta*, vol. 4, Editori Riuniti, Rome.

Bruno, Edoardo, 1972, 'Prefazione', in G. Della Volpe et al. (eds), *Teorie e prassi del cinema italiano: 1950–1970*, Mazzotta Editore, Milano, pp. I–XVIII.

Bruno, Giuliana, 1993, *Streetwalking on a Ruined Map*, Princeton University Press, Princeton.

Bruno, Giuliana, 2007, *Atlas of Emotion*, Verso, London.

Brunsdon, Charlotte, 1989, 'Problems with quality', *Screen*, no. 1, pp. 67–90.

Bryson, N. 1990, *Looking at the Overlooked: Four Essays on Still Life Painting*, Harvard University Press, Cambridge.

Bruzzone, M.G., 1989, 'Produttori alla riscossa per "salvare il cinema"', *La Stampa*, 28 May.

Buoanno, Milly, 2005, 'The "sailor" and the "peasant": The Italian police series between foreign and domestic', *Media International Australia*, no. 115, pp. 48–59.

Burke, Frank, 1996, *Fellini's Films: From Postwar to Postmodern*, Twayne, New York.

Caponio, Tiziana, Nielsen, Annette and Ribas Mateos, Natalia, 2000, 'The policy mirror mechanism: The case of Turin', *Papers 60,* available www.bib.uab.es/pub/papers/02102862_n60p67.pdf. Accessed April 2006.

Cappellieri, Alba, 2007, *Moda e Design: il progetto dell'eccellenza*, Franco Angeli, Milan.

Caratozzolo, Vittoria Caterina, 2006, *Irene Brin: Italian Style in Fashion*, Marsilio, Venezia.

Cardini, Francesco, 1997, *L'ombra del tempo: Memoria e passato dei programmi televisi*, RAI VQPT, no. 146, RAI Radiotelevisione Italiana, Roma.

Cassano, Franco, 2007 [1996], *Pensiero meridiano*, Laterza, Bari.

Castoriadis, Cornelius, 1997, *The Castoriadis Reader*, Blackwell, Oxford.

Cereda, Giuseppe, 1996, 'Piccoli schermi e grandi antenne', in M. Sesti (ed.), *La 'scuola' italiana: Storia, strutture e immaginario di un altro cinema (1988–1996)*, Marsilio, Venezia, pp, 239–47.

Chabod, F. 1976, *Storia della politica estera italiana: dal 1870 al 1896*, Laterza, Roma-Bari.

Ch, P. 1979, 'Noi orfani', *L'espresso*, n. 11, 18 March, pp. 98-105.

Clark, Martin, 1996, *Modern Italy 1871–1995*, Longman, London.

Bibliography

Clarke, David B., 1997, *The Cinematic City*, Routledge, London.

Clerici, S. and Di Pietro, A., 1991, '1951: C'è una speranza per gli italiani, è la seicento', *il Venerdì di la Repubblica*, 18 October.

Coe, Neil M., 2000, 'On location: American capital and the local labour market in the Vancouver film industry', *International Journal of Urban and Regional Research*, vol. 21, no. 1, March, pp. 79–94.

Cohen, Robin and Kennedy, Paul 2000, *Global Sociology*, Macmillan, London.

Corrigan, Timothy, 1991, *A Cinema without Walls: Movies and Culture after Vietnam*, Rutgers University Press, New Brunswick, NJ.

Coletti, Elisabetta Anna, 2000, '"Made in Italy" label gains celluloid cachet', *Christian Science Monitor*, 4 October.

Contini, G., 1997, *La memoria divisa*, Rizzoli, Milano.

Cooke, Philip and Lazzeretti, Luciana (eds), 2008, *Creative Cities, Cultural Clusters and Local Economic Development*, Edward Elgar, Cheltenham, UK.

Cosolovich, G., 2002, 'Italian producer sets up local production', *The Age*, 5 March.

Council of Europe/ERI/Carts, 2002, *Cultural Policies in Europe: A Compendium of Basic Facts and Trends: Italy*. Available from: www.culturalpolicies.net. Accessed 20/3/2006.

Crary, J. 1990, *Techniques of the Observer: On Vision and Modernity in the Nineteenth Century*, MIT Press, Cambridge, MA.

Cremonini, G. 1987, *Storia generale del cinema*, Lucarini, Roma.

Crespi, Alberto, 1990, 'RAI: I politici della produzione', in *Sperduti nel buio*, supplement to *Cineforum*, no. 292, March.

Crofts, Stephen, 1992, 'Reconceptualizing national cinema/s', *Quarterly Review of Film & Video*, vol. 14, no. 3, pp. 49–67.

Croteau, David and Hoynes, William, 2003, *Media Society: Industries, Images and Audiences*, Pine Forge Press, Thousand Oaks, CA.

Cucchiarelli, P. and Giannuli, A., 1997, *Lo stato parallelo*, Gamberetti Editrice, Roma.

D'Agostini, P. 1996, 'Un altro cinema. Voci e segnali del nuovo', in M. Sesti (ed.), *La 'scuola' italiana: Storia, strutture, immaginario di un altro cinema*

1988–1996, Marsilio, Venezia, pp. 39–47.

De Martino, Ernesto, 1961, *La terra del rimorso*, Il Saggiatore, Milan.

Della Volpe, Galvano et al., 1972, *Teorie e prassi del cinema italiano: 1950–1970*, Mazzotta Editore, Milano.

Di Giovanni, E.M. and Ligini, M., 2000, *La strage di stato. Controinchiesta*, Odradek, Roma.

Di Stefano, John, 2002, 'Moving images of home', *Art Journal*, vol. 61, no. 4, pp. 38–51.

Diamante, Ilvo and Lazar, Marc, 1997, *Stanchi di miracoli: Il sistema politico italiano in cerca di normalità*, Guerini e Associati, Milano.

Dianese, M. and Bettin G., 1999, *La strage: Piazza Fontana. Verità e memoria*, Feltrinelli, Milano.

Eco, Umberto, 1983, 'New developments in the mass media of contemporary Italy', *Altropoto*, pp. 109–25.

Elsaesser, Thomas, 1998, 'Digital cinema: Delivery, event, time', in T. Elsaesser and K. Hoffmann (eds), *Cinema Futures: Cain, Abel or Cable? The Screen Arts in the Digital Age*, Amsterdam University Press, Amsterdam, pp. 201–22.

Elsaesser, Thomas, 1989, *New German Cinema: A History*, Rutgers University Press, New Brunswick, NJ.

Emmer, Luciano and Gras, Enrico, 1947, 'The film renaissance in Italy', *Hollywood Quarterly*, vol. 2, no. 4, pp. 353–58.

Engelmeier, Regine and Engelmeier Peter W., 1997, *Fashion in Film*, Prestel, Munich.

European Audiovisual Observatory, 2002, *Imbalance of Trade in Films and Television Programmes between North America and Europe Continues to Deteriorate*, Available www.obs.coe.int/about/oea/pr/desequilibre.html. Accessed 8/10/2007.

European Audiovisual Observatory, 2006, *Rapporto Italia Francia, Prima parte.*

European Cinema Journal – MEDIA Salles, 2003, 'Multiplexes: A research study by the Bocconi University using MEDIA Salles data', no.1, February.

Fantoni Minnella, Maurizio, 2004, *Non riconciliati: Politica e società nel cinema italiano dal neorealismo a oggi*, UTET, Torino.

Bibliography

Fasanella, G., Sestieri, C. and Pellegrino, G., 2000, *Segreto di stato: la verità da Gladio al caso Moro*, Einaudi, Torino.

Ferrero, Adelio, 1972, 'La critica e l'organizzazione del pubblico', in A. Ferrero et al., *Responsabilità sociali e culturali della critica cinematografica*, Marsilio Editori, Padova, pp. 9–18.

Ferrero-Regis, Tiziana, 2004, 'Pizza Down-Under: Italo-Australian co-productions', in E. Davies and A. Moran (eds), *Film and Television in Context: Working Papers in Communications*, nos. 4/5, pp. 79–82.

Ferrero-Regis, Tiziana, 2006, '*Open City*: Rossellini and neorealism, sixty years later', *Screening the Past*, December, no. 20, December.

Ferrucci, Riccardo, 1995, 'A journey to the south', in R. Ferrucci and P. Turini (eds), *Paolo and Vittorio Taviani: Poetry of the Italian Landscape*, Gremese, Roma, pp. 126–28.

Finney, Angus, 1996, *The State of European Cinema: A New Dose of Reality*, Cassell, London.

Florida, Richard 2002, *The Rise of the Creative Class: And How It's Transforming, Work, Leisure, Community and Everyday Life*, Basic Books, New York.

Fofi, Goffredo, 1994, 'Cinema: raccontare il paese e la società', in P. Ginsborg (ed.), *Stato dell'Italia*, Il Saggiatore/Mondadori, Milano, pp. 593–96.

Fofi, Goffredo, 1997, 'Regista fa rima con conformista', *Panorama*, no. 36, pp. 150–51.

Folli, S., 1995, 'De Felice né rosso né nero', *Corriere della Sera*, 2 September.

Foucault, Michel, 1977, 'What is an author?', in D.F. Bouchard (ed.), *Language, Counter-Memory, Practice: Selected Essays and Interviews*, Cornell University Press, Ithaca, NY, pp. 113–38.

Friendly, Alfred, 1970, 'Laurentiis quits making films: Woes mount for Italian industry', *New York Times*, 31 January.

Fröbel, F., Heinrichs, J. and Kreye, O., 1980, *The New International Division of Labour*, Cambridge University Press, Cambridge.

Fusco, M.P. 1998, 'Noi, dilettanti della guerra', *la Repubblica*, 20 August.

Galimberti, Mario, 1996, 'Minimalismo', in M. Sesti (ed.), *La 'scuola' italiana: storia, strutture e immaginario di un altro cinema (1988–1996)*, Marsilio,

Venezia, pp. 365–72.

Galt, Rosalind, 2002, 'Italy's landscapes of loss: Historical mourning and the dialectical image in *Cinema Paradiso*, *Mediterraneo* and *Il postino*', *Screen*, no. 432, Summer, pp. 158–73.

Garofalo, Pietro, 2002, 'Seeing red: The Soviet influence on Italian cinema in the thirties', in J. Reich and P. Garofalo (eds), *Re-viewing Fascism: Italian Cinema, 1922–1943*, Indiana University Press, Bloomington and Indianapolis, pp. 223–49.

Giannuli, Aldo, 2001, 'L'insostenibile leggerezza del revisionismo storico', *Libertaria*, no. 1, January/March, pp. 58–64.

Gili, Jean A., 1988, 'Le nouveau cinéma italien au bout du tunnel', *Positif*, no. 333, November, pp. 39–40.

Ginsborg, Paul, 1990, *A History of Contemporary Italy: Society and Politics 1943–1988*, Penguin, London.

Ginzburg, C. and Prosperi, A., 1975, *Giochi di pazienza: Un seminario sul Beneficio di Cristo*, Einaudi, Torino.

Goldsmith, Ben and O'Regan, Tom, 2003, *Cinema Cities, Media Cities: The Contemporary International Studio Complex*, Australian Film Commission, Sydney, Australian Key Centre for Media and Cultural Policy, Brisbane, and Creative Industries Research and Applications Centre, Brisbane.

Goldsmith, Ben and O'Regan, Tom, 2005, *The Film Studio: Film Production in the Global Economy*, Rowman & Littlefield, Lanham, NJ.

Grassi, Raffaella, 1997, *Territori di fuga. Il cinema di Gabriele Salvatores*, Edizioni Falsopiano, Alessandria.

Grasso, Aldo, 2000 [1992], *Storia della televisione italiana*, Garzanti, Milan.

Guback, Thomas H., 1969, *The International Film Industry: Western Europe and America since 1945*, Indiana University Press, Bloomington, IN.

Gundle, Stephen, 2000, *Between Hollywood and Moscow: The Italian Communists and the Challenge of Mass Culture, 1943–1991*, Duke University Press, Durham, NC.

Günsberg, Maggie, 2005, *Italian Cinema: Gender and Genre*, Palgrave Macmillan, New York.

Harvey, David, 1990, *The Condition of Postmodernity: An Inquiry into the Origins of Cultural Change,* Blackwell, Cambridge. MA.

Harvey, Silvia, 1996, 'What is cinema? The sensuous, the abstract and the political', in C. Williams (ed.), *Cinema: The Beginnings and the Future,* Westminster, London, pp. 228–52.

Hayward, Susan, 1993, *French National Cinema,* Routledge, London.

Higson, Andrew, 1989, 'The concept of national cinema', *Screen,* vol. 30, no. 4, pp. 36–46.

Higson, Andrew, 1993, 'Re-presenting the national past: Nostalgia and pastiche in the heritage film', in L. Friedman (ed.), *Fires Were Started: British Cinema and Thatcherism,* University College Press, London.

Hill, John, 'The future of European cinema: The economics and culture of pan-European strategies', in J. Hill, M. McLoone and P. Hainsworth (eds), *Border Crossing: Film in Ireland, Britain and Europe,* Institute of Irish Studies in association with the University of Ulster and the British Film Institute, London, pp. 53–80.

Hope, William, (ed.), 2005, *Italian Cinema: New Directions,* P. Lang, Frankfurt.

Huyssen, Andreas, 1986, *After the Great Divide: Modernism, Mass Culture, Postmodernism,* Indiana University Press, Bloomington, IN.

Il settore cinematografico italiano: *Analisi strutturale e identificazione strategie di marketing per un newcomer,* 1998, Rapporto finale di ricerca. Una ricerca ISICULT (Istituto Italiano per l'industria culturale) per Mediaset.

Irish Times, 'Italian Stallion', 9 February, p. 8.

Ires Piemonte 2004 *Ricerca Atlas,* 'Dinamiche socio-economiche', Part 2. Available: www.ires-biblioteca.it/sito%20Atlas%(html)_agosto2004/file %20Atlas/Rapporti/DinamicheSocioEconomiche.pdf. Accessed 15/2/ 2007.

Italian Film Commission, 2007, *A Production Guide,* Available: www.filminginitaly.com. Accessed 30/3/2007.

Jameson, Fredric, 1979, 'Reification and Utopia in Mass Culture', *Social Text,* no. 1, pp. 130–48.

Jäckel, Anne, 1996, 'European co-production strategies: The case of France and Britain', in A. Moran (ed.), *Film Policy: International, National and Regional Perspectives,* Routledge, London, pp. 85–97.

Jäckel, Anne, 2003, 'Dual Nationality Film Productions in Europe after 1945', *Historical Journal of Film, Radio and Television*, vol. 23, no. 3, pp. 231–43.

Jarvie, Ian, 1994, 'The postwar economic foreign policy of the American film industry: Europe 1945–1950', in D.W. Ellwood and R. Kroes (eds), *Hollywood in Europe: Experiences of a Cultural Hegemony*, VU University Press, Amsterdam, pp. 155–75.

Jarvie, Ian, 1998, 'Free trade as cultural threat: American film and TV exports in the post-war period', in G. Nowell-Smith and S. Ricci (eds), *Hollywood and Europe: Economics, Culture, National Identity 1945–1995*, BFI, London.

Jowett, G. 1975, *Film: The Democratic Art*, Little, Brown and Co., Boston.

Jones, Anne and Whyte, Robert, 1987, 'Life After De Laurentiis', *The Sydney Morning Herald*, 12 December, p. 78.

Kersevan, Alexandra, 1997, 'Lettere a *Panorama*', *Panorama*, no. 35, p. 5.

Kezich, Tullio, 1997, 'Sangue ed effetti speciali, questa malga è da spot', *Corriere della Sera*, 1 September.

Kundera, Milan, 1995, *Slowness*, Faber and Faber, London.

La Capra, D. 1994, *History, Theory, Trauma: Representing the Holocaust*, Cornell University Press, Ithaca and London.

Laura, Ernesto G., 1971, 'Ipostesi per una politica culturale', in A. Ferrero et al. (eds), *Responsabilità sociali e culturali della critica cinematografica*, Marsilio Editori, Padova, pp. 29–42.

Lefebvre, Henry, 1991, *The Production of Space*, Blackwell, Oxford.

Leitch, Alison, 2003, 'Slow food and the politics of pork fat: Italian food and European identity', *Ethnos*, vol. 68, no. 4, December, pp. 437–62.

Levi, Primo, 1979, *If This is a Man* and *The Truce*, combined volume, Penguin, New York.

Levi, Primo, 1984, *The Periodic Table*, Schocken Books, New York.

Levi, Primo, 1987, *Opere*, vol. 1, Einaudi, Torino.

Levi, Primo, 1988, *The Drowned and the Saved,* Simon and Schuster, New York.

Loshitzky, Y., 1997, 'Holocaust others: Spielberg's *Schindler's List* versus Lanzmann's *Shoah*', in Y. Loshitzky (ed.), *Spielberg's Holocaust: Critical*

Perspectives on Schindler's List, Indiana University Press, Bloomington, IN, pp. 105–18.

Mai, Nicola, 2001, ''Italy is beautiful': The role of Italian television in Albanian migration to Italy', in R. King and N. Wood (eds), *Media and Migration: Construction of Mobility and Difference*, Routledge, London, pp. 95–109.

Manin, Giuseppe, 1994, 'Tornatore: i francesi mi stroncano, amano solo Moretti', *Corriere della Sera,* 17 May, p. 33.

Manin, Giuseppe, 1997, 'Gelo alla Mostra: Porzûs divide ancora', *Corriere della Sera*, 1 September.

Marcus, Millicent, 2002, *After Fellini: National Cinema in the Postmodern Age*, John Hopkins, Baltimore, MD.

Marin, Dalia, 2005, 'A New International Division of Labor in Europe: Outsourcing and Offshoring to Eastern Europe', paper prepared for the Papers and Proceedings of the European Economic Association Congress, Amsterdam, August 2005.

Marshall, P. David, 2001, *Celebrity and Power: Fame in Contemporary Culture*, University of Minnesota Press, Minneapolis.

Martinelli, Renzo, 'Non è revisionismo, è una storia che va raccontata', *L'Unità*, 12 August, p. 3.

Martini, Andrea, 1995, *De Santis and Moretti: Citizens and Filmmakers*, VHS, 54 min.

Martini, Emanuela, 1987a, 'Segre: dobbiamo diventare anche dei buoni imprenditori', *Cineforum*, no. 5, May, pp. 45–50.

Martini, Emanuela, 1987b, 'Il malinconico destino dei "prodotti e abbandonati"', *Cineforum*, no. 5, May, pp. 38–44.

Martini, Emanuela, 1987b, 'Il futuro nascosto in una selva di sigle produttive', *Cineforum*, no. 3, March, pp. 22–52.

Marrone, Gaetana (ed.), 1999, *New Landscapes in Contemporary Italian Cinema*: *Annali d'Italianistica*, vol. 17.

Masi, Stefano, 1987, 'Le scuole di cinema, le caste e la truffa della gavetta', *Cineforum*, January–February, pp. 50–55.

Mason, T., 1986, 'The great economic history show', *History Workshop Journal*, Spring, no. 21, pp. 3–35.

Masoni, T. and Vecchi, P. 1995, 'Quest'Italia del duemila', *Cineforum*, no. 6,

July/August, pp. 35–39.

Mazierska, Ewa and Rascaroli, Laura, 2004, *The Cinema of Nanni Moretti: Dreams and Diaries*, Wallflower Press, London.

Melchiori, Paola, 1988, 'Women's cinema: A look at female identity', in G. Bruno and M. Nadotti (eds), *Off Screen: Women and Film in Italy*, Routledge, London, pp. 25–35.

Mele, Marco, 2005, 'E Cinecittà si batte per le produzioni USA', *Il Sole 24 Ore*, 28 April. Available from http://global.factiva.com/ha/default.aspx. Accessed 23/04/2007.

Miccichè, Lino, 1975, *Il cinema italiano degli anni sessanta*, Marsilio, Venezia.

Miccichè, Lino, 2002 [1975], *Il cinema italiano: Gli anni '60 e oltre*, Marsilio, Venezia.

Miller, Toby, 1996, 'The crime of Monsieur Lang: GATT, the screen and the new international division of labour', in A. Moran (ed.), *Film Policy: International, National and Regional Perspectives*, Routledge, London, pp. 72–84.

Miller, Toby 2006, 'Global Hollywood 2010', Guest Lecture, Centre for Critical and Cultural Studies, University of Queensland, Brisbane, 9 May.

Miller, Toby, Nitin, Govil, McMurria, John and Maxwell, Richard, 2001, *Global Hollywood*, BFI Publishing, London.

Miller, Toby, Nitin, Govil, McMurria, John and Maxwell, Richard, 2005, *Global Hollywood 2*, BFI Publishing, London.

Milvy, E., 1998, 'I wanted to make a beautiful movie', *Salon*, 30 October. Available from www.salonmag.com?ent/movies/int/1998/10/30int.html. Accessed 10/12/2000.

Miscuglio, Annabella, 1988, 'An affectionate and irreverent account of eighty years of women's cinema in Italy', in G. Bruno and M. Nadotti (eds), *Off Screen: Women and Film in Italy*, Routledge, London, pp. 151–64.

Misler, Nicoletta, 1973, *La via italiana al realismo: La politica culturale artistica del P.C.I. dal 1944 al 1956*, Gabriele Mazzotta Editore, Milano.

Mitchell, Tony, 1995, 'Questions of style: notes on Italian hip hop', *Popular Music*, vol. 14, no. 3, pp. 333–48.

Moran, Albert, 2004, 'Crossroads and connections: An introduction', in T.

Ferrero-Regis and A. Moran (eds), *Placing the Moving Image, Working Papers in Communications*, no. 3, pp. 1–7.

Morandini, Mario, 1990, 'Quante "balle" per Tornatore', *Cinema Lombardia*, no. 4, April.

Morandini, Mario, 1996, 'Paradise lost', *Sight & Sound,* June, pp. 18–21.

Moravia, Alberto, 1977, 'Il cinema specchio involontario della società italiana', *Bianco e Nero*, January/February, pp. 6–9.

Moretti, Franco, 2000, 'Conjectures on world literature', *New Left Review*, January–February, pp. 54–68.

Moretti, Franco, 2001, 'Planet Hollywood', *New Left Review*, May–June, pp. 1–8.

Morreale, Emiliano, 1996, 'Sud', in M. Sesti (ed.), *La 'scuola' italiana: Storia, strutture e immaginario di un altro cinema (1988–1996)*, Marsilio, Venezia, pp. 415–21.

Moss, David, 2001, 'The gift of repentance: A Maussian perspective on twenty years of *pentimento* in Italy', *Journal of European Sociology*, no. 2, pp. 297–331.

Moulaert, Frank and Wilson Salinas, Patricia, 1983, *Regional Analysis and the New International Division of Labour: Applications of a Political Economy Approach*, Kluwer Nijhoff, Boston.

Mowlana, Hamid, 1997, *Global Information and World Communication*, Sage, London.

Mumford, Lewis, 1961, *The City in History*, Penguin, New York.

Muscio, Giuliana, 1988, 'Tutto fa cinema: La stampa popolare del secondo dopoguerra', in V. Zagarrio (ed.), *Dietro lo schermo: Ragionamenti sui modi di produzione cinematografici in Italia*, Marsilio, Venezia, pp. 105–15.

Muscio, Giuliana, 2000, 'Invasion and counterattack: Italian and American film relations in the postwar period', in R. Wagnleitner and E.T. May (eds), *Here, There and Everywhere: The Foreign Politics of American Popular Culture*, University Press of New England, Hanover, pp. 116–31.

Museum of Broadcast Communications, 2005, 'Coproductions International', 2005. Available www.museum.tv/archives/etv/C/html/coproductions/coproductions.htm. Accessed 21/11/2005.

Neale, Steve, 1981, 'Art cinema as institution', *Screen*, vol. 20, no. 1, pp. 11–39.

Nido, Roberto, 2007, 'Rutelli mette a dieta Cinecittà Holding', *MF — Mercati finanziari*, 12 January.

Nowell-Smith, Geoffrey, Hay, James and Volpi, Gianni, 1996, *The Companion to Italian Cinema*, British Film Institute, London.

Orr, John, 1993, *Cinema and Modernity*, Polity Press, Cambridge.

Ortoleva, Peppino, 1996, 'A geography of the media since 1945', in D. Forgacs and R. Lumley, *Italian Cultural Studies*, Oxford University Press, Oxford.

Paggi, L. (ed.), 1996, *Storia di un massacro ordinario*, manifestolibri, Roma.

Passerini, Luisa, 2002, 'Utopia and desire', *Thesis Eleven: 1968*, no. 68, Sage, London, pp. 11–30.

Paternò, Cristiana, 2006, 'Un cinema al femminile', in V. Zagarrio (ed.), *La meglio gioventù: Nuovo cinema italiano 2000–2006*, Marsilio, Venezia.

Pavone, Claudio, 1998 [1991], *Una guerra civile: Saggio storico sulla moralità nella Resistenza*, 2nd ed, Bollati Boringhieri, Torino.

Per fare spettacolo in Europa: Manuale per gli operatori italiani dello spettacolo, dell'audiovisivo e dell'industria culturale, 1996, Presidenza del Consiglio dei Ministri, Dipartimento per l'informazione e l'editoria, Roma.

Petro, Patrice 1996, 'Historical *ennui*, feminist boredom', in V. Sobchack (ed.), *The Persistence of History. Cinema, Television and the Modern Event*, Routledge, New York, pp. 187–200.

Pezzino, Paolo, 1997, *Anatomia di un massacro: controversie sopra una strage*, Il Mulino, Bologna.

Piedmont Cultural Monitoring System, 2001, *Annual Report*.

Pilati, Antonio, 1992, 'L'economia televisiva negli anni '80: risorse, strategie, prospettive', in A. Silj (ed.), *La nuova televisione in Europa*, vol. II, *L'esperienza italiana*, Gruppo Fininvest, Milano.

Pillitteri, Paolo, 1992, *Cinema come politica: Una commedia all'italiana*, Franco Angeli Editore, Milano.

Piperno, Franco, 1979, 'E gli accusati come rispondono?', *L'espresso*, 15 April, p. 20.

Polo, G., 1997, La storia e il fango', *il manifesto*, 9 August, p. 5.

Portelli, Alessandro, 1985, 'Oral Testimony, the law and the making of history:

The "April 7 Murder Trial"', *History Workshop Journal*, no. 20, Autumn, pp. 5–35.

Presidenza del Consiglio dei Ministri, Commissione per la garanzia dell'informazione statistica, 2004, *Statistiche sulle attività culturali*, Roma.

Prono, Franco, 1999, 'Rimozioni, ellissi, assenze in una città metaforica', in *Così ridevano*, Lindau, Torino.

Quaresima, Leonardo, 1991, 'Non è carino', *Cinema & Cinema*, no. 62, September/December, pp. 31–40.

Rapporto sullo stato dell'editoria audiovisiva in Italia, 2006. Available at www.anica.it.

Rentschler, E., 1989, *West German Film in the Course of Time*, Redgrave, New York.

Rodowick, D.N. 1988, *The Crisis of Political Modernism*, University of Illinois Press, Urbana.

Rooney, David, 2000, 'Growing Medusa heads into new plan', *Variety*, June.

Rossellini, Roberto, 1973 [1963], 'Sulla cultura e sul cinema', in G. Della Volpe et al. (eds), *Teorie e prassi del cinema italiano: 1950–1970*, Mazzotta Editore, Milano, pp. 55–58.

Ruberto, Laura E. and Wilson, Kristi M., 2007, *Italian Neorealism and Global Cinema*, Wayne State University Press, Detroit.

Rusconi, Gian Enrico, 1998, 'La politica della storia', *Il Mulino*, July–August, pp. 603–11.

Said, Edward W., 1978, *Orientalism: Western Conceptions of the Orient*, Routledge, London.

Santoro, Vincenzo and Torsello, Vincenzo, 2002, 'Interview with Edoardo Winspeare', in V. Santoro and V. Torsello (eds), *Il ritmo meridiano: La pizzica e le identità danzanti del Salento*, Edizioni Aramiré, Lecce.

Sassen, Saskia, 1988, *The Mobility of Labor and Capital: A Study in International Investment and Labor Flow*, Cambridge University Press, Cambridge.

Sassen, Saskia, 2001, *The Global City: New York, London, Tokyo*, Princeton University Press, Princeton.

Sassoon, Donald, 1981, *The Strategy of the Italian Communist Party: From the Resistance to the Historic Compromise*, Frances Pinter, London.

Scoppola, Pietro, 1995, *25 aprile. Liberazione*, Einaudi, Torino.

Scott, Allen J., 2000, *The Cultural Economy of Cities*, Sage, London.

Serenellini, Mario, 1985, *I diseducatori: Intellettuali d'Italia da Gramsci a Pasolini*, Dedalo, Bari.

Sesti, Mario, 1994, *Nuovo cinema italiano: Gli autori, i film, le idee*, Theoria, Rome, Naples.

Sesti, Mario, 1995, 'Non sono bambini, sono persone di pochi anni — Dichiarazioni di Francesca Archibugi raccolte da Mario Sesti', in C. Proto (ed.), *Francesca Archibugi*, Dino Audino Editore, Roma.

Sesti, Mario (ed.), 1996a, *La 'scuola italiana': Storia, strutture e immaginario di un altro cinema (1988–1996)*, Marsilio, Venezia.

Sesti, Mario, 1996b, 'Il nuovo, il cinema. Altre avventure', in M. Sesti (ed.), *La 'scuola italiana': Storia, strutture e immaginario di un altro cinema (1988–1996)*, Marsilio, Venezia, pp. 3–24.

Sgorlon, Carlo, 1997, 'Sgorlon su Porzûs', *Panorama*, no. 37, p. 7.

Shaeffer, Peter V. and Mack, Richard S., 1996, 'The new international division of labor: An appraisal of the literature', presented at the Regional Science Association, 36th European Congress ETH, Zurich, Switzerland, 26–30 August.

Sharrock, David, 2005, 'Hollywood takes the road to Morocco', *The Times*, 22 January, p. 59.

Sheldon, Peter, Thornthwaite, Louise and Ferrero-Regis, Tiziana, 1997, 'The Federmeccanica: Its changing commitment to collectivism and the remaking of industrial relation in Italy, 1980–1995', in D. D'Art and T. Turner (eds), *Collectivism and Individualism: Trends and Prospects*, Proceedings of the Fifth IIRA European Regional Industrial Relations Congress — 'The employment relationship on the eve of the Twenty-first century', Dublin, 26–29 August, Oak Tree Press, Dublin, pp. 77–97.

Sheraton, Mimi, 1983, 'Mimi Sheraton reviews DDL Foodshow', *New York Times*, 4 May, p. 1.

Shiel, Mark and Fitzmaurice, Tony (eds), 2001, *Cinema and the City*, Blackwell, Oxford.

Il Sole 24 Ore, 1994, 'Ente Cinema's three-year plan proposes creation of communications centre in Rome', 7 December, p. 9.

Bibliography

Sorlin, Pierre, 1996, *Italian National Cinema 1896–1996*, Routledge, London.

Souhail, Karam, 2005, 'Cinema, Dino De Laurentiis apre studios in Morocco', Reuters, 19 January. Available at http://global.factiva.com/ha/default. aspx. Accessed 23/04/2007.

Srivastava, Siddarth, 2004, 'Hollywood forays into India', *Asia Times*, 10 February. Available at www.atimes.com/atimes/South_Asia/FB10Df04. html. Accessed 18/2/2007.

Storper, Michael, 1989, 'The transition to flexible specialisation in the US film industry: External economies, the division of labour, and the crossing of industrial divides', *Cambridge Journal of Economics*, no. 13, pp. 273–305.

Te Koha, Nui, 1998, 'Power of contradiction', *The Courier Mail* (Brisbane), 29 December, p. 15.

van der Burg, Tsjalle, Dolfsma, Wilfred and Wilderom, Celeste P.M., 'Raising private investment funds for museums', *International Journal of Arts Management*, vol. 6, no. 3, pp. 50–59.

Vattimo, Gianni and Rovatti, Pier Aldo, 1983, *Il pensiero debole*, Feltrinelli, Milano.

Vivarelli, Nick, 1999, 'Cinecittà back in black after a string of losses', *Hollywood Reporter*, 19 July, vol. 358, no. 36.

Vivarelli, Nick, 2004, 'Salvatores minds Baby', *Variety*, November 8.

Wagstaff, Christopher, 1995, 'Italy in the post-war international cinema market', in C. Duggan and C. Wagstaff (eds), *Italy in the Cold War: Politics, Culture and Society 1945–58*, Berg, Oxford.

Wagstaff, Christopher, 1998, 'Italian genre films in the world market', in G. Nowell-Smith and S. Ricci (eds), *Hollywood and Europe: Economics, Culture, National Identity: 1945–95*, BFI, London.

Winterhalter, C., 1996, 'L'immagine della Resistenza nella radio e nella televisione. Un'analisi quantitativa', in G. Crainz, A. Farassino, E. Forcella and N. Gallerano (eds), *la Resistenza italiana nei programmi della Rai*, RAI VQPT no. 142, RAI Radiotelevisione Italiana, Roma, pp. 127–50.

Wood, Mary, 2005, *Italian Cinema*, Berg, Oxford.

Yomiuri Shimbun/Daily Yomiuri, 2000, 'Cultures linked by sun & sea'. Available at http://global.factiva.com/ha/default.aspx. Accessed 7/9/2007.

Zagarrio, Vito (ed.), 1988, *Dietro lo schermo: Ragionamenti sui modi di produzione cinematografici in Italia*, Marsilio, Venezia.

Zagarrio, Vito, 1998, *Cinema Italiano anni novanta*, Marsilio, Venezia.

Zagarrio, Vito (ed.), 2000a, *Il cinema della transizione: Scenari italiani degli anni Novanta*, Marsilio.

Zagarrio, Vito, 2000b, "'Il cinema della transizione: cronache di fine secolo'", in V. Zagarrio (ed.), *Il cinema della transizione: Scenari italiani degli anni Novanta*, Marsilio, pp. 1–29.

Zagarrio, Vito (ed.), 2006, *La meglio gioventù: Nuovo cinema italiano 2000–2006*, Marsilio, Venezia.

Zanardi, Francesco Lamberto, 2005, "Quando sei nato non puoi più nasconderti", *il Venerdì di Repubblica*, 6 maggio.

Zincone, Giuliano, 1979, 'Orfani', *Corriere della Sera*, 20 February.

Zucotti, S., 1987, *The Italians and the Holocaust: Persecution, Rescue and Survival*, Peter Halban, London.

INDEX

CPSIA information can be obtained at www.ICGtesting.com
Printed in the USA
LVOW081746140911

246286LV00002B/63/P